THE GOSPELS WITH SALT: JESUS WILDMAN—JESUS WOMAN

Meditations on the Gospels

Francis Gross

Francis Gross

who trusts;
you will smile
when you read
this book,

Hamilton Books
A member of
The Rowman & Littlefield Publishing Group
Lanham · Boulder · New York · Toronto · Oxford

Dedicated

to my sons Joe and Matt
to my daughters-in-law Johanna and Angela
to their friends

Jesus said to them,

"Who do you say that I am?"

They replied,

*"You are the eschatological
manifestation of the ground
of our being, the kerygma of
which we find the ultimate
meaning in our interpersonal
relationships."*

And Jesus said,

"What?"

—Anonymous sage

Contents

PART TWO—JOHN'S GOSPEL

PART FOUR—LUKE'S GOSPEL

PART FIVE—REFERENCES YOU MIGHT FIND USEFUL TO READ, SEE OR HEAR,
Listed According to Gospel Theme (Confer Index)

Introduction

I am writing this series of comments on the gospels, because I have read these scriptures all my life, and because I am aware that many of my dear friends a generation or two down from me have found Christianity a distasteful religion or perhaps a religion with no taste at all. Somehow they do not get translated into a language that touches them. This work is written in an informal, even slangy mode; it is concerned with the message of the gospels as a person might meditate on that message today. I'm writing for people who are unacquainted with the basic salty nature of the gospels and the person of Jesus which lies behind them. The churches and biblical scholars have sometimes been hard on the gospels. My own experience with the gospels is that translators and commentators on the gospels often write and comment on them in a language and sentiment far from the earthy style in which they themselves are written .

My heartfelt thanks to the few movie makers and playwrights who have actually tried to do what I am trying to do and done it better. I refer to those who have succeeded in showing both the grit of the gospel's words and the kind of people to whom it originally made sense. I owe special reverence to Pier Paulo Passolini for his film "The Gospel According to Matthew", to Tom Key and Harry Chapin for their play and the film made from that play, "Cotton Patch Gospel". Denys Arcand's film "Jesus of Montreal" has impressed me as capturing the gospel spirit in its unvarnished audacity. All three of these films seem to me to capture the grit and radical spirit of the gospels. I feel as well a real kindred spirit with Lawrence Ferlinghetti when he writes about Jesus in his "A Coney Island of the Mind."

My heartfelt thanks to Andrew Senesi-Good and Barbara Bauman for proofing this manuscript. I am grateful to my sons Joe and Matt, and to my daughter-in-law Johanna, for reading it with a critical eye when it was still in manuscript form and to Bob Simmermon who encouraged me. Acknowledgement is made to Sharon Wollman for permission to use her illustrations in this book as well as the book's cover. I want very much to thank Dorothy Albritton for taking a somewhat bedraggled manuscript and preparing it with great care and accuracy for the publisher.

Last but not least is Dr. Janaan Manternach, who has not only been a thorough critic of this book in its final form, but wonderfully believable in her encouragement.

Francis Gross
April 28, 2004

Part One

The Gospel According to Mark

Reader Please Note:

I am aware that the gospels are not biographies. The person of Jesus does, however stand behind each gospel narrative, as do the people of the first Christian communities.

F.G.

1. Mark 1:1-13
John the Baptist and Jesus: Wildmen

The Passage

The beginning of the good news of Jesus Christ, the Son of God. As it is written in the prophet Isaiah,

> "See, I am sending my messenger
>   Ahead of you,
> who will prepare your way;
> the voice of one crying out in the
>   wilderness
>   'Prepare the way of the Lord,
>   make his paths straight,'"

John the baptizer appeared in the wilderness, proclaiming a baptism of repentance for the forgiveness of sins. And people from the whole Judean countryside and all the people of Jerusalem were going out to him, and were baptized by him in the river Jordan, confessing their sins. Now John was clothed in camel's hair, with a leather belt around his waist, and he ate locusts and wild honey. He proclaimed, "The one who is more powerful than I is coming after me; I am not worthy to stoop down and untie the thong of his sandals. I have baptized you with water; but he will baptize you with the Holy Spirit."

In those days Jesus came from Nazareth of Galilee and was baptized by John in the Jordan. And just as he was coming out of the water, he saw the heavens torn apart and the Spirit descending like a dove on him. And a voice came from heaven. "You are my son, the Beloved; with you am I well pleased."

And the Spirit immediately drove him out into the wilderness. He was in the wilderness forty days, tempted by Satan; and he was with the wild beasts; and the angels waited on him.

Commentary

Mark's gospel beginning with the heavens torn open at the baptism of Jesus. Jesus, who had been in the desert for forty days, like the Jews, his ancestors were, for forty years. An account, rough as a cob, of torn skies and desert, and the adversary, Satan. I think of sand and dust and a blazing sun, the desert wilderness, the banks of a river. Jesus is the Wildman who could live in such places, with the wild beasts. He does not do his work clad in soft garments. He is not the pampered son of a king. I don't know who he reminds me of. I've never met anybody quite that wild. Maybe the American frontiersmen were a little like that. There's a bit of that in the very old Hispanic village people of northern New Mexico, the ones Robert Coles writes about.[1] Hard people, close to the earth, making almost everything they need to live. A relationship with trees and winds, with sand and heat, with thirst and hunger that is so very elemental. They wrested their lives from the ground itself. Their faces like mirrors of the hard and rocky soil, carved by wind and sun. And the one who first introduced him, his cousin John, is even more of a wildman, wearing his camel's hair tunic and living off the land, baptizing people right there outside in the River Jordan. Wild honey and insects were his food!

_____

1. Robert Coles, *The Old Ones of New Mexico*

2. Mark 2:1-12
The Meaning of Healing

The Passage

When he returned to Capernaum after some days, it was reported that he was at home. So many gathered around that there was no longer room for them, not even in front of the door; and he was speaking the word to them. Then some people came, bringing to him a paralyzed man, carried by four of them. And when they could not bring him to Jesus because of the crowd, they removed the roof above him; and after having dug through it, they let down the mat on which the paralytic lay. When Jesus saw their faith, he said to the paralytic, "Son, your sins are forgiven." Now some of the scribes were sitting there, questioning in their hearts. "Why does this fellow speak in this way? It is blasphemy! Who can forgive sins but God alone?" At once Jesus perceived in his spirit that they were discussing these questions among themselves; and he said to them, "Why do you raise such questions in your hearts? Which is easier, to say to the paralytic, 'Your sins are forgiven,' or to say, 'Stand up and take your mat and walk?' But so that you may know that the Son of Man has authority on earth to forgive sins"—he said to the paralytic—"I say to you, stand up, take your mat and go to your home." And he stood up, and immediately took the mat and went out before all of them; so that they were all amazed and glorified God, saying, "We have never seen anything like this!"

Commentary

Mark's story of the paralyzed man has had a place in my heart for a long time. I'm not sure why. Taking the tiles off the roof and letting the stricken one down. This is a dramatic entrance! The cure touches me too, for he cures the whole person, not just a piece of him. The idea of the division between body and soul has seemed false to me for a long time. I'm quite sure the Jews did not think that way. It's a Greek way of thinking, that separation.

I know that for me, when my old bag of bones hurts, then I myself hurt. The inventors of Prozac know that. To do something about depression you take a pill or go out and run your ass ragged on a road or trail. Brother Ass is an integral part of our ups and downs.

So Jesus forgave the man's sins and did something for his maimed and crippled limbs as well. The guy tossed his pallet over his shoulder and walked home. I think of healing as a form of recognition, a welcoming an embrace, a touch of real hands on a real body, a touch of real words into real ears. It says, "You are worthwhile!" It says, "Welcome, my dear." That's how I see it.

3. Mark 2:23-28
The Root of Bad Habits in Dealing with the Law

The Passage

One Sabbath he was going through the grainfields; and as they made their way, his disciples began to pluck heads of grain. The Pharisees said to him, "Look, why are they doing what is not lawful on the sabbath?" Ad he said to them, "Have you never read what David did when he and his companions were hungry and in need of food? He entered the house of God when Abiathar was high priest, and ate the read of the Presence, which it is not lawful for any but the priests to eat, and he gave some to his companions." Then he said to them, "The sabbath was made for humankind, and not humankind for the sabbath; so the Son of Man is lord even of the sabbath."

Commentary

You've just read about Jesus and his followers picking some kind of grain to eat out in the field on the Sabbath. And we get his famous retort to the scandalized pious ones, "The Sabbath was made for people and not the other way round!" It's an old story, making an idol of a rule or a custom. I know something about this. Almost every bad habit you have was a good one once. Almost all wooden interpretations of the law began as something good. People who love too much almost surely found pleasing others as a good way to get along as kids. Pleasing mom or dad or your small friends is a pretty good strategy for getting noticed, even for being loved. It gives you a place in the family, a niche, a role to play. You are the good guy. You make up for the bad guys, even if the bad guys are rambunctious other kids in the family. Being nice or reliable or compliant is okay unless it becomes something too out of touch with its beginnings and too unbending. Keeping the Sabbath law of rest ahead of cooking breakfast might be an example.

I think of the famous episode in the book of Exodus, the one about the people worshiping a golden calf. Gold indeed is a valuable substance. Calves are precious as well to those who are wandering herdsmen as were the Jews at this time. I'm thinking of the almost comical scene of Moses is on the mountain top receiving the law from God while his brother Aaron is down there in the valley leading people to worship golden statue of a bull calf. Laws and perspectives *do* get turned around.

So often good and respectable people become unknowing experts at turning good sense and good law into something destructive.

Pleasing other people, to return to my earlier example, is not the pearl of great price. There are times when all it amounts to is a desperate attempt not to make waves, to be liked at any cost, to keep on being liked or admired. Giving up your own needs or worth in order to please other people or to keep the rules is not smart—and Jesus knew that.

4. Mark 3:1-6
The Anger of Jesus

The Passage

And again he entered the synagogue, and a man was there who had a withered hand. They watched him to see whether he would cure him on the sabbath, so that they might accuse him. And he said to the man who had the withered hand, "Come forward." Then he said to them, "Is it lawful to do good or to do harm on the sabbath, to save life or to kill?" But they were silent. He looked around at them with anger; he was grieved at their hardness of heart and said to the man, "Stretch out your hand." He stretched it out and his hand was restored.

Commentary

Mark's gospel says, "He looked around at them with anger; he was grieved at their hardness of heart." And so, his anger. Well, there it is. He was just plain pissed and upset. At issue was a man with a withered hand who wanted it to be healed. It was the Sabbath; according to Jewish law, one should not work on that day. Should Jesus heal him on the Sabbath? That was the question.

There was a lot going on here, but I am concerned with just one thing. Can I imagine Jesus as a person with a short fuse? Can I say he was volatile or testy? Mark's terse story telling doesn't qualify or soften his anger. He was angry for a reason; that's true. He was concerned with the hardness of heart of the people there in the synagogue on that Sabbath morning. But my gentle Jesus on the holy cards from the funeral parlor, the one with the lamb on his shoulders, looking so peaceful and soft, well, he is just not here, not on this day, not in this town.

I'm really not sure what to make of this, unless it be that he reminds me of the men I loved most as a young man in the Jesuit Order. They were fiery people. You saw that anger just beneath the surface of their faces and the way they carried themselves. They stood up straight, their eyes looking right at you. I think of the Jesuit priest I knew informally as Charlie Clark, calling the governor of Missouri on the phone and reading him out in no uncertain terms, because he as governor had not stayed the execution of a certain convict condemned to death. I have never known the name of the condemned man who was executed the day of Father Clark's phone call; and it doesn't matter either. It was Charlie's bile that mattered. For years he fought for the convicts in prison within the grim penitentiary walls, there in Jefferson City, Missouri. He saw them as people held in contempt by those righteous ones charged with enforcing the law. He knew the prisoners as people without influence or hope, sometimes guilty, sometimes not, but always with muted voices and without much of a hearing among the power elite of my state, almost always poor, usually black—they were Charlie's people and he fought for them with a kind of rage that I see here in Jesus. This One, it seems to me, is *a man*.

5. Mark 3:13-19
In the Desert, In the Hills

The Passage

He went up the mountain and called to him those whom he wanted, and they came to him. And he appointed twelve, whom he also named apostles, to be with him and to be sent to proclaim the message, and to have authority to cast out demons. So he appointed the twelve: Simon (to whom he gave the name Peter); James son of Zebedee and John the brother of James (to whom he gave the name Boanerges, that is Sons of Thunder); and Andrew, and Philip, and Bartholomew, and Matthew, and Thomas, and James son of Alphaeus, and Thaddeus, and Simon the Cananaean, and Judas Iscariot who betrayed him.

Commentary

He went up a mountain to choose the twelve apostles. I'm not all that aware of the geography of the gospels; I mean the shape of the land, the flora, the fauna. I do know that mountains are important all through both the Hebrew scriptures and the gospels. I've a feeling that most of the mountains weren't very big when compared to the Rocky Mountains in America. Like—he'd not climbed the Grand Teton to pick the twelve, because you don't just stroll up the Grand. I know; I climbed it when I was nineteen years old and am not likely to forget dangling from a rope over a precipice; or the cold, the rain, and sleet that greeted our group of five climbers we shakily signed our names on a little scroll and returned it to its cannister on top of that great peak, fourteen thousand feet above sea level. It was an awesome adventure on an awesome mountain.

He picked the twelve from some mount a lot lower, chances are. Maybe like Clingman's Dome in the Smokies of Tennessee, with the sand and color of the Sangre de Cristos in New Mexico. Still, he chose the wilderness and a high place for this powerful moment, the twelve being like Jacob's twelve sons, the figurative poppas of the twelve tribes of Israel. He didn't pick them in the temple in Jerusalem, or on the shore of a lake, or in a town square, or at some famous well. I think of the Jews as being very much in touch with the wildness of nature, not today's urban Jews but yesterday's Chosen People, the ones who lived in Palestine two thousand and more years ago. God was close to them in the desert and on the hills. They often conversed with God away from the cities, in high places out in the country.

What I'm reminded of is my own inclination when in need of restoration, to head for my twenty acres of woods ten miles out of town. No mountains there, but no crowds either. By and large, nobody at all but a Barred Owl, the deer and wild turkeys, and all what one might call "the little people of the forest." Stones and trees are my close companions there. Neither the stones nor the trees are talkative in the ordinary sense. But I do feel them and see them, the weight and beauty of the stones, the incredible dances of the trees on windy days. The feel of being high in a tree, the swing and movement of it, the danger and the intimacy of clinging to a branch while cutting the grape vines up there. The heft of the great stones, scattered eons ago in the forests of Michigan by glaciers. I use my body strenuously there. The stillness and company of my silent companions are part and parcel of healing for me. I know as well that groves of trees and arrangements of stones are sacred to many peoples— and I lacking mountains or oceans, am healed there. They wash me clean. There I feel chosen, just as truly as one of the twelve on that hill in Galilee long ago.

6. Mark 4:35-41
Jesus Calms the Storm

The Passage

On that day, when evening had come, he said to them, "Let us go across to the other side." And leaving the crowd behind, they took him with them in the boat, just as he was. Other boats were with him. A great windstorm arose, and the waves beat into the boat, so that the boat was already being swamped. But he was in the stern, asleep on the cushion; and they woke him up and said to him, "Teacher, do you not care that we are perishing?" He woke up and rebuked the wind and said to the sea, "Peace! Be still!" Then the wind ceased and there was a dead calm. He said to them, "Why are you afraid? Have you still no faith?" And they were filled with great awe and said to one another, "Who is this, that even the wind and the sea obey him?"

Commentary

And so, Mark's story of the storm at sea. It doesn't say which ones were with him in the boat, some of his chosen ones it seems to me. And there were other boats with them. I never noticed that before, maybe a small flotilla of boats carrying those hairy, grubby men, fishermen, mostly, who were his disciples. And then comes the storm and; they are terrified. He's sleeping in the back of the boat. They say, "Do you not care that we are perishing?" What's the message? He does calm things down. He asks them why they are afraid and then do they have no faith. It seems they *were* afraid and they didn't have faith in him. I'm thinking of the second of the twelve steps of Alcoholics Anonymous, "Came to believe that a power greater than ourselves could restore us to sanity." I think this story and the second step are both about surrender.

And I do wonder sometimes about my own small ups and downs, for example my hip is sore on the left side this morning. That's a small down. And this evening I must face a seminar right upstairs from where I am writing this. Among the students is my son Matt, two personal friends: John Foley and Mary McCoy, a Baptist minister who is also president of the local chapter of the N.A.A.C.P., and six very bright undergraduates. I know they will see me as I am, sometimes a good teacher, sometimes not, and that scares me. I can be a great teacher, a tower, even an icon, if I live by reputation and not face to face with real faces for two and a half hours each Monday night. They'll know that I sometimes talk too much; and that sometimes I tell the same stories two classes in a row. Sometimes the readings I have chosen for each class are boring. They'll know for sure that every class is not some kind of orgasm of insights. Not every time do we ascend to the top of the mountain together. That doesn't happen often. They'll know that this is merely a good class tonight taught by a good teacher. And of course I would love to be *The Messiah* asleep in the boat, who awakens and stills the storms . . . even the wind and the waves obeying me. The wind and the waves, however are not what I do, well, maybe a little. I am more like those panicky guys in the boat, saying, "Oh shit! This time I'm going to really get clobbered, I just *know* it." I know all about being scared spitless; I wrote the book on that. That's my second home. That's why I like this story.

7. Mark 5:21-24; 35-43
The Daughter of Jairus

The Passage

When Jesus had crossed again in the boat to the other side, a great crowd gathered around him; and he was by the sea. Then one of the leaders of the synagogue named Jairus came and, when he saw him, fell at his feet and begged him repeatedly, "My little daughter is at the point of death. Come and lay your hands on her, so that she may be made well, and live." So he went with him. And a large crowd followed him and pressed in on him.

* * *

While he was still speaking, some people came from the leader's house to say, "Your daughter is dead. Why trouble the teacher any further?" But overhearing what they said, Jesus said to the leader of the synagogue, "Do not fear, only believe." He allowed no one to follow him, except Peter, James, and John the brother of James. When they came to the house of the leader of the synagogue, he saw a commotion, people weeping and wailing loudly. When he had entered, he said to them, "Why do you make a commotion and weep? The child is not dead but sleeping." And they laughed at him. Then he put them all outside and took the child's father and mother and those who were with him, and went in where the child was. He took her by the hand and said to her, "Talitha cum," which means, "Little girl, get up!" And immediately the girl got up and began to walk about (She was twelve years of age). At this they were overcome with amazement. He strictly ordered them that no one should know this, and told them to give her something to eat.

Commentary

The story of the daughter of the synagogue leader is a tender story, quite different from the preceding tales of the demoniac and the woman with the issue of blood. There is the derisive laughter of the crowd when he says this little girl is only sleeping. The wails of the paid mourners make one hear this scene as well as see it. And his voice, "Talitha cum" taking her hand meant of course that he was defiled for touching a dead person. He gets defiled a lot in this gospel, giving us always the irony of breaking the law and healing at the same time. He takes her hand. He says that she should be given something to eat. She is twelve years old. Twelve year-old girls then as now, are part girl and part woman. There is sometimes a kind of radiant naivety about them, a woman's body and a little girl's spirit and mind. So, we hear the words and feel the touch of this man. He is not always fierce and angry, even here in Marks's gospel. You and I need to know his tenderness; do we not? Oh yes, we need to know this.

8. Mark 6:31-44
Loaves and Fishes

The Passage

He said to them (the apostles), "Come away to a deserted place all by yourselves and rest a while." For many were coming and going, and they had no leisure even to eat. And they went away in the boat to a deserted place by themselves. Now many saw them going and recognized them, and they hurried there on foot from all the towns and arrived ahead of them. As he went ashore he saw a great crowd; and he had compassion for them, because they were like sheep without a shepherd; and he began to teach them many things. When it grew late, his disciples came to him and said, "This is a deserted place and the hour is now very late; send them away so that they can go into the surrounding country and villages and buy themselves something to eat." But he answered them, "You give them something to eat." They said to him, "Are we to go and buy two hundred denarii worth of bread, and give it to them to eat?" And he said to them, "How many loaves have you? Go and see." When they had found out, they said, "Five, and two fish." Then he ordered them to get all the people to sit down on the green grass. So they sat down in groups of hundreds and fifties. Taking the five loaves and the two fish, he looked up to heaven and blessed and broke the loaves, and gave them to his disciples to set before the people; and he divided the two fish among them all. And all ate and were filled. And they took up twelve baskets full of broken pieces and of the fish. Those who had eaten the loaves numbered five thousand men.

Commentary

Sometimes when I read the gospel, it seems all jumbled, as it did just now. Nothing came to me as good or lovely or significant. The story of the multiplication of the loaves and fishes caused me to wonder, "What does this mean?" I know that the signs Jesus did are not at the very heart of his message. But they are very important in all the gospels, including Mark's, whom I am reading each morning during Lent this year.[2] I

---

2. I have written this entire commentary in short bits, reading a bit of a given gospel each morning until I find a story which resonates. Then I write my thoughts, which have been crystalizing as regards the gospels for more than six decades

quote Black Elk, the Lakota holy man, "I don't know whether all these things happened or not, but I know that they are true."[3]

So, what *is* the truth, what is the meaning of the feeding of the five thousand? I know that there is a long cord tying this story to the manna which the ancestors of these people ate in the desert long before. And I know that feeding people has to do with caring for them, and that it is quite clear in Mark that those closest to him did not understand what this sign was all about. Only later, after the resurrection, do they understand that this remarkable dinner is a foreshadowing of the Eucharist and the triumph of good over evil. And so, this morning, this day, this minute, I feel a kinship with his confused inner circle, those who were afraid and turned around in their minds. And I think of the words of a wise old bishop to a struggling young priest, "None of us knows much, only enough to hold a hand out in the dark."[4] Those words go straight to my heart, both the darkness and being able to hold a hand out to someone else. I can do that. "Yes, my Lord."

3. *Black Elk Speaks* as told through John G. Neihart.
4. *I Heard the Owl Call My Name* by Margaret Craven.

9. Mark 7:1-23
What Makes You Unclean?

The Passage

Now when the Pharisees and some of the scribes who had come from Jerusalem gathered around him, they noticed that some of his disciples were eating with defiled hands, that is, without washing them. ('For the Pharisees and all the Jews do not eat unless they thoroughly wash their hands, thus observing the tradition of the elders; and they do not eat anything from the market unless they wash it; and there are also many other traditions that they observe, the washing of cups, pots, and bronze kettles.) So the Pharisees and the scribes asked him, "Why do your disciples not live according to the tradition of the elders, but eat with defiled hands?" He said to them, "Isaiah prophesied rightly about you hypocrites, as it is written,

> 'This people honors me with
>   Their lips,
> But their hearts are far
>   from me;
> in vain do they worship me,
>   teaching human precepts as
>   doctrines.'

You abandon the commandment of God and hold to human tradition."

Then he said to them, "You have a fine way of rejecting the commandment of God in order to keep your tradition! For Moses said, 'Honor your father and your mother'; and 'Whoever speaks evil of father or mother must surely die.' But you say that if anyone tells father or mother, 'Whatever support you might have had from me is from Corban' (that is an offering to God)—then you no longer permit doing anything for a father or mother, thus making void the word of God through your tradition that you have handed on. And you do many things like this."

Then he called the crowd together and said to them, "Listen to me, all of you, and understand: there is nothing outside a person that going in can defile, but the things that come out are what defile."

When he had left the crowd and entered the house, his disciples asked him about the parable. He said to them, "Then, do you also fail to understand? Do you not see that whatever goes into a person from the outside cannot defile, since it enters not the heart but the stomach, and goes out into the sewer?" He said, "It is what comes out of a person that defiles. For it is from within, from the human heart, that evil intentions come: fornication, theft, murder, adultery, avarice, wickedness, deceit, licentiousness, envy, slander, pride, folly. All these evil things come from within, and they defile a person."

The Commentary

An amazing passage in chapter seven about what makes a person un-clean. And I have a personal reaction to it. I've wondered most of my adult life, "Why do the Jews have all those rules about eating, menstru-ating, keeping the Sabbath, indeed about everything one can look at or touch; there is an incredible mass of rules about matters of what seem to me things of small import. And then I remember that when I was a boy, a young kid growing up as a Roman Catholic in the nineteen thirties and forties, we also had an incredible set of rules concerning our bodies. You weren't supposed to eat meat on Fridays. The grownups fasted during the forty days of Lent. If you didn't go to Mass on Sundays, that was a serious breach of law. If it was your fault that you didn't get your body to church and you died unrepentant, you went to hell . . . and there was an exact moment in the ritual of the Mass you had to be there for or it didn't count. That was when the priest took the veil off the chalice after the sermon. You had to be there by then or it was no soap, your atten-dance didn't count.

And the toughest rules were about sex. There seemed to be a zillion ways you could blacken your soul there. No masturbation, no seeking sexual pleasure through fantasy, no kissing or dancing which was sexu-ally arousing. As a matter of fact you just couldn't get through a week unscathed if you danced with your girl friend or boy friend, or for that matter, if you bathed in a bath tub alone . . . dear God . . . we had a tough set of rules about our bodies. If I'd known a little more about being Jewish and had been given the option, I'd have traded our rules for theirs in a trice! I don't think the Jews were as strict about sex as we were, and kosher food, no matter how complex the rules of preparation, was and still is, good stuff!

I think Jesus would have been just as scornful about what makes a person unclean as evidenced by many of our Catholic rules as he was about Jewish rules. There's no doubt in my mind. Man, it would have been great if he had showed up in St. Louis, right in my parish church on some Sunday in the nineteen forties to speak of what indeed makes a person unclean. I think he would have told us single ones all not to sleep with our girl friends boyfriends, that sexual expression should be a form of love, but not to sweat the small stuff. Life would have been easier for us had we kept our rules of morality rooted in the law of love. But of course nobody, but nobody would have suggested that the Lord himself would have been so easy going. You just would not have had such a thought. It's taken me most of a lifetime to figure this out.

I remember a cartoon in the *New Yorker* which appeared shortly the Roman law forbidding Catholics to eat meat on Fridays was abolished. The scene in the cartoon was that of a conversation between two devils in hell. One devil says to another one, "What do we do with all the Catholics who ate meat on Fridays?" Well, Jesus, how about it? (To be continued, I trust.)

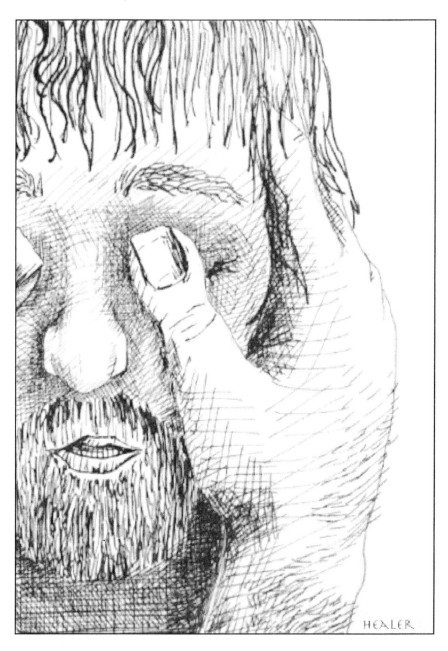

10. Mark 8: 22-26
The Blind Man

The Passage

They came to Bethsaida. Some people brought a blind man to him and begged him to touch him. He took the blind man by the hand and led him out of the village; and when he had put saliva on his eyes, and laid his hands on him, he asked him, "Can you see anything?" And the man looked up and said, "I can see people, but they look like trees walking." Then Jesus laid his hands on his eyes again; and he looked intently, and his sight was restored, and he saw everything clearly. Then he sent him away to his home, saying, "Do not even go into the village."

Commentary

I've just read the eighth chapter of Mark's gospel—feeding a multitude in the desert, a blind man, the apostles' continued obtuseness. Peter calls him the Messiah. A lot about food and blindness. He does want to feed them. He does want them to see. These are issues still—nourishment and blindness. For decades I've loved the blind men of the gospels. I have felt them to be my kin. I've seen myself as the blind man, and I still do; Jesus is the one who can help me see. In this particular case it takes two tries for Jesus to bring sight to the blind one. The first attempt, the man says he can see all right, but people look like trees walking. So Jesus tries again, using spit on the man's eyes, a gesture, a small rite.

So what does it mean? It surely means that we need Him in order to understand what Muslims call "surrender". It's such a conundrum to me, this business of surrendering, as if I wasn't supposed to stand up and look after myself. I'm sure that surrender means more than becoming a jelly fish, something quite different in fact. "Acceptance" seems a good word here, or "receptivity". It's as if the Lord is with me all day long, and I need to accept what he gives me. I need to rely on what comes, not to ask for a different life or a different self, as if these are the conditions for being healed or whole or able to see. It means being willing to wait and to trust . . . to trust that what comes to me is all right.

We're not talking about a lack of initiative here. We're talking about openness to what comes. We're talking about not fretting or worrying. We're talking about the famous Buddhist parable of the monkey who made his own cage by fretting about freedom. The word "serenity" is here apropos; doing what you can and then saying, "That's that!" right in the face of the smallness of your own daily striving and the not very big quality of your life. It is knowing that you're not a big deal, but believing that being a small deal is a divine gift. It's about avoiding being nervous about not being Florence Nightingale or Gandhi; and yet accepting the real beauty of your small gift and being grateful for it, knowing that it is in large part a gift. It has been given to you, your own genius, just as surely as the blind man's gift of being able to see. Healing and seeing are here and now, not tomorrow and not yesterday. Today is the gift I have, right now, this moment, this body, these eyes here, this body now, this job, this house, this day.

11. Mark 9:2-8
The Transfiguration

The Passage

Six days later, Jesus took with him Peter and James and John, and led them up a high mountain, apart, by themselves. And he was transfigured before them, and his clothes became dazzling white, such as no one on earth could bleach them. And there appeared to them Elijah with Moses, who were talking with Jesus. Then Peter said to Jesus, "Rabbi, it is good for us to be here; let us make three dwellings, one for you, one for Moses, and one for Elijah." They did not know what to say, for they were terrified. Then a cloud overshadowed them, and from the cloud there came a voice, "This is my Son, the Beloved, listen to him!" Suddenly when they looked around they saw no one with them any more, but only Jesus.

Commentary

The Transfiguration. I've loved this story since I was a teenager. I remember a little log cabin church near the Grand Teton in Wyoming called the chapel of the Transfiguration. The summer before I entered the Jesuit Order I climbed the Grand with my two boyhood friends and my cousin Tom Scott—that high mountain. There was no transfiguration for us at the summit. It was raining and snowing up there. You were lucky to see your hand in front of your face!

Still, we were high up and we got there on our own steam. It was tough work, and scary. I think now of how the air is thinner when you get that high up. High mountains are places I associate with fields of purple flowers, so very rich and unexpected. I have seen shepherds with their flocks in both the Himalayas of India and the Sangre de Cristo mountains of New Mexico. There is something about the wailing sound of a flock of sheep on the move which makes me think of another world. The shepherds themselves, so removed from ordinary life in general, and mine in particular. Seeing a shepherd in New Mexico, way up high on the Santa Barbara divide, above timber line, that was something! He was riding a bay horse and carrying an old octagonal barreled rifle across the pommel of his saddle, his face a very deep, rich brown, a battered black fedora on his head. I wondered if I was dreaming. Up high things really *are* different.

And so I think of Peter, James, and John there on Mount Hermon, for a very short time in that other world that holy people sometimes speak of. I think of the great Jewish founder of the movement of the Hasidim, the man called The Baal Shem Tov, who seems to have spent as much time in that other world as he spent in this one. I think of Jesus' clothing shining and white there in the cold mists of the mountain, having pierced the veil between one life and another one. And his three closest friends there with him, in that moment the joy of the Resurrection, time having become a secondary matter. It was a vision of triumph and hope, I think, there in the thin air with the cold wisps of clouds touching their faces and hands.

And I know now just how much you need those whiffs of hope, those moments of clairvoyance. They are vital to me; to feel that clean, cold air, to be apart from all the *stuff* for a while. Christianity being a religion of triumph in the midst of hurt and sorrow. I'd never get out of bed in the morning without my own experiences of transfiguration. I know that.

12. Mark 9:14-29
A Son Possessed

The Passage

When they came to the disciples, they saw a great crowd around them, and some scribes arguing with them. When the whole crowd saw him they were immediately overcome with awe, and they ran forward to greet him. He asked them, "What are you arguing about with them?" Someone from the crowd answered him, "Teacher, I brought you my son; he has a spirit that makes him unable to speak; and whenever it seizes him, it grinds his teeth and becomes rigid; and I asked your disciples to cast it out, but they could not do so." He answered them, "You faithless generation, how much longer must I be among you? How much longer must I put up with you? Bring him to me." And they brought the boy to him. When the spirit saw him, immediately it convulsed the boy, and he fell on the ground and rolled about foaming at the mouth. Jesus asked the father, "How long has this been happening to him?" And he said, "From childhood. It has often cast him into the fire and into the water to destroy him; but if you are able to do anything, have pity on us and help us." Jesus said to him "If you are able—All things can be done for the one who believes." Immediately the father of the child cried out, "I believe; help my unbelief!" When Jesus saw that, a crowd came running together, he rebuked the unclean spirit, saying to it, "You spirit that keeps this boy from speaking and hearing, I command you, come out of him, and never enter him again.!" After crying out and convulsing him terribly, it came out, and the boy was like a corpse, so that most of them said, "He is dead." But Jesus took him by the hand and lifted him up, and he was able to stand. When he had entered the house, his disciples asked him privately, "Why could we not cast it out?" He said to them, "This kind can come out only through prayer."

Commentary

The father of the boy who was held by an unclean spirit. He is afraid, that father. This fear reminds me of the time when I was making my very first closed religious retreat, I was a senior in high school. All of us in my class made retreats in groups of thirty or so at the White House Retreat outside St. Louis on a bluff overlooking the Mississippi River.

The priest giving the retreat said of Jesus in the Garden of Olives, the night he was to be betrayed, "Thank God, he was afraid!"

The father of the possessed boy was afraid as well. Thank God for him too.

Fear is as much a part of my own life as having breakfast in the morning. I have often been terrified. You're not supposed to admit being like that, I think. You and I cover our fears with all sorts of fronts, which is all right as long as we do know that we are afraid. I can remember my terror at being a contestant for three years in the statewide boxing tournament in Missouri called The Golden Gloves. You fought in a ring at the center of a huge sports palace called the St. Louis Arena. There you were in front of more than ten thousand people. For months before the tournament there was a sign, a big one, on the front of The Arena, something like *Golden Gloves Boxing Tournament, February 4-8.* In the months before the tournament I passed that sign every morning as I rode to school with my dad. I dreaded even seeing that sign, tried to pretend it wasn't there as we drove by. My dad liked to point it out, knowing it would get a rise out of me. He wasn't a mean man, my father, it was just a bit of needling on his part. He knew that my cousins and I were all deathly afraid of that tournament, of which we were somehow condemned to be a part.

Well, so Jesus knew fear too, just as many of the people around him did. It's a simple lesson, this, a reminder that people faced with disease or danger or things they don't understand are usually afraid. The people in the gospels are not plaster saints or folks immune to emotion. Mark does not bother to lard over the fears of those who people his gospel. I'm glad of that.

13. Mark 10:13-16
Children

The Passage

People were bringing little children to him in order that he might touch them; and the disciples spoke sternly to them. But when Jesus saw this, he was indignant and said to them, "Let the little children come to me; do no stop them; for it is to such as these that the kingdom of God belongs. Truly I tell you, whoever does not receive the kingdom of God as a little child will never enter it." And he took them up in his arms, laid his hands on them, and blessed them.

Commentary

So, I continue to read Mark's gospel. Here in chapter ten is a famous passage about children, the little ones. They have a place of privilege in the Kingdom. People with little power or influence are an important part of Mark's rendition of the gospel. They are not only welcome in the Kingdom; they are central. I am touched by the notion of Jesus' kingdom being a kingdom of nuisances and nobodies.[5] I've wondered about that with regard to the people in the world around me; it can apply to me as well, and perhaps to you. I am a gifted teacher in a not very well known state university. I love my work and my family, but I know that it is likely that neither I nor those I hold most dear will make a huge splash when we move away from the places where we work. You can turn that lack of great influence on its head and say that this very smallness makes me and mine very respectable in the Kingdom, for it is they as we whom the Lord prefers. If being a nobody is important there in his kingdom, well, then we'll be right at home. We have a place by the fire and a good bed to sleep in.

I am not at all sure why Jesus singled out children and other folk who had little of rank or privilege in the world they lived in. I wonder, "Why them? Why them?" just as I wonder, "Why me and mine?" Is it that he saw the hollowness of many people in positions of power and influence?

---

5. The Kingdom of Nuisances and Nobodies is the title of chapter three of John Dominic Crossan's book, *Jesus, a Revolutionary Biography*. It is a lovely chapter in a lovely book by an honest man.

Or did he see that money doesn't make you honest or kind or generous? I don't know. I do know that he saw beauty in the lives of very ordinary people, including people who were not even ordinary, people who stood out because of what they didn't have, people whose claims to fame were minuses rather than pluses. He clearly was pointing to something other than being a big deal, as being important. I don't think he just meant that failure or lack of talent was something to be longed for or cultivated. I think he was pointing to another way of measuring who is or is not a big deal. I'm quite aware that honesty is not the same thing as success. Generosity is not something that puts your obituary notice in big print in the New York Times. It's something else he is pointing to, something frequently not recognized by people of ambition or talent. But what is it? I'm certain there's a connection with honesty and fairness and caring, those rock-bottom small potatoes qualities that lie at the root of good people rather than influence, power or talent. There is, I think, even a quality of naivety here, a quality of innocence, of going your own way seeking the small beauties of the world, whether they be flowers or trees or people. How keen is his insight here. The kingdom does not lay great store in "making it". Think about that, Francis.

14. Mark 10:35-45
The Servant

The Passage

James and John ask for special places of honor in the Kingdom. This is how he replies:

But Jesus said to them, "You do not know what you are asking. Are you able to drink the cup that I drink, or be baptized with the baptism that I am baptized with?" They replied, "We are able." Then Jesus said to them, "The cup that I drink you will drink; and the baptism with which I am baptized, you will be baptized; but to sit at my right hand or at my left is not mine to grant, but it is for those for whom it has been prepared."

When the ten heard this, they began to be angry with James and John. So Jesus called them and said to them "You know that among the Gentiles those whom they recognize as rulers lord it over them, and their great ones are tyrants over them. But it is not so among you; but whoever wishes to become great among you must be your servant, and whoever wishes to be first among you must be slave of all. For the Son of Man came not to be served but to serve, and to give his life a ransom for many."

Commentary

In Mark's chapter ten, the theme of the Servant. "Whoever wishes to become great among you must be your servant and whoever wishes to be the first among you must be the slave of all."

I've known about the Servant for a long time. It is so very beautiful and central a gospel motif, and so very difficult a role to play. I wonder if anyone has ever done it well, lived it well. You can be a smarmy and unctuous imitation easily enough. You can use the Servant to somehow be the slave of all with a *very* bad temper. You can learn to despise other people out of resentment while acting as a servant. Who is more condescending than the servant who knows he is better than the ones he serves? The Pharisee and the Servant can appear to be nearly identical. They drink at the same well and wear the same clothing.

It's what's inside that counts. And even there inside, on a given day you might confuse them, could you look into the heart of each. Is not the Pharisee the dark side of the Servant? It seems so to me. Charles Dickens' Uriah Heep called himself "the 'umble servant" and he was nothing of the sort. So who's the real McCoy? Frankly, I don't think there is one. The Pharisee lives very close to the Servant; they are often the same person. It is the tug of war between these two that is the battle which that those who would keep the law must fight. It is easy to see them as disparate persons, these two, easy and wonderfully deceptive to think of yourself as one or the other rather than both. Divide them and you will surely be fooled. Most Pharisees think of themselves as Servants, and sometimes they are! It is surely important to know that the publican and the pharisee in the famous parable are not two people but one. It is in the tension between these two where I live. It is helpful to know that. I think that the story teller is especially acute when he puts both of them in the same parable . . . "Two men went up to the temple to pray" is how that famous gospel passage begins.[6] It takes a while to see why they are both in the same story, *a while* meaning years, decades of not seeing how closely they are joined. After all, who doesn't want to be the publican who stands afar off and says, "Lord, be merciful to me, a sinner." And the one who stands afar off looks especially good when appearing in such close proximity to the one who pays tithes of all his possessions, fasts twice a week, and of course "is not like the rest of men". Specifically not like the Publican, visible, because both are in the temple at the same time. Indeed they *are* in the same temple, always. I know that first hand.

---

6. I know it is unpardonable to quote one gospel, even one of the synoptics in commenting on another, but this I unrepentantly do. The reference to the story of the publican and the pharisee is Luke 18:9-14.

15. Excursus (Not in Mark) Am I holy?

I'm not reading Mark today. Something down there deep is lodged with me. I wonder about three of the men in my circle of friends whom I admire most We'll call them L. B., G.M. and T.L Two of them were the pillars of the local chapter of The American Association of University Professors, a.k.a., AAUP, our union of professors at Western Michigan University, where I teach. The third is the university provost, the officer in the university administration actually charged with running the teaching and research end of the university endeavor. All of them are my friends. Perhaps they esteem me as I do them. Sometimes I think they do, and that is confusing.

It seems strange to me. Do they think that I am a holy man? I chuckle and think, "I've struggled just to be sane and operational most of my life . . . and the holy stuff I do is an attempt to keep me from going bananas: seeking to work through depression, fear, worry, and being anxious to point of paralysis. I spend a lot of time with these lethal companions. This is not just pious bull shit; it's true. I know this. I'm not in love with God, like Rumi.[7] I think of myself as having a name once given to my father by some Indians he knew, *Little old man going along picking up sticks*.[8] It's a good name for me. My Lord might say to me, "Well, Francis, so what? Do you think you are some sort of spiritual big deal?"

"Maybe, maybe not, Lord", says I, but I am aware of this: it's a very bad idea to spend a lot of time looking in the mirror, saying "Mirror, mirror on the wall, am I the holiest one of all?"

So Jesus says to me, and perhaps to you, "Remember, my friend, for you to ask for some romantic, double- barreled holiness, is not of much use. I told you years ago, 'All I want is you.' That includes whatever form of holiness you have or don't have. So keep on doing what comes to you, the regular things. They are enough. You really don't need to know how far up the Divine Richter Scale you measure."

---

7. Rumi is the name of the famous Muslim Sufi mystic of centuries past, whose works are quite the rage these days, among those who know what he's talking about and those who don't. It is very chic to quote him, which gets us back to Pharisees!

8. Yes, I know I'm supposed to use the term *Native American* when referring to indigenous American people.

"You know that if you are a football player, you do best if you just play the game. It doesn't make you better or worse to know how high you rank in the world of football. If that were an overwhelming concern of yours, you'd do well to remember that it's the joy of playing the game that counts, and not where the sportswriters rank you. So, play your game; take the praise and blame that come your way and know that neither of these forms of recognition have much to do with whether you play well or not. True, there is no real harm in wondering how good you are. You won't be cursed by wondering, but there is something of the high school 'grade hound' in too much concern. Remember those kids you taught who knew their G.P.A.s down to a hundredth of a point? They weren't bad kids, but they were stuck on themselves, and less interesting as people because of all that self-absorption, and surely quite a ways away from their true worth as students because of this obsession. What to do? Just let it be, knowing that such an attitude is really only poisonous if over-indulged."

"Yes, my Lord," I say. "I guess it wouldn't do to ask how you learned so much about football and the minds of high school students. And I think we're still talking about the publican and the pharisee, don't you? (I received no answer to this last question.)

16. Mark 12:28-34
The Two Great Commandments

The Passage

One of the scribes came near and heard them disputing with one another; and seeing that he answered them well, he asked him, "Which commandment is the first of all?" Jesus answered, "The first is 'Hear, O Israel: the Lord our god, the Lord is one; you shall love the Lord your God with all your heart, and with all your soul, and with all your mind, and with all your strength.' The second is this, 'You shall love your neighbor as yourself.' There is no other commandment greater than these." Then the scribe said to him, "You are right, Teacher; you have truly said that 'he is the one, and besides him there is no other'. And 'to love him with all the heart, and the strength,' and 'to love one's neighbor as oneself,'—this is much more important than all whole burnt offerings and sacrifices." When Jesus saw that he answered wisely, he said to him, "You are not far from the kingdom of God." After that no one dared to ask him any question.

Commentary

The first is, 'Hear, O Israel: the Lord our God, the Lord is one; you shall love the lord your God with all your heart, and with all your soul and with all your mind and with all your strength.' The second is this, 'You shall love your neighbor as yourself.' There is no other commandment greater than these.

These two commandments summarize the whole of Christian life. I've known that for a very long time. What a great help it is to know that every law, every rule, each regulation I know, large and small, sacred and profane—all of them are applications of these two. Without these two, "Love your God and love your neighbor as you love yourself," without them, all other rules are tinsel and wrapping paper. They *are* the law. There is no other, not here, not there, not yesterday, not tomorrow. They are the ageless summary of it all.

I do know that it took millennia for humans to see the rock bottom simplicity of this summary of the law . . . I think of the Hebrew scriptures in their entirety as a struggle to reach these two. I think of the history of the world as the same kind of struggle. It's been a losing battle, I fear. My country is at war, breaking yet again the second of these ancient foundation stones of morality. In my own life I have lived through, God knows, a large number of hate- generated wholesale executions: the Nazi holocaust, the Khmer Rouge in Cambodia, the years of genocide in Indonesia, the current simmering feud between Serbs and the Albanians. I devoutly hope that the tragedy of the mass killings in New York and Washington, D.C. are not the opening chorus of yet another genocidal war, this time between my country and the Islamic Near East. I wish I could say that we are better for knowing these two great foundations stones of all morality. Better than we were a hundred years ago, or a thousand years ago, or ten thousand years ago.

And what do we do, we who are so very small in the large scheme of things? What can we do? We can get up each morning and greet our work, our colleagues, our families with joy. What did the lama say about doing something about the long history of hatred? "Take a friend to lunch." I can do that. I can yell pretty loud too, when it comes to raising my voice against hatred. Perhaps you can do the same. Peace, after all, begins at home.

17. Mark 16
The Passion

I am not going to reproduce here the Passion of Jesus according to Mark. What I have to say by way of commentary concerns the gospels in general. I'll reflect on the Passion and Resurrection of Jesus in connection with another gospel, later in this book.

Commentary

I finished reading Mark's gospel this morning. This gospel, this and the other three, moved me deeply when I was a Jesuit novice fifty years ago. I had a small book called *A Harmony of the Gospels* that put all four together in one narrative; I read it over and over. I read Alban Goodier's *The Public Life of Jesus*, as well, all four volumes of it. So warm and heartening it was. The Lord was right there, right there for me. I devoured those four volumes; I read them again and again. Here was my Lord.

And today? I sit writing at the kitchen table in a silent house, my wife Toni having gone to work, I'm late getting up because I had a seminar last night right here in the house, eleven people there. It runs until 9:30 P.M. starting at 7:00, and I am bushed when it's over. The new day starts more slowly usually, today being no exception.

What role does the gospel play for me now? The passion and the resurrection of Jesus? Today my reading of the gospels is flatter, thinner, less filled with the blood of my emotions. I know that the gospels themselves are not biographies of Jesus of Nazareth. He stands behind them; it is true, but He is more elusive than I once thought. Still and all, those old words float before my eyes each and every day My heart does not jump today as it once did when I first got to know them. It's not that I have no heart or that I have no faith. It's just flatter.

I think if I were an old baseball player and today was the season's opening day in St. Louis or Detroit, well, as I sat in the dugout watching a young pitcher take his warmup pitches, it would be like a movie I had seen many times. Short on surprises. And there is a quality of silence there, a kind of utter familiarity. I don't think it likely that this is unusual, entirely unique to me. Lots of people have described the religion of old people, and now I am one of them. This game is called the desert by some, the dark night by others. It has a dry quality, like very old paper. There is little wind and no thunder. Even its quality of doubting this and being unsure of that is very familiar. It is not overly cynical nor overly enthusiastic. It is certainly aware that faith wears many garments . . . but my own robe of faith is soft, like old denim, the color faded, the cloth very thin in places.

Is there sadness? Well, yes there is some of that. There's life too, and joy. I've had joy off and on all my life. I'm better at being alone now than at any other time in my life, but it's not dramatic. I am thinking of an old stone mason I know, a man in his late seventies, who tuck pointed the brick walls of our house six years ago, and did a good job too. The lobes of his ears were so thin as to be translucent, very fine and brown. Old ears are thin, and sometimes very fine. They don't hear a whole lot that is completely new. They don't hear things that don't interest them at all!

Part Two

John's Gospel

18. John 1:1-18
The Prologue

The Passage

In the beginning was the Word, and the Word was with God, and the Word was God. He was in the beginning with God. All things came into being through him, and without him not one thing came into being. What has come into being with him was life, and the life was the light of all people. . . . The light shines in the darkness and the darkness did not overcome it.

There was a man sent from God, whose name was John. He came as witness to testify to the light, so that all might believe through him. He himself was not the light, but he came to testify to the light. The true light which enlightens everyone was coming into the world.

He was in the world and the world came into being through him; yet the world did not know him. He came to what was his own, and his own people did not accept him. But to all who received him he gave power to become children of God, who were born, not of blood or the will of the flesh or the will of man, but of God.

And the Word became flesh and lived among us, and we have seen his glory, the glory as of the Father's only son, full of grace and truth.

Commentary

I am going to read and meditate on John's gospel much as I read and meditated on Mark, just prior to this. So . . .

The prologue of John's gospel, quoted above, was read at the end of Sunday Mass when I was a boy. We all stood up for it, as we did for the regular gospel reading early in the Mass. One does not sit when the gospel is being read. I'd forgotten this old custom of reading John's prologue until I read those solemn verses this morning and wondered why they were so totally familiar to me.[1] They begin just like the book of Genesis begins, "In the beginning . . . " only here it is the story of The Word rather than the creation of the world, "In the beginning was the Word," it says, extending Jesus all the way back in history to the eons before there was history. I think of the dim, early pages of Christian history, it was before that. I think of Moses and Abraham; it was before that. I think of Adam and Eve and the creation story, before even that. And whatever old and purple pages there were before there was time or measurement, way back there, before them too. Before there was a *before* or an *after*, for that matter, "In the beginning was the Word." That's what it says.

I know that there are other ways to think of the beginning times of the cosmos, scientific ways and other more measured and practical ways, the ways in which such earliness is described in other religions. And I know there are circular ways to see the beginning, if you can use that word *beginning* in this context. (John's way is a very linear one.) There are ways of describing it all that would never use the phrase "In the beginning". This one, however, is precious to me, for of course in my own beginning years it was read out loud every Sunday in Latin, "In principio erat Verbum" it went in the Latin.

It puts my own Jesus' spirit and soul back there before the ages, right when it ought to be. He may have had company, surely did, in fact. So The Prophet was there and the Buddha was there and Lord Shiva was there, these last two in not so linear a fashion, but in a cyclic way, because that's how Hindus and Buddhists express this most inexpressible moment. Sofia was there too, if she or anyone had a there in which to be.[2] Proverbs says in her voice:

----

1. The reading of John's prologue at the end of Mass was discontinued when the Roman liturgy was overhauled at the Second Vatican Council in the nineteen sixties.

2. Sofia is the female personification of divine Wisdom in the wisdom books of the Bible.

> . . . then I was beside him like a
> master worker;
> and I was daily his delight,
> rejoicing before him always . . .[3]

There is a kind of permanence beyond the failure of words and ideas to wrap up this beginning; there is a kind of centered and central quality that touches me, a kind of *always* at the heart of everything I know and don't know. A pervasiveness is there . . . there in the Word. And I am grateful for it, and grateful to John for saying it so boldly and with such abandon, and yet so serenely.

---

3. Proverbs 8:22-31

19. John 1:19-34
John the Baptist

The Passage

This is the testimony given by John when the Jews sent priests and Levites from Jerusalem to ask him, "Who are you?" He confessed and did not deny it, but confessed, "I am not the Messiah." And they asked him, "What then? Are you Elijah?" He said,

I am not." "Are you the prophet?" He answered, "No." Then they said to him, "Who are you? Let us have an answer for those who sent us. What do you say about yourself?" He said,

> "I am the voice of one crying out
> In the wilderness
> 'Make straight the way of the Lord.'"

Now they had been sent from the Pharisees. They asked him, "Why then are you baptizing if you are neither the Messiah, nor Elijah nor the prophet?" John answered them, "I baptize with water. Among you stands one whom you do not know, the one who is coming after me; I am not worthy to untie the thong of his sandal." This took place in Bethany across the Jordan where John was baptizing.

Commentary

John then, the Baptist John, not the writer John. John the cousin of the Bridegroom. I've always loved this John. His roughness, his bluntness, the one who is not the Christ nor The Prophet nor Elijah. The one who quotes Isaiah's great theme of the road back to Israel for the Exiled Jews more than five hundred year earlier—"Make straight the path.' He is the one crying out in the wilderness. I've noted in my comments on Mark's gospel that if there has ever been an archetypal Wildman in the gospels, John is surely he. He is crazy and untamed, maybe not *the* prophet but unquestionably a prophet.

He reminds me of my Jesuit heroes when I was in my training in the Society of Jesus, those testy men who were such an amazing mixture of loyalty to the church and the Order as well as outspoken critics of anything or anyone not truthful or true. Bill Wade criticized the neo-Thomist philosophy we all studied. Charlie Clark, as I have mentioned before, blistered anyone right up to the governor of the state of Missouri, anyone who was a part of the brutality, callousness and meanness of the state's prison system, who called the governor on the phone whenever a convict was executed, and blasted that Brahmin of whatever political party for daring to acquiesce to the execution of any man or any woman.[4] Harold Rahm who somehow by charm, cajolery and threats turned the Mexican-American teen-aged gangs into baseball players, cooks, scouts, both boy and girl, dancers, and even a few priests! And John Corridan, S.J. about whom Elia Kazan made a movie, who stood up for the common long-shoremen against their mob affiliated bosses.[5]

There were others, but these are the principal fierce and gentle holy men whom I looked up to as a young Jesuit. They *were* a testy lot; they certainly scared me and awed me, these heroes; they were warriors all. I'd have killed to be one of them. They remind me to this day of John the Baptist, all that ferocity, impatience, compassion and plain talk. "Soldiers be content with your pay" is one of John's plain admonitions. That quality of trusty trueness went to anyone not getting a fair deal, including us young Jesuits. Smoother teachers never dared speak clearly to us of the flaws in St. Thomas Aquinas' philosophy or about the flaws and callous strictures of our church as regards sexual morality. I refer here to the inevitability of the practice of masturbation among young celibates as also the rigidity of the church laws of those days on divorce and remarriage of Roman Catholics. To this day I prefer the company of such persons, male or female, to the smooth prophets among clergy and teachers. Which one of those choleric truth tellers was it who said, "I dearly love a fight!"? It could have been any one of them. They were my heroes. How lovely that the friend of the Bridegroom should be one of them.

---

4. I mention the Jesuits in the section on Jesus' anger, number four in this book.

5. I have mentioned some of these men before in my commentary on Mark's gospel. All were Jesuits; all were Catholic priests working in various places during the fifteen years of my Jesuit training. Some of them are still at it! They were the revered elder brothers of us Jesuits in the making. All of them courted danger and were in trouble with various authorities, both civil and churchly as a part of their daily lives. Elia Kazan's movie mentioned here is entitled *On the Waterfront*. Karl Malden, Marlon Brando and Eva Marie-Saint were the starring actors in the film.

20. John 1:35-51
Calling the First Disciples

The Passage

The next day, John again was standing with two of his disciples, and as he watched Jesus walk by, he exclaimed, "Look, here is the Lamb of God!" The two disciples heard him say this, and they followed Jesus. When Jesus turned and saw them following, he said to them, "What are you looking for?" They said to him, "Rabbi" (which translated means Teacher), "where are you staying?" He said to them, "Come and see." They came and saw where he was staying, and they remained with him that day. It was about four o'clock in the afternoon. One of the two who heard John speak and followed him was Andrew, Simon Peter's brother. He first found his brother Simon and said to him, "We have found the Messiah" (which is translated Anointed). He brought Simon to Jesus, who looked at him and said, "You are Simon son of John. You are to be called Cephas" (which is translated Peter).

The next day Jesus decided to go to Galilee. He found Philip and said to him, "Follow me." Now Philip was from Bethsaida, the city of Andrew and Peter. Philip found Nathanael and said to him. "We have found him about whom Moses in the law and also the prophets wrote, Jesus son of Joseph from Nazareth." Nathanael said to him, "Can anything good come out of Nazareth?" Philip said to him, "come and see. "When Jesus saw Nathanael coming toward him, he said of him. "He is truly an Israelite in whom there is no deceit!" Nathanael, asked him, "Where did you get to know me? Jesus answered, "I saw you under the fig tree before Philip called you." Nathanael relied, "Rabbi, you are the Son of God! You are the King of Israel. Jesus answered, "Do you believe because I told you that I saw you under the fig tree? You will see greater things than these," And he said to him, "Very truly I tell you, you will see heaven opened and the angels of God ascending and descending upon the Son of Man."

Commentary

The calling of the first disciples: Andrew, Philip, Peter, and Nathaniel. I remember when I was nineteen years old, during what we Jesuits called The Long Retreat, a stretch of thirty silent days in which recently recruited novices of the Society of Jesus got their first real taste of silence and meditation. I remember our Master of Novices telling us this story in John's gospel, the calling of Jesus' first followers. I remember being told of Jesus' comment to the young man Nathaniel. Jesus said that he had seen Nathaniel "under a fig tree." And it was then quite clear to me that this magic man had seen Nathaniel under that fated tree without actually being physically present. It was the wonder of that moment that I remember. This was my Lord and he could do anything, anything at all.

And there I was, another version of Nathaniel, called as well to his service. There were at least fifty of us listening to Nathaniel's story. We all wore the long, black soutane of the Jesuit Order, held together in the front by a sash we called a cincture. None of us had worn those magic garments very long. We sat at our desks in a large room called an ascertary, the spelling of which eludes me to this day, with Father Joseph Gschwend, S.J. sitting up front and facing us at a table with his notes. His table and chair were on a raised, wooden platform, perhaps a foot high, enough to give him a commanding view of the fifty young men's faces and postures, we who sat facing him, taking notes from his talks. Each one of those talks was followed by a period of meditation a little less than an hour in length. We went through this ritual three times each day of the thirty days of the retreat. We kept silence all day during that month, broken only by three break days, occurring every week or so during the thirty days of the retreat. On those days we took walks together in threes down the country roads around the seminary. We were allowed to talk during those walks. Those were amazing times, my early Jesuit days, and the long retreat was the most concentrated and the most amazing time of those times. We meditated on heaven and hell and the life of Jesus, from his birth to his death and resurrection. All this was done during the month of October, the month which marked the end of the Missouri summer. I had no doubt that I was another Nathaniel, magically called to serve my Lord as a member of the coolest of all the Catholic religious Orders, the Society of Jesus. Wow![6]

---

6. I use the word *cool* to describe the Jesuits because that's what we thought of our new organization; it was the coolest group in the world and we knew it.

21. John 2:1-12
The Wedding at Cana

The Passage

On the third day there was a wedding in Cana of Galilee, and the mother of Jesus was there. Jesus and his disciples had also been invited to the wedding. When the wine gave out, the mother of Jesus said to him, "They have no wine." And Jesus said to her, "Woman, what concern is that to you and me? My hour has not yet come." His mother said to the servants, Do whatever he tells you." Now standing there were six stone jars for the Jewish rites of purification, each holding twenty or thirty gallons. Jesus said to them, "Fill the jars with water." And they filled them up to the brim. He said to them, "Now draw some out and take it to the chief steward." So they took it. When the steward tasted the water that had become wine, and did not know where it came from (though the servants who had drawn the water knew), the steward called the bridegroom and said to him,"Everyone serves the good wine first, and then the inferior wine after the guests have become drunk. But you have kept the good wine until now." Jesus did this, the first of his signs, in Cana of Galilee, and revealed his glory; and his disciples believed in him.

Commentary

The wedding feast at Cana. I've known this passage most of my life as well, like the one I spoke of above. It was read at my wedding.[7] I remember that because Pat McAnany, my best man and a fellow former Jesuit, said by way of commentary on that reading, "They saved the best wine until last." I was forty years old at that wedding. Pat's words were lovely to hear, there in the living room of a United Church of Christ minister, who officiated over the ceremony. I had not yet obtained permission to marry from church authorities in Rome. My wife and I could not be married in front of a priest for that reason. Nor did I mind in the

---

7. I spent twenty years in the Jesuit Order and was ordained a priest towards the end of those twenty. I left the Jesuits to marry. It was a hard choice, for I am fond of those men to this day, as is evident throughout this book. They still command my respect and awe.

least being compared to the miraculous wine whose presence marked Jesus advent into public life in John's gospel.

The resonance of that story is one of unexpected joy. It still surprises me that a wedding was the occasion for his first sign in John's gospel—and that the sign was about a large quantity of water made into wine. This was not a penny-sized sign. The wine holds resonance surely for the principal Christian rite of remembrance of the Savior, the celebration of the Lord's Supper. This first miracle stands as an almost brazen signal of bodily joy as part of the Christian message. You just can't get out of that. And I am grateful that in the centuries of Christianity this day has stood up to a recurrent Christian embarrassment about what Francis of Assisi called Brother Ass. I mean of course that one's body, warts and all is underlined with an unembarrassed ease and pride, right there at the start of John's gospel. It does make you wonder about institutionalized Christianity's recurring fears of sexuality, alcohol, and whatever goes with having a good time. John, I love you!

22. John 2:13-21
Jesus Cleanses the Temple

The Passage

The Passover of the Jews was near and Jesus went up to Jerusalem. In the temple he found people selling cattle, sheep, and doves, and the money changers seated at their tables. Making a whip of cords, he drove all of them out of the temple, both the sheep and the cattle. He also poured out the coins of the money changers and overturned their tables. He told those who were selling the doves, "Take these things out of here! Stop making my Father's house a marketplace!" His disciples remembered that it was written, "Zeal for your house will consume me." The Jews then said to him, "What sign can you show us for doing this?" Jesus answered them, "Destroy this temple and in three days I will raise it up. The Jews then said, "This temple has been under construction for forty-six years, and will you raise it up in three days?" But he was speaking of the temple of his body.

Commentary

The cleansing of the temple. What pious person has not worried about this passage? Perhaps I am not the only one whose personal image of Jesus was once that of a man of kindness only. When reading this fierce passage of the gospel I have thought "This is not my Jesus!" I've thought that not once but many times throughout my life. I wonder what it is that brought me to that, I, the one whose heroes in the Jesuit Order were nearly all men with piercing eyes and short fuses.

I know as well that neither this gospel of Johns's nor any of the other three are biographies in the modern sense. They are not profiles of my Lord, even though I read them as such for years. They are more message than biography. They are not intentionally unbiographical either. There is the man Jesus standing behind all of them. And it seems to me that the man had a temper, just as I do.

Today, when I am old, I know that the whole Christian message is one of emotion, a call to love others, a call to serenity through suffering, sometimes even a call to anger at injustice or callousness. It's not the kind of message you could deliver casually or glibly like a singing telegram or an ad for Gillette Razor Blades. So when he tore up things in the temple in protest against the commercialism of the most sacred space of his people, he was, as I have noted before, *pissed*. I've come to accept him as a real human being these last decades of my life, a fiery man, knocking over the tables with coins on them with a home-made whip in his hand and anger in his eyes. He was the kind who made enemies among the respectable, pious people, who themselves did not want to make waves and were leery of other people who caused commotion or trouble in the name of honesty or justice.

In this context I remember seeing the ushers at Sunday Mass when I was a boy. They sat in the back of the church at little tables covered with green felt. There were piles of dimes and quarters on those tables, arranged in small stacks on the green table tops neat as pie. You paid a small fee on a Sunday morning, you or your dad, as you entered the building right after blessing yourself with holy water at the holy water font next to the entryway. The men who collected money for admission wore suits and ties and had their hair slicked back as they silently made change for you from those neat and very shiny piles of coins. I have wondered what Jesus would have done about all *that* had he been the man in front of my father and me as we entered the church with my two sisters. St. Mary Magdalene Church was the name of the place on the corner of Brentwood Boulevard and Manchester Road in St. Louis County. There might have been some fireworks right inside the church; and it wasn't the fourth of July. I wonder about that.

23. John 3:1-3, 17-21
Nicodemus

The Passage

Now there was a Pharisee named Nicodemus, a leader of the Jews. He came to Jesus by night and said to him, "Rabbi, we know that you are a teacher who has come from God; for no one can do these signs that you do apart from the presence of God." " Jesus answered him, "very truly, I tell you, no one can see the kingdom of God without being born from above.

* * *

"Indeed, God did not send the Son into the world to condemn the world, but in order that the world might be saved through him. Those who believe in him are not condemned; but those who do not believe are condemned already because they have not believed in the name of the only Son of God. And this is the judgement, that the light has come into the world, and people loved darkness rather than light because their deeds were evil. For all who do evil hate the light and do not come to the light, so that their deeds may not be exposed. But those who do what is true come to the light, so that it may be clearly seen that their deeds have been done in God."

Commentary

Nicodemus comes to visit Jesus at night. In this conversation with Nicodemus the Pharisee Jesus refers to himself as the light, a recurring image in this gospel. Nicodemus comes at night; it is dark outside. I can see the two of them talking with the shadows of the night around them and the brightness of an oil lamp illuminating the two of them as they converse, a tableau in a warm evening in Jerusalem. Darkness and light play on the two faces—and I know that these two will always be together thus, neither making sense without the other. Light without darkness would not be precious or joyful or sweet. Darkness without light would be the dark and rank despair without hope. And so in this gospel of John they are always together, each deriving meaning from the other.

I think of my life that way: light and darkness, never far apart, joy and sorrow, peace and war, the ups and the downs I know every day. I have always wished that there could only be light, but I know better, even if on every sunny day I think that my days will always be bright; it just seems that's the way it should be. The dark days, of course, seem endless as well. I know now, having had lots of each, that they go together. They are twins; they are of a piece, a simple and seamless robe; that's what they are. Sunshine and shadow are one. I know that, for this moment at least. There would be no Jesus without darkness. Perhaps you know that too.

24. John 4:1-30; 39-42
The Woman at the Well

The Passage

So he came to a Samaritan village called Sychar, near the plot of ground that Jacob had given to his son Joseph. Jacob's well was there and Jesus, tired out by his journey, was sitting by the well. It was about noon.

A Samaritan woman came to draw water, and Jesus said to her, "Give me a drink." (His disciples had gone to the city to buy food.) The Samaritan woman said to him, "How is it that you, a Jew, ask a drink of me, a woman of Samaria?" (Jews do not share things in common with Samaritans.) Jesus answered her, "If you knew the gift of God, and who it is that is saying to you, 'Give me a drink,' you would have asked him, and he would have given you living water." The woman said to him, "Sir, you have no bucket, and the well is deep. Where do you get that living water? Are you greater than our ancestor Jacob, who gave us the well, and with his sons and his flocks drank from it?" "Jesus said to her, "Everyone who drinks of this water will be thirsty again, but those who drink of the water that I will give them will never be thirsty. The water that I will give will become in them a spring of water gushing up to eternal life." The woman said to him, "Sir, give me this water, so that I may never be thirsty or have to keep coming here to draw water."

Jesus said to her, "Go, call your husband and come back." The woman answered him, "I have no husband." Jesus said to her, "You are right in saying, 'I have no husband; for you have had five husbands, and the one you have now is not your husband. What you have said is true!" The woman said to him, "Sir, I see that you are a prophet. Our ancestors worshiped on this mountain, but you say that the place where people must worship is Jerusalem." Jesus said to her, "Woman, believe me, the hour is coming when you will worship the Father neither on this mountain nor in Jerusalem. You worship what you do not know; we worship what we know, for salvation is from the Jews. But the hour is coming, and is now here, when the true worshipers will worship the Father in spirit and truth, for the Father seeks such as these to worship him. God is spirit, and those who worship him must worship in spirit and truth." The woman said to him, "I know that Messiah is coming" (who is called Christ). "When he comes, he will proclaim all things to us." Jesus said to her, "I am he, the one who is speaking to you."

Just then, the disciples came. They were astonished that he was speaking to a woman, but no one said, "What do you want?" or, "Why are you speaking with her?" Then the woman left her water jar and went back to the city. She said to the people, "Come and see a man who told me everything I have ever done!" He cannot be the Messiah, can he?" They left the city and were on their way to him.

* * *

Many Samaritans from that city believed in him because of the woman's testimony, "He told me everything I have ever done." So when the Samaritans came to him, they asked him to stay with them; and he stayed there two days. They said to the woman, "It is no longer because of what you said that we believe, for we have heard for ourselves and we know that this is truly the Savior of the world."

Commentary

Jesus visits the woman at the well. Oh my, when have I not known this story? Peter, Paul and Mary, the folk singers, had a wonderful sung version of this encounter that not only touched me, but reminded me that this is an ironic story, as close to humor as anything in the gospels. She is a great lady, this woman with all her "husbands". So often it is the outcasts who know him first: blind people, lepers, paralytics, tax collectors and women in all walks of life. The stories about these people in John's gospel are especially pleasing to me because they are longer and more detailed than similar stories in the other three gospels. They are long enough for you to get into them, getting the feel of the characters and the surroundings.

This one is a story of Jesus' encounter with a woman, and he had many encounters with women and many disciples who were women. Here, he flouts the customs of his day, talking, a rabbi, in a public place in the heat of the day to a lady whose reputation was pretty shady—and a Samaritan to boot. Jews didn't talk to Samaritans. He broke a lot of rules, this man. I have always delighted in that—a Messiah with the guts of a burglar. I've never once in all my life seen an image of him that reflected that puckish side of him. I've seen pictures of him laughing, pictures of him looking fiercely at Pontius Pilate, and, my God!, stacks of pictures that made him look like a bearded lady, soft and melancholy and sweet, pointing to his exposed heart mounted on the front of the folds of his ample tunic. I'm grateful to gospels for showing him in other poses. In this story he is a mysterious and ironical bad ass!

I know very well that you just don't use words like *bad ass* for Jesus, and I wonder why that is. Maybe because he is almost always portrayed by people who belong to the churches. Churches, like almost all organizations, like their models to be company men or nice ladies. One doesn't want to encourage the members to be strange or deviant in imitation of the Boss. The official models are seldom people who rock the corporate boat. Come to think of it, I know George Washington as the one who never told a lie, and Abraham Lincoln as Honest Abe. There's good reason to believe that both these American saints were a lot saltier than the images we have of them in the official legends told in their regard. So, good for John in those early days of gospel writing, for not whitewashing my man. Thank you, Jesus, for not being one of the straights. That gives me hope.

25. Various Places in John's Gospel: The Trickster

Here, having just treated John's story of the woman at the well, I want to make a note about humor and the archetypal image of the trickster. There is lots of irony in John's gospel. Jesus' remark to the woman at the well, in response to her statement that she had no husband is a humorous and ironic retort, He says, "You are right in saying 'I have no husband'; for you have had five husbands, and the one you are living with now is not your husband. What you have said is true!" Later on in our treatment of John we will take the story of the man born blind. At one point in that story, after Jesus has healed the blind man, the formerly blind man is closely questioned by the Pharisees, in response to their queries, he asks, "Do you also want to become his disciples?" I still grin when I read that jibe. It reminds me that there is humor in John's gospel. I wonder then, "Is it Jesus who has the ability to make the humorous cutting remark, or is it John the author of the gospel? Surely it is one of them, perhaps both.

I am also reminded that one of the time-honored and nearly universal images of those who speak for God is what C.G. Jung calls "The Trickster." The trickster is often the messenger between God and us humans. Organized religion, so often bureaucratic in its nature, does not take kindly to sly critics and usually plays down the role of the trickster. Tricksters, after all, are people who rock the boat by poking fun at those who are supposed to be above reproach, priests, ministers, bishops, rabbis, imams, and even Zen masters. It has always been a scandal to well organized religious bodies that God seems to have often chosen tricksters for his messengers. I am delighted to see this image occur in this gospel, because trickery is so often the tool of the prophet. Here it is, irony, cleverness, ridicule. I am glad to see it here. Those of us who are irreverent by nature derive hope from the trickster. It is nice to see the sly one appear in John's narrative. It is understandable that I have never once in my life heard a sermon on Jesus as sly or tricky or possessed of an ability to ridicule. Not surprising, this. Most sermons are given by the holy ones, the untouchables, indeed the very ones whom Jesus so often lampooned. All right!

26. John 4:46-54
The Royal Official's Son

The Passage

Then he came again to Cana in Galilee where he had changed the water into wine. Now there was a royal official whose son lay ill in Capernaum. When he heard that Jesus had come from Judea to Galilee, he went and begged him to come down and heal his son, for he was at the point of death. Then Jesus said to him, "Unless you see signs and wonders you will not believe." The official said to him, "Sir, come down before my little boy dies." Jesus said tho him. "Go; your son will live." The man believed the word that Jesus spoke to him and started on his way. As he was going down, his slaves met him and told him that his child was alive. So he asked them the hour when he began to recover, and they said to him, "Yesterday at one in the afternoon the fever left him." The father realized that this was the hour when Jesus had said to him, "Your son will live." So he himself believed. along with his whole household. Now this was the second sign that Jesus did afer coming from Judea to Galilee.

Commentary

Jesus comes back north to Galilee, his home country, a hundred miles north as the crow flies. from Jerusalem. He heals the son of a man who was probably a member of Herod Antipas' court. Healing is a huge part of his work. I'm aware as well that children have a special place in his message. Kids, who were so very vulnerable just about everywhere in the Roman empire of Jesus' day. They were chattel, like their mothers. Whether they lived or died depended on their fathers' good will. I remember Erik Erikson once saying that you can tell the health or sickness of any society when you see how the adults in that society take care of their children. Who was it who said, "Healing is never a private matter."? Whoever it was, she was surely right. Let me explain.

I see Jesus healing a little boy while talking to the boy's father, the child not being there. Jesus ties the boy's healing to the father's faith, so I think of that small boy's healing as a lovely symbol of Jesus' attitude toward children. They are precious. He knows that. He reaches out to them down the centuries all the way to the children I know today.. My own boys, so recently children, are grown now. They've always been dear to me. I am so grateful for having learned from my Lord how very precious they were and are, and for reminding me that even now my own faith has a lot to do with how they live. The royal official is all the fathers of the world. I am glad to be in that company.

27. John 5:1-18
Healing on the Sabbath

The Passage

After this there was festival of the Jews, and Jesus went up to Jerusalem.

Now in Jerusalem by the Sheep Gate there is a pool, called in Hebrew Bethzatha, which has five porticoes. In these lay many invalids—blind, lame, and paralyzed. One man was there who had been ill for thirty-eight years. When Jesus saw him lying there and knew hat he had been there a long time, he said to him, "Do you want to be made well?" The sick man answered him, "Sir, I have no one to put me into the pool when the water is stirred up; and while I am making my way, someone else steps down ahead of me." Jesus said to him, "Stand up, take your mat and walk." At once the man was made well, and he took up his mat and began to walk.

Now, that day was a sabbath. So the Jews said to the man who had been cured, "It is the sabbath; it is not lawful for you to carry your mat." But he answered them, "The man who made me well said to me, 'Take up your mat and walk.'" They asked him, "Who is the man who said to you, 'Take it up and walk'?" Now the man who had been healed did not know who it was, for Jesus had disappeared in the crowd that was there. Later Jesus found him in the temple and said to him, "See, you have been made well! Do not sin any more, so that nothing worse happens to you." The man went away and told the Jews that it was Jesus who had made him well. Therefore the Jews started persecuting Jesus, because he was doing such things on the sabbath. But Jesus answered them, "My Father is still working, and I also am working." For this reason he Jews were seeking all the more to kill him, because he was not only breaking the sabbath, but was also calling God his own Father, thereby making himself equal to God.

Commentary

We are back to the sabbath business here and the laws that concerned the sabbath. The man who had been healed was not supposed to carry his pallet after Jesus healed him, because it was the sabbath, and Jews did not carry things around on that day. It was a sacred day, a day of rest. In response to those who wondered how Jesus could order a man to break the sabbath rest, he replied, "My father is still working, and I am working." Obviously if you put yourself above the sabbath, that means trouble, for the sabbath rest is a divine law, well attested to in the Hebrew scriptures.[8]

I think of those words, "My father is still working" as a reminder that the God of Israel was an active God, even after the work of creation was finished. This is a God who interferes in the affairs of the world, who is present in the workings of the people. Thomas Jefferson and the Deists neglected that age-old mystery, because they were very conscious of scientific explanations for the events of the world. I know what they were doing; I sympathize with them. But there is no reason at all why God cannot be at the heart of it all, the center, the active force underneath all scientific reasoning about cause and effect, of which we know so much today. Either my Lord is present in all of it or none of it. The poet Gerard Manley Hopkins says, "The world is charged with the grandeur of God. It will shine out like shining from shook foil."

I think of that "grandeur" as at the center, not only of the universe around me, but at my own center as well. The world is, I think, an incredibly magical place, shot though with that divine grandeur. The Father is at work indeed. I think that when I am most alive, most myself, most receptive to all the millions of small things which come to me each day, at those holy times I am most aware of that Presence. It is at the heart of everything I know, everything I do, the whole shebang, all of it. Every day, every moment, every place is holy. Every movement is sacramental. Every *where* is as holy as the tabernacle holding the hosts in my parish church. Every movement is sacramental. There is no sacred, no profane, the division between divine things and other things, just this immense shadow over us all. Hopkins says in the same poem, "The Holy Ghost over the bent world broods." Oh my, that is my main mystery, my base, my fulcrum of belief. That's is how I read, "My father is still working" in St. John's gospel.

As for Jesus' apparent license telling the man to carry his pallet and leave the pool where he had rested, we have seen conflict over the sabbath before in the gospels. In this particular instance, Jesus justified his advice to the cripple by saying that he, along with his father in heaven, was lord of the sabbath.

---

8. See the book of Nehemiah 13: 51 and Jeremiah 17: 19-27.

28. John 6:1-14
Feeding the Five Thousand

The Passage

After this Jesus went to the other side of the Sea of Galilee, also called the Sea of Tiberias. A large crowd kept following him, because they saw the signs that he was doing for the sick. Jesus went up the mountain and sat down there with his disciples. Now the Passover, the festival of the Jews, was near. When he looked up and saw a large crowd coming toward him, Jesus said to Philip, "Where are we to buy bread for these people to eat?" He said this to test him, for he himself knew what he was going to do. Philip answered him, "Six months wages would not buy enough bread for each of them to get a little." One of his disciples, Andrew, Simon Peter's brother, said to him "There is a boy here who has five barley loaves and two fish. But what are they among so many people?" Jesus said, "Make the people sit down." Now there was a great deal of grass in he place; so they sat down, about five thousand in all. Then Jesus took the loaves, and when he had given thanks, he distributed them to those who were seated; so also the fish, as much as they wanted. When they were satisfied, he told his disciples, "Gather up the fragments left over, so that nothing may be lost." So they gathered them up, and from the fragments of the five barley loaves, left by those who had eaten, they filled twelve baskets. When the people saw the sign that he had done, they began to say, "this is indeed the prophet who is to come int the world."

Commentary

All the overtones and richness of the barley loaves, the proximity of Passover, the mountain. One thinks of the manna in the desert, God's guiding hand feeding Jesus' ancestors all those years ago—the Jews wandering, free from the Egyptians, but still lost, fed by the Father. One thinks as well of the bread of the Eucharist to come as nourishment for the early Christian community. So often the gospel collapses time, so that in the same moment there is the past feeding of God's people, the present marvelous meal in the Galilean hill country, and the future meals in memory of the Lord's supper.

I am reminded of the paintings of Marc Chagall, especially the ones in the Chagall museum in Nice, where in those huge blue and red canvasses about the stories of Genesis and the Song of Songs the artist mixes past and present with such deftness.[9] I think of the quality of dreams in my own life where elements of my childhood and young adulthood rub shoulders with my present fears and joys, and how things that have not yet happened in my own life are interspersed with ease and abandon with my past and present circumstances.

I have been taught since childhood to reach back to gospel scenes and to live them again, bringing them into the present time of my own mind, so that they occur again with all the power of the time when first they happened: at Christmas, Easter, and at the other great Christian feast days, all those heavy and beautiful events happening again as I say the rosary or listen to the gospels read at church or home. What was long ago is now, what has not happened is now in the beautiful and sometimes scary landscape of my mind until I wonder if time itself is not some artificial and thin deception, and the real world a melange of all times floating before me, touching me, calling me. Thank you, Lord of time, for that heavy richness of my heritage.

---

9.   There is a museum in the south of France, in the city of Nice, devoted nearly entirely to two series of paintings by Marc Chagall. The one, all done in blues, consists of depictions of the great stories of Genesis. The other, done in reds, are pictures inspired by The Song of Songs, Solomon's great love poem. In both series the artist brings yesterday to now, the past to the present, as though these things are happening right in front of the viewer.

29. John 6:22-59
A Long Discourse

The Passage

The next day the crowd that had stayed on the other side of the sea saw that there had been only one boat there. They also saw that Jesus had not got into the boat with his disciples, but that his disciples had gone away alone. Then some of the boats from Tiberias came near the place where they had eaten the bread after the Lord had given thanks. So when the crowd saw that neither Jesus nor his disciples were there, they themselves got into the boats and went to Capernaum looking for Jesus.

When they found him on the other side of the sea, they said to him, "Rabbi, when did you come here?" Jesus answered them, "Very truly I tell you, you are looking for me, not because you saw signs, but because you ate your fill of the loaves. Do not work for the food that perishes, but for the food that endures for eternal life, which the Son of Man will give you. For it is on him that God the Father has set his seal." Then they said to him, "What must we do to perform the work of God?" Jesus answered them, "This is the work of God, that you believe in him whom he has sent." So they said to him, "What sign are you going to give us then, so that we may see it and believe you? What work are you performing? Our ancestors ate the manna in the wilderness; as it is written, 'He gave them bread from heaven to eat.'" Then Jesus said to them, "Very truly, I tell you, it was not Moses who gave you the bread from heaven, but it is my father who gives you the true bread from heaven. For the bread of God is that which comes down from heaven and gives life to the world." They said to him, "Sir, give us this bread always."

Jesus said to them, "I am the bread of life. Whoever comes to me will never be hungry, and whoever believes in me will never be thirsty. But I said to you that you have seen me and yet do not believe. Everything that the Father gives me will come to me, and anyone who comes to me I will never drive away; for I have come down from heaven not to my own will, but the will of him who sent me. And this is the will of him who sent me, that I should lose nothing of all that he had given me, but raise it up on the last day. This is indeed the will of my father, that all who see the son and believe in him may have eternal life; and I will raise them up on the last day."

Then the Jews began to complain about him because he said, "I am the bread that came down from heaven." They were saying, "Is not this Jesus, the son of Joseph, whose father and mother we know? How can he now say, 'I have come down from heaven'?" Jesus answered them, "Do not complain among yourselves. No one can come to me unless drawn by the father who sent me; and I will raise that person up on the last day. It is written in the prophets, 'And they shall all be taught by God.' Everyone who has heard and learned from the Father comes to me. Not that anyone has seen the Father except the one who is from God; he has seen the Father. Very truly, I tell you, whoever believes has eternal life. I am the bread of life. Your ancestors ate the manna in the wilderness and they died. This is the bread that comes down from heaven so that one may eat of it and not die. I am the living bread that come down from heaven. Whoever eats of this bread will live forever; and the bread that I will give for the life of the world is my flesh.

The Jews then disputed among themselves, saying, "How can this man give us his flesh to eat?" So Jesus said to them, "Very truly, I tell you, unless you eat the flesh of the son of Man and drink his blood, you have no life in you. Those who eat my flesh and drink my blood have eternal life, and I will raise them up on the last day; for my flesh is true food and my blood is true drink. Those who eat may flesh and drink my blood abide in me, and I in them. Just as the living Father sent me, and I live because of the Father, so whoever eats me will live because of me. This is the bread that came down from heaven, not like that which your ancestors ate, and they died. But the one who eats this bread will live forever." He said these things while he was talking in the synagogue at Capernaum.

Commentary

A long discourse. There are a number of these long discourses in John. They are rich in sacramental themes of bread and wine, flesh and blood. They speak of his relationship with the Father; they look forward to his crucifixion and death. They tell us that he is the way to the Father. There is really nothing in the three other gospels parallel to these long discourses. They remind me of the first creation account in Genesis, the list of days and what was created in each of them ending with God's rest on the seventh day, the Sabbath.

Here is a new creation, a new order with the addition of the Son to the Father, the place of the Son in the ongoing creation, the unfolding of the divine plan. Here there is a truly terrible naming of those who do not believe—and the mention of the one who is to betray him. What is here for me, and perhaps you? John never leaves out the power of evil; and that has bothered me for most of my life, even if I know that there cannot be any freedom or choice that amounts to much without the possibility of choosing what is false or untrue or crass and self-serving. My own life has been, by most standards, an easy one. There is a cocoon-like quality in the ease of Americans of the upper middle class. We do not want. We are well schooled and well fed and well off. Those of us who have not been in the army or navy, those who have not seen war and its horror, we are even more protected.

If your entire life spreads out before and behind you, there is work, perhaps the challenge of marriage, the small betrayals and picayune bad choices of those who have security and will always have it. For us, the mention of faithlessness and punishment doesn't have much real resonance. Starvation, ethnic cleansing, air raids are simply not ours to deal with. I think John's gospel gets a better hearing from those whose lives have been uprooted and shredded like the Albanians who have been removed one way or another from their native parts of what was once Yugoslavia, despite NATO's bombs and a terrible financial squeeze applied by the outside nations of the world. It is nearly impossible for me to imagine the life of the Albanians of Kosovo, the victims of the Khmer Rouge or the Nazis, or even the victims of our own home-grown Ku Klux Klan.

The world of evil, so familiar to the writer of John's gospel, is not all that familiar to me. Even the recent attacks on the World Trade Building and the Pentagon, shocking as they are, still seem far away to me.

30. John 7:25-31
Who is the Messiah?

The Passage

Now some of the people of Jerusalem were saying, "Is not this the man whom they are trying to kill? And here he is, speaking openly, but they say nothing to him! Can it be that the authorities really know that this is the Messiah? Yet we know where this man is from; but when the Messiah comes, no one will know where he is from." Then Jesus cried out as he was teaching in the temple, "You know me, and you know where I am from. I have not come on m own. But the one who sent me is true, and you do not know him. I know him, because I am from him, and he sent me." Then they tried to arrest him, but no one laid hands on him, because his hour had not yet come. Yet many in the crowd believed in him and were saying, "When the Messiah comes, will he do more signs that this man has done?"

Commentary

What a vexing question! Who is the Messiah? We still ask who will lead us out of the tangles and tragedies of our lives. "Are you the One?" we ask. We look and we look, at this one and that one. We search; we scramble we push and shove. We do anything but wait. We don't want to be still or silent. We find the Messiah here; we reject him there. We adore and we curse by very close turns. We think that we will decide who the Messiah is, but the Messiah is who he or she is, no matter how much noise we make, no matter who we pick or don't pick. It's not up to us. The Messiah is not a will o' the wisp, coming and going, appearing and disappearing. The Messiah is here all the time, day in and day out, at night, in the early morning and the heat of the day—the Messiah is always here. It is not the Messiah who has a demon. It is not the Messiah who is evasive and slippery and two-faced. No Francis, it is not.

31. John 7:1-9 and 25-26[10]
Whence Comes the Prophet?

After this Jesus went about in Galilee. He did not wish to go about in Judea because the Jews were looking for an opportunity to kill him. Now the Jewish festival of Booths was near. So his brothers said to him, "Leave here and go to Judea so that your disciples also may see the works you are doing; for no one who wants to be widely known acts in secret. If you do these things, show yourself to the world." (For not even his brothers believed in him.) Jesus said to them, "My time has not yet come, but your time is always here. The world cannot hate you, but it hates me because I testify against it that its works are evil. Go to the festival yourselves. I am not going to this festival, for my time has not yet fully come." After saying his, he remained in Galilee.

* * *

Now some of the people of Jerusalem were saying, "Is not this the man whom they are trying to kill? And here he is, speaking openly, but they say nothing to him! Can it be that the authorities really know that this is the Messiah?"

Commentary

Whence comes the prophet?[11] *They* did not think that the prophet could come from Galilee. Who is this *they?* I find myself thinking of what you might call the religious bureaucracy. There's little question that you must have such a body of people, whether it is called the Sanhedrin or the body of governing bishops. Whether it is the Roman curia or the college of Cardinals, such people exist in all but the very smallest organizations,

---

10. These two passages in John deal only indirectly with the problem, "Whence comes the prophet. You will remember that early in Mark's gospel, Nathaniel queries, "Can any good come out of Galilee?" That's a pithy statement of the problem.

11. The word *prophet* in both Old and New Testament means someone who speaks for God. Jesus was certainly a prophet, and, Christians believe, much more.

whether they are churches or not. Businesses have them, the state has them, the armed forces have them. Even good bureaucrats, the ones who stick to what their appointed tasks are, even they have so often have a certain built in callousness, a certain endemic proclivity to miss the point. They ask, "Can the prophet come from Galilee?" The prophet often *does* come from Galilee or some other unlikely place. And most of the time, prophets being what they are, they have a tough time with the bureaucracy, the organization. Government, after all, is meant to keep order; prophets usually disrupt order.[12] Dostoevsky knew damn well that the Inquisition, which kept very good order indeed, would not recognize Jesus.[13] Even the Grand Inquisitor himself would not, and indeed did not, recognize his dominion in that famous passage from *The Brothers Kharamasov*.

What am I saying? I'm saying that we need order to avoid chaos. We really do, but we should not look for the prophet in civil servants, bishops, or the members of the Congress of these United States, even if there is the rare exception. The higher you go in any kind of bureaucracy, the fewer prophets you will find. They are usually going to ask, "Can the prophet come from Galilee? Or Peoria? Or Paw Paw? Or Bad Axe? Or Wounded Knee? I think it's important to know the limits of governments of any kind, but I'm thinking here in this context of religious government. Prophets come from all sorts of places and they are not popular with those who keep order. And that is *that!*

I wonder, "Do prophets always get crucified?" I think that the Jesuits invented casuistry in order to keep prophets from getting crucified; casuistry is the art of bending the law while showing the appearance of keeping it. One learns, as Teresa of Avila did, that sometimes one must lie when there's something important at stake. Ignatius Loyola told his

---

12. I don't know who it was who initially began the recent revelations of priestly pedophilia in our country, but I do know that the bishops of my church, good bureaucrats that they are, have tried their level best to keep such scandal concealed. Whoever has brought these things to light is surely a prophet, don't you think?

13. I'm referring here to the famous passage in Dostoevsky's *The Brothers* Karamasov. The passage is know as "The Grand Inquisitor". The grand inquisitor, the church official charged with keeping order in the church, condemns a modern version of Jesus to death.

sons, "Go in their door in order to come out your own." I do believe that prophets who stay alive, are often a little bit slippery. They know the limits of organization.

I'm not at all sure where to put Jesus in all this, because he himself did not last very long as a prophet. Can it be that the great prophets are especially bold? Especially uncaring as to whether they survive or not? Is that what "a stand up guy" is? Today, I have more understanding of the slippery prophets, I must admit, because they know the limits of systems. Jesus was not a slippery prophet.

32. John 8:1-11
The Woman Taken in the Act of Adultery

The Passage

Then each of them went home while Jesus went to the Mount of Olives. Early in the morning he came again to the temple. All the people came to him and he sat down and began to teach them. The scribes and the Pharisees brought a woman who had been caught in adultery; and making her stand before all of them, they said to him, "Teacher this woman was caught in the very act of committing adultery. Now in the law, Moses commanded us to stone such women. What do you say?" They said this to test him so that a they might have some charge to bring against him. Jesus bent down and wrote with his finger on the ground. When they kept on questioning him, he straightened up and said to them. "Let anyone of you who is without sin be the first to throw a stone at her." And once again he bent down and wrote on the ground. When they heard it they went away, one by one, beginning with the elders; and Jesus was left alone with the woman standing before him. Jesus straightened up and said to her, "Woman, where are they? Has no one condemned you?" She said, "No one sir." And Jesus said, "Neither do I condemn you. Go your way and from now on do not sin again."

Commentary

So, the story of the bad lady, much spoken of then and now, a marvelous story. It certainly is about his attitude toward the law . . . and that he knew well that all the people who wished to throw stones at her were not one whit better than she was. Who will ever know what he wrote in the sand? That's part of the power of this story. Was it their names? Was it what they had done? We don't know, but we do know the wonderful drama of it all. It is the irony of sinners punishing a person no worse than they are, and likely much better, because she doesn't have their righteous anger, their power, or their essential dishonesty. It seems to me that all Jesus really asks of us is to admit what we are. That's a lot, but it is not impossible to do. He is hard on those who sit in judgement on others rather than sitting in judgement on themselves.

33. John 8:12
Jesus as Light

The Passage

Again Jesus spoke to them, saying, "I am the light of the world. Whoever follows me will never walk in darkness, but will have the light of life."

Commentary

This is the motif of light, Jesus as light of the world. It's another of those really central themes in John's gospel. I think of candles and my life-long habit of lighting candles in churches. I think of those great womb-like interiors of the Greek Orthodox churches in Athens that so stunned me years ago with their warmth and light. The light and warmth came not from windows so much as from the hundreds of long tapers lit, each one by some person who needed to see and feel the light of their own dear Lord. I think of the whole service dedicated to light at the vigil of Easter, a service going all the way back to the seventh century in Rome, the ceremony whose great empowering weight the church still feels each Easter, the prime service, the great symbol of going from death to life.[14]

At the Easter Vigil, celebrated at night, the church building is entirely dark before the new fire comes, starting from a single great candle which stays in the front of the church all year long, burning at each Eucharist, reminding us all that Christianity is a religion of liberation through suffering, reminding us that we are a people who know both darkness and light as sisters, the one a function of the other. They are always together. One can no more exist without the other than waking can be without sleeping.

---

14. I am speaking here of the Easter Vigil service held in the dark the night before Easter in Catholic and Orthodox churches the world over.

34. John 8:31-40; 56-59
Vexing Problems:
Hatred and the Divinity of Jesus

The Passage

Then Jesus said to the Jews who had believed in him, "If you continue in my word, you are truly my disciples; and you will know the truth, and the truth will make you free." They answered him, "We are descendants of Abraham and have never been slaves to anyone. What do you mean by saying, "You will be made free?"[15]

Jesus answered them, "Very truly I tell you, everyone who commits sin is a slave to sin. The slave does not have a permanent place in the household; the son has a place there forever. So if the Son makes you free, you will be free indeed. I know that you are descendants of Abraham; yet you look for an opportunity to kill me, because there is no place in you for my word. I declare what I have seen in the Father's presence; as for you, you should do what you have heard from the Father."

They answered him, "Abraham is our father." Jesus said to them, "If you were Abraham's children, you would be doing what Abraham did, but now you are trying to kill me, a man who has told you the truth that I heard from God. This is not what Abraham did. You are indeed doing what your father does." They said to him, "We are not illegitimate children; we have one father, God himself." Jesus said to them, "If God were your father, you would love me, for I came from God and now I am here. I did not come on my own, but he sent me. Why do you not understand what I say? It is because you cannot accept my word. You are from your father the devil, and you choose to do your father's desires. He was a murderer from the beginning and does not stand in the truth because there is no truth in him."

* * *

---

15. Very frequently the expression "The Jews" refers to the elite ruling class among the Jews of Jesus' day. It is only rarely used for the common people within Jewry.

"Your ancestor Abraham rejoiced that he would see my day; he saw it and was glad." Then the Jews said to him, "You are not yet fifty years old, and have you seen Abraham?" Jesus said to them, "Very truly I tell you, before Abraham was, I am." So they picked up stones to throw at him, but Jesus hid himself and went out of the temple.

Commentary

The awful bitterness between Jesus and the Jewish authorities reminds me that this gospel was written after the destruction of Jerusalem in 70 A.D. The Romans really took Jerusalem apart after a Jewish revolt against the hegemony of Rome. The community of Christian Jews for the most part left Jerusalem before it was destroyed. The non-Christian Jews stayed in Jerusalem and many of them were slaughtered by the Roman army under Titus. The survivors regarded the Christian Jews as traitors for deserting the holy city in time of need. In the process the Christian Jewish community and the non-Christian Jews learned to hate each other. I know that all the gospels are as much the story of the early church as they are a story of Jesus' own life. This terrible rift between two communities, begins from the very beginning of the Christian movement. Both were Jewish in their roots and practice.

If it is true, as many scholars say, that the crucifixion was more the work of suspicious Roman overlords than it was of the Jewish governing leadership, then we must account for this hatred between Jews and Christians. Whether this explanation of the causes of Jesus' execution is true or not, we have a hatred between two sets of Jews going back nearly all the way to the life of Jesus. The first Christians then, were nearly all Jews. This 2000 year-old legacy is an awful tear in the robes of two ancient religious traditions, or perhaps only one tradition, depending on how one looks at it. This body of people whose basic teachings are brotherly and sisterly love combined with the love of God. This curse has been so very long lasting, so horribly durable throughout twenty centuries; it is nearly as old as Christianity itself. Sometimes it leaks backward, as it were, into John's gospel.

I myself know that hatred which lasts is *always* a two-sided affair. I really don't know of any lasting hatred in which there is only one guilty party. That's a hard thing to say, I know, but I am sure now at this late point in my life that the exceptions to two-sided hatred are very rare. It takes a great deal of wisdom and forbearance to be able to bring two hating parties together seriously, to really listen to both sides of the tangled skein of hatred in hopes of bringing them back to mutual respect for each other.

I do know as well that sometimes one party contributes more to a hatred between two than the other. Often the more guilty party is the one with more strength or power, the sharpest tongue or the support of more powerful allies or friends. Just to admit that it takes two to dance the tango of hatred is very hard, for it robs you of your right to righteous anger; it demeans your attempts at revenge if you yourself are one of the provocateurs. I think the Christian hatred for Jews and Judaism is surely two-sided in its genesis. Does that mean that Jesus must have taunted some of the Jews in his community, or at least the Romans? The Jesus in John's gospel seems to have done exactly that . . . or does the blame lie more with those who have told the story of Jesus, and that would include the author of John's gospel. The hatred in John's gospel would then have been caused in part by the enmity between the two communities after the sack of Jerusalem rather than any such bitterness on the part of Jesus himself.

What a mess this is, Christians regard the gospels as part of the inspired word of God. See the problem? What *is* clear to me is this: in every conflict, in every violent death, you simply do not know what happened without hearing both sides of the story, without listening carefully to *all* the facts.

There have been lots of examples of Christian hatred toward Jews and for Jewish hatred of Christians throughout the centuries of the Christian movement; and that is humbling for both Jews and Christians. In sum I find it unlikely that Jesus hated the leaders of his people as John portrays him. His bitterness reflects rather the enmity between the two peoples when John was writing his gospel.

As for the divinity of Jesus, let me only say that I am from a generation which has reclaimed the humanity of Jesus: his tears and anger, his fear, his disappointments, his joy. And here I am flat up against the Jesus of St. John's gospel who says clearly, "I AM." That's what God said to Moses from the burning bush when Moses wished to know God's name. It is, in the long tradition of Jewish scriptures, an unequivocally divine name; there is no hidden or cryptic language here in John. There it is; take it or leave it. And here as well is the context of bitter hatred between "The Jews" and Jesus. We have seen that this is the last gospel to be written. It was written in the light of the bitterness between Christian

Jews and the Jews who did not convert in Jerusalem . . . and this shows up in John's gospel, a later enmity being written into the gospel story. I have no quarrel with all the gospels reflecting the early days of Christianity as well as the times of Jesus himself. Much of the Bible is written with past and present events collapsed into one story. That is a very Semitic way of writing. Historians today are quite aware that even the so-called objective writers of history in our own day do not escape imposing present realities in their descriptions of the past. "History," we say, "is usually written by the victors in any time of conflict. What they write is written from the perspective of battles won and cultures which have prevailed."

Still I am shocked by the painting of "The Jews" as devils in this gospel. Still, I am aware that the divinity of Jesus seems quite clearly to have been a later belief of Christians, later than his own lifetime. John's gospel reflects that developing divinization. What do I do with this hatred between Jesus and the Jews? What do I do, for that matter, with the divinity of Jesus? Both are clear in John's gospel. And I *do* see the gospels as inspired documents, among my religion's sacred books.

I am reminded, first of all, that this is a document of the church, for it *was* chosen from among many other versions of the good news of Jesus by church officials at the end of the first four centuries of the Christian movement. I am reminded that the church even in its early years was flawed and sinful, even the church which chose this gospel as inspired. The hatred between two sets of Jews over the destruction of Jerusalem, one set of them demonizing the other, is inescapable. I've loved the image of the church as a pilgrim people for a long time. I see the church as a people on a journey, a people striving to live the message of Jesus but always with a shadow side. If it shocks me to see some of this shadow right in the gospel, then I have not taken that pilgrim title of my people seriously.

As far as the divinity of Jesus goes, well, I do lean, in the mystery of his existence, to his human side. And if St. John emphasizes a divine side of him, it does point out to me that nobody's words have ever been able to capture this great and mysterious person. I know that other religions have deified their founders and even other important people in their histories. The Romans deified Augustus, for example. The Buddhists deified The Buddha in trying to describe the mysterious greatness of his person. Part of the greatness of Islam is surely that somehow the prophet Muhammad has stayed just Muhammad, the prophet.

I do think that Jesus was indeed divine, but not in the sense that John makes him so. More in the sense of the other three gospels, who leave him more undefined, more mysteriously human and something else. Someone more divine than I or any of those who followed him, but of the same substance as us, hence we call him our *brother.* If no one has ever adequately described him down the centuries, seeing him now a rabbi, now as warrior or bridegroom, and most recently as the liberator of oppressed peoples . . . well, I am content that the centuries have seen him in many suits of clothes, and that neither the early interpreters nor those of today will ever penetrate his mystery. If he were somehow captured by this or that image, then he would not be our savior still. He would have died and been forgotten long ago. Yes, I do think that.

35. John 9:1-12
The Blind Man

The Passage

As he walked along, he saw a man blind from birth. His disciples asked him, "Rabbi, who sinned, this man or his parents, that he was born blind?" Jesus answered, "Neither this man nor his parents sinned; he was born blind so that God's works might be revealed in him. We must work the works of him who sent me while it is day; night is coming when no one can work. As long as I am in the world, I am the light of the world." When he had said this, he spat on the ground and made mud with the saliva and spread the mud on the man's eyes, saying to him, "Go wash in the pool of Siloam (which means sent). Then he went and washed and came back able to see. The neighbors and those who had seen him before as a beggar began to ask, "Is this not the man who used to sit and beg?" Some were saying, "It is he." Others were saying, "No, but it is someone like him." He kept saying, "I am the man." But they kept asking him, "Then how were your eyes opened?" He answered, "The man called Jesus made mud, spread it on my eyes and said to me, 'Go to Siloam and wash.' Then I went and washed and received my sight." They said to him, "Where is he?" He said, "I do not know."

They brought to the Pharisees the man who had formerly been blind. . . .

Commentary

I have loved this blind man of John's for most of my life. Long ago, in 1968, when I was 38 years old, I made a weekend retreat called an Antioch weekend, in New York City. I was a graduate student there, at Fordham University. The retreat was one of those high-powered deals, where they keep everyone up half the night. The four young men who gave it were the four who started the Charismatic movement among American Catholics. At the end of the weekend, we were assembled in a large room. We knelt on the floor there, a hard floor made of flagstones joined with mortar and polished to a high sheen. We were all in a circle around the sides of the room, facing the center. There was a small book of the gospels being passed from person to person around the room. When it was passed to you, you had the chance to pray out loud.

When the book came to me, I spoke as one who identified with the blind man in John's gospel. I spoke as one who was still blind, there on the stones of that floor. I asked that I might see. Speaking there on that floor was a holy moment for me, filled as I was with the knowledge of my blindness, yet hoping to see, drawn to the light there in the gloom of the room. We were there for a couple of hours, yet the time passed very quickly. It was a long time to be on your knees, yet I felt no stiffness or pain.

Most of the fifteen or twenty people in that room spoke when the book came to them, but I was not bored or jumpy. It was all of a piece, that time. Perhaps it was what the Australian aborigines call "the dream time." I was the blind man there, kneeling, hoping with the others. The others were mostly students at Columbia University, with a few from Fordham, like me, intermingled. It was a deep time, nothing else mattered to us except our presence there together. We were swept up in the moment, most of us. Nothing else mattered. I knew I *was* that blind man. That was me, unseeing yet hoping. And that is who I still am now, more than thirty years later. The story fits me, and I do think I have company. So if the blind man actually received his sight in the story, I was hopeful of receiving mine some day via the same Jesus who enabled the blind man to see, and I am hopeful still!

36. John 10:1-18
The Good Shepherd

The Passage

"Very truly, I tell you, anyone who does not enter the sheepfold by the gate but climbs in by another way is a thief and a bandit. The one who enters by the gate is the shepherd of the sheep. The gatekeeper opens the gate for him and the sheep hear his voice. He calls his own sheep by name and leads them out. When he has brought out all his own, he goes ahead of them and the sheep follow him because they know his voice. They will not follow a stranger, but they will run from him because they do not know the voice of strangers." Jesus used this figure of speech with them, but they did not understand what he was saying them.

So again Jesus said to them, "Very truly I tell you, I am the gate for the sheep. All who came before me are thieves and bandits; but the sheep did not listen to them. I am the gate; whoever enters by me will be saved, and will come in and go out and find pasture. The thief comes only to steal and destroy. I came in order that they may have life and have it abundantly.

"I am the good shepherd. The good shepherd lays down his life for his sheep. The hired hand, who is not the shepherd and does not own the sheep, sees the wolf coming and leaves the sheep and runs away because a hired hand does not care for the sheep. I am the good shepherd. I know my own and my own know me, just as the Father knows me and I know the Father. And I lay down my life for the sheep. I have other sheep that do not belong to this fold. I must bring them also, and they will listen to my voice. So there will be one flock, one shepherd. For this reason the father loves me, because I lay down my life in order to take it up again. No one takes it from me, but I lay it down of my own accord. I have power to lay it down and I have power to take it up again. I have received this command from my Father."

Commentary

I gave a homily on this passage in Brussels, Belgium, years ago, in French! I recall saying that it was interesting that Jesus picked sheep as a metaphor for his followers, because, as I said, "Les agneaux sont stupides!"[16]

This was a brief homily to my fellow students at Mass in an international center for pastoral studies affiliated with the Gregorian University in Rome. Its name was Lumen Vitae. I was one of about a hundred and fifty students there from forty different countries, studying pastoral psychology, new approaches to scripture study and new ways of teaching religion. If there was anybody stupid in that group, I don't know who it was. In any event, they loved my homily and promptly gave me the nick name of "L'Agneau."

So, why did they like what I had to say? I think it was because my remarks were earthy and picaresque. So often preachers about the Good Shepherd wax eloquent and pious, gushing this way and that about this gospel metaphor for Jesus. The followers of the shepherd were the elect after all, the chosen, the best, just as Jesus was the best, and yet the gospel message makes those early ones out as a pretty rough lot: blind guys, beggars and such, and it wasn't just "The Jews" who didn't get the message, it was his own followers as well, dumb country folk who wanted him to be some kind of hot-shot king, so that this hairy lot could eat at linen covered tables, drink lots of wine and just generally live it up in the face of the smart ones, the rich ones, anybody in fact who was privileged by class or power, any of those who looked down their noses at this raggedy prophet and his equally raggedy followers.

Now that was food for thought! The stupid ones were the chosen ones. How very odd! Now I note that anyone whose thinking of churchy things was to the left of center looked attractive to my fellow students. The ones among my fellows there in Belgium whom I loved best were a rambunctious and even raggedy lot: lay women from Central and South America, young priests who had a bit of the rascal in them. They were not the "best" students in the school. These were the ones who threw a dance at the Jesuit house on boulevard St. Michel at the end of the school year. They didn't mind being called "Les Agneaux" one single bit. They knew, I think, that being one of the smart ones was not the key to the kingdom Jesus spoke of.

---

16. "Lambs are stupid!"

37. John 11:32-44
The Raising of Lazarus

The Passage

When Mary came where Jesus was and saw him, she knelt at his feet and said to him, "Lord, if you had been here, my brother would not have died."[17] When Jesus saw her weeping, and the Jews who came with her also weeping, he was greatly disturbed in spirit and deeply moved. He said, "Where have you laid him?" They said to him, "Lord, come and see." Jesus began to weep. So the Jews said, "See how he loved him!" But some of them said, "Could not he who opened he eyes of the blind man have kept this man from dying?"

Then Jesus, again greatly disturbed, came to the tomb. It was a cave, and a stone was lying against it. Jesus said, "Take away the stone." Martha the sister of the dead man, said to him, "Lord, already there is a stench, because he has been dead four days." Jesus said to her, "Did I not tell you that if you believed you would see the glory of God?" So they took away the stone and Jesus looked upward and said, "Father, I thank you for having heard me. I knew that you always hear me, but I have said this for the sake of the crowd standing here, so that they may believe that you sent me." When he had said this, he cried out with a loud voice, "Lazarus, come out!" The dead man came out, his hands and feet bound with strips of cloth, and his face wrapped in a cloth. Jesus said to them, "Unbind him, and let him go."

Commentary

What a rich story! I think of Lazarus as standing for all of us who would be free, all of us who have died one way or another. The picture of Lazarus coming out of the tomb, almost a mummy, with burial cloths still hanging on his body, strikes me still as both terrifying and hopeful, striking ever so close to the core message of Christianity, the coming from death to life. I think of the way Central Park in New York City looks in the winter time, trees blackened with the soot of Manhattan. The

---

17. The Mary referred to is neither Mary Jesus' mother nor Mary Magdalene. This Mary is the sister of Jesus' friend Lazarus, whom he raised from the dead.

grass, the bushes, brown and dead. The park's paths strewn with thrown away candy wrappers, cardboard boxes flattened by the snow and ice, old and empty cigarette packages, everything grimy and gritty. Yet Spring, when it comes, emerges from all that death. It comes impossibly, surely, deliberately, breaking through the black bindings of winter's desolation and dirt. The black trees leaf out and flower; the grass is once again green; the birds return from the South; the park is once again, impossibly beautiful.

Lazarus, like Spring, gives me hope. G.K. Chesterton once said in a poem about this story, "My name is Lazarus and I am free!" Lazarus is my brother. He is perhaps yours as well.

38. John 12:1-8
Mary of Bethany Washes his Feet

The Passage

Six days before the Passover Jesus came to Bethany, the home of Lazarus, whom he had raised from the dead. There they gave a dinner for him. Martha served, and Lazarus was one of those at table with him. Mary took a pound of costly perfume made of pure nard, anointed Jesus' feet, and wiped them with her hair. The house was filled with the fragrance of the perfume. But Judas Iscariot, one of his disciples, (the one who was about to betray him), said, "Why was this perfume not sold for three hundred denarii and the money given to the poor?" (he said this not because he cared about the poor, but because he was a thief; he kept the common purse and used to steal what was put into it.) Jesus said, "Leave her alone. She bought it so that she might keep it for the day of my burial. You always have the poor with you, but you do not always have me."

Commentary

This passage was read at Mass during a retreat I made with nuns, priests and lay people in Belize City, 1966. I had been sent to the tiny Central American country of Belize to teach in the Jesuit high school there. I had gotten close to a nun, a Sister of Mercy, during the discussions which we had during the retreat. The retreat was held at St. Catherine's Convent in Belize City. It was very hot there and I was worn down from the long and difficult year in the blistering heat and humidity of that country.

When that story of Mary's anointing Jesus' feet was read, these words struck me: "The house was filled with the fragrance of the perfume." It seemed to me that the small church where we worshiped somehow contained that scene in John's gospel again. That the perfume filled every inch of that chapel—this woman's courage and love coming right with the smell of the perfume. I gave the homily at public worship that day. In it I spoke of my sense of how that profound gesture was with us that day, there in the heat, touching us all. As I spoke I was just overcome by that scene. It sometimes happens when you're tired or not well, or just plain down, that there's a special window of your heart open. That window is quite firmly shut in ordinary times, when things are going well, and you're not scared of what tomorrow may bring, or the day after that, or the weeks still to be played out in the sadness of that time.

It is on such days that this window of your heart sometimes opens; and readings or perhaps the people with whom you are at the moment take on a special intimacy, because you're just too tired and down to keep up your normal and every day defenses. That reading and the friendship of a young nun I'd never seen before reached right into my heart and suffused all of me with a sense of beauty and closeness. It carried with it no guarantee that I'd get over my bone-deep fatigue or that I'd be all right somehow there, a lonely young priest in the stifling heat of that a tropical country. It was just a brief and touching moment of reprieve. I was grateful that it enveloped me that day, crowding out all the heaviness of that year and all the worry about what would come to me next. I can feel that moment still. And I am glad it is still with me.

39. John 12:12-16
His Triumphal Entry into Jerusalem

The Passage

The next day the great crowd that had come to the festival heard that Jesus was coming to Jerusalem. So they took branches of palm trees and went out to meet him, shouting,

> "Hosanna!
> Blessed is the one who comes in
> The name of the Lord—
> The King of Israel!"

Jesus found a young donkey and sat on it; as it is written:

> "Do not be afraid, daughter of
> Zion.
> Look, your king is coming,
> Sitting on a donkey's colt!"

His disciples did not understand these things at first; but when Jesus was glorified, then they remembered that these things had been written of him and been done to him.

Commentary

This is another story of hope for me, and perhaps for you. In a way I have always dreaded Jesus' Passion, the tale of his suffering and death. It is so sad and heavy; none of the gospels treat it lightly. Each gives the dark details of the supper, the betrayal, and all the ghastly and loaded bits of this and that which surround the event we call "The Passion". The gospels go through the Passion in slow-mo, perhaps to let us all know inescapably and forever that there are forces of evil which grow and flourish in the presence of someone good. There is a kind of inevitability there in the gospels. There is a collision course. He has told his friends and followers that it is coming, but they have not wanted to believe it, neither they nor I. The gospels' trick of twinning the people whose story it tells, with all those who have come later is never clearer than in the passion. They are not just *they*. He is not just *He*. They are also us; He is also now. I'd known that in my heart long before I read Edouard Schweiser and the other scripture scholars who write about the literary forms in the gospels.

They who explained how time in the gospels is so often not just then alone, but both earlier and later than the time of writing, echoing back and forth through the centuries, and lived again in the lives of the people who came later.

This is why the Transfiguration and the joyous entry into Jerusalem are so very important. We need them to balance what is to come. They give us a bit of Easter . . . and the gospel writers knew that those who later read these stories would need that. As I write these notes, I think of Joe and Matt and Johanna, my two sons and my daughter-in-law to whom I have dedicated this book and for whom I have written it. They are with me as dear ones whom I hope will learn to look for joy and hope in times of sorrow. My family has always done that. There is always a clown at family funerals, and there must be, because as a clan we've never been half-way people. We are a vulnerable people, often unguarded. We are high or low, but not often in the middle in the gamut lines of joy and sorrow. "In medio stat virtus" was written for somebody else.[18] So, to see him on a donkey's back, with kids singing, with people waving palms and making rude, unfettered noises, oh we do need that. My God, do we need that. And I do not think we are alone in this need.

---

18. This old Latin aphorism is translated "Virtue lies in the in the center, in a balance of joy and sorrow, feast and famine."

40. John 12:23-26
The Grain of Wheat

The Passage

"The hour has come for the Son of Man to be glorified. Very truly, I tell you, unless a grain of wheat falls into the earth and dies, it remains just a single grain, but if it dies, it bears much fruit. Those who love their life lose it, and those who hate their life in this world will keep it for eternal life. Whoever serves me must follow me, and where I am there will my servant be also. Whoever serves me, the Father will honor."

Commentary

This is another old image, old in my heart that is. The grain of wheat must be put into the ground and die before it can sprout with new life. These words sound almost oriental to me. This saying could be a koan offered by a Zen master to one of his young monks in training. What does it mean? Indeed what *does* it mean, this paradox, this juxtaposition of life and death?

Something in us all must die if something else can come to birth. This aphorism contains the center of Christianity within itself: the Passion, the Death, the Resurrection, His and also mine. The scripture scholar David Stanley once put it this way, "Christianity is a religion of liberation through suffering;" I tucked that short sentence into my heart and mind more than thirty years ago. It was said by Stanley in a large lecture class devoted to St. Paul's letters at Fordham University in the summer of 1968. William James said something like it in *The Varieties of Religious Experience* when he compared Christianity to Buddhism. "Both religions," he noted, "have suffering at their very heart."

I note that the first of the four noble truths of Buddhism states baldly, "Life is suffering." I muse that this is not a very cool thing for the Buddha to have said. Cool in the sense of how we often use that word today in a consumer society. The advertising people like to gloss over the dark side of life when they want to sell you a new Buick or a miraculous hair conditioner. Many of the ads I see and hear on the tube, on the radio, and in the daily paper hint broadly that this beer or that car, this shampoo or that razor blade will produce in its owner an absence of suffering. Yup, they really do that. And if I try out the new triple blade approach to shaving and find that my life is even remotely better today than it was yesterday, then I can take this grain of falsehood tucked in to a mountain of lies and somehow keep my own illusion that somehow, some way, if I use enough of the right stuff, it will all be well with me, Jesus and the Buddha not withstanding.

The older hucksters, Jesus and Buddha, are more honest than the new ones. They do offer triumph and joy but they don't let me have it for free, or for a very small cost. The freedom they offer is a very costly freedom. So far, I have had only glimpses of it, but those patches of peace really are touched with the serene. An old man's serenity is dearly paid for. It is the result of a thousand doubts and sad moments, a thousand sweet and joyful times. When you are old, you have a little higher ground from which to view the sorrows and joys of the world. This is a certain detachment in old age. Most of your job is done. Perhaps you have more time to be still, to listen, to observe. It is a special time in one's life. Serenity is not by any means something which envelops me. It is a beautiful, some-time thing. I have more of it than when I was younger . . . it is not as flashy as the hots of younger times . . . but it is very, very beautiful.

41. John 13:3-17
Jesus Washes the Feet of his Disciples

The Passage

Jesus, knowing that the Father had given all things into his hands, and that he had come from God and was going to God, got up from the table, took off his outer robe, and tied a towel around himself. Then he poured water into a basin and began to wash the disciples' feet and to wipe them with the towel that was tied around himself. He came to Simon Peter, who said to him, "Lord, are you going to wash my feet?" Jesus answered, "You do not know what I am doing, but later you will understand." Peter said to him, "You will never wash my feet." Jesus answered, "Unless I wash you, you have no share with me." Simon Peter said to him, "Lord, not my feet only, but also my hands and my head." Jesus said to him, "One who has bathed does not need to wash, except for the feet, but is entirely clean. And you are clean, though not all of you." For he knew who was to betray him; for this reason he said, "Not all of you are clean."

After he had washed their feet, had put on his robe, and had returned to the table, he said to them, "Do you know what I have done to you? You call me teacher and Lord—and you are right, for that is what I am. So if I, your Lord and Teacher, have washed your feet, you also ought to wash one another's feet. For I have set you an example, that you also should do as I have done to you. Very truly, I tell you, servants are not greater than their master, nor are messengers greater than the one who sent them. If you know these things you are blessed if you do them.

Commentary

One of the old, old rituals of Christianity has its roots in this story. When the ceremonies of Easter time began to be revised among Roman Catholics in the mid nineteen hundreds of the century just past, I was studying philosophy at St. Louis University, a Jesuit in training. I was assigned to help in the rituals of the Easter triduum at the neighboring St. Malachy's parish. I was about twenty-four years old then. St. Malachy's was a largely African-American parish run by the Jesuits. Father Fred Zimmerman, S.J. was the pastor there. A young woman from this parish had broken the color bar for undergraduate students at St. Louis University some years before, with the help of Claude Heithaus, S.J. and John

Markoe, S.J., over the objections of the president of the university. Claude, for his pains was given a public penance in front of the entire Jesuit community attached to the university during the evening meal. He was on a train headed for a different Jesuit house far from St. Louis the next day. A distinguished scholar, he did not return to the university for decades. He was there as an old man when I taught here as a young priest in the late sixties, a warrior who had paid his dues.

St. Malachy's then, has a special place in the history of racial integration at St. Louis University. I'm glad to have been there when the ancient practice of foot-washing again became a part of the church ceremonies on Holy Thursday. Fred Zimmerman washed the feet of his black parishioners that evening for the first time, in the sanctuary of that old church as a part of the evening's liturgy. Everybody there knew what that meant. I'm proud to have been there, witnessing a distinguished white man washing the feet of his parishioners.

The theme of that washing in St. John's gospel is that of Servant. Jesus washed the feet of his followers, pointing out to them in this ritual cleansing that this is how one acted as Boss in the Kingdom of God. The church has never lived up to that ceremony, but I'm still glad we do it. There's no escaping its meaning: those closest to the Christian message are to serve the others. I think of eating lunch with my son Matt and a street guy we both know just last Saturday. The street guy is a middle-aged black man named Jim. For a few dollars he had helped me clean the basement of our house. I hope that the years of being a part of the ceremony of foot washing, known as The Maundy, had something to do with my cooking lunch for Him. I'm proud of *that* too!

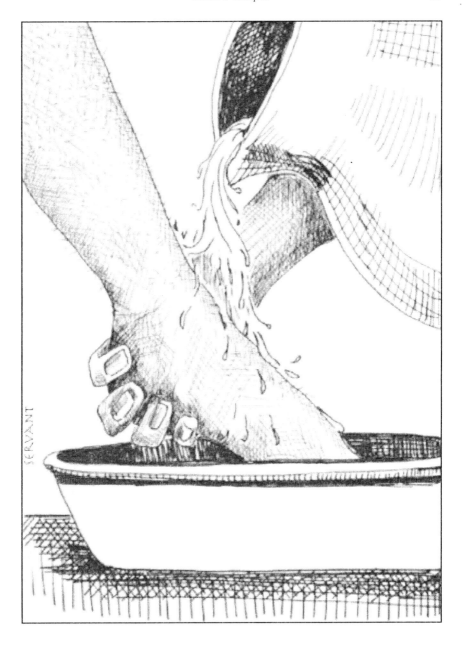

42. John 13:34-41
The New Commandment

The Passage

"I give you a new commandment, that you love one another. Just as I have loved you, you also love one another. By this everyone will know that you are my disciples, if you have love for one another."

Commentary

Well, here it is, the heart of it all, "By this shall everyone know you, by the love you have for one another." Everything in the Christian message comes back to this one thing. It is the heart, the center, the *sine qua non* of the gospel. I was teaching in St. Louis at the Jesuit university when this came home to me with a thump. Here's how I put it in an under-graduate class on the Christian Tradition: "You can do anything you want, and if it doesn't hurt anyone, it's not wrong. That *is* the Christian code of ethics." "Anything?" a student asked. "Yes, anything at all," was my answer.

Today, it still seems amazing to me that the whole moral law could reduce itself to this one sentence. It has stood there carved in the stone of St. John's gospel down through the centuries while thousands upon thousands of books have been written about morality, about the law, this and that fine distinction about this or that case of conscience. My moral theology text in the seminary was bound in two thick volumes of the thinnest paper, paper so thin it was hard to turn the pages without wetting your finger. A certain Genicot-Salzman, S.J. was the author. Every word of the text was written in Ciceronian Latin sentences. One whole volume of the set was on the niceties of sexual morality. And so I wonder, "Was there any sense in all that commentary?" And in addition to such heavy texts on moral theology there was and is in my church, another heavy volume which contains the particular laws binding all members of the Roman Catholic Church, in addition to what Jesus had to say. That book and revisions of it is called the *Codex Juris Canonici,* in English *The Code of Canon Law.* Its many pages required of us an entire full year's course of study.

There is a terrible irony in all this. I do know that one can defend these laws and rules as merely spelling out the one great law of love, but I'm not at all sure I looked at it that way during those long years of study at St. Mary's College, the divinity school of St. Louis University. I almost forgot to mention all the rules and rubrics for the celebration of Roman ritual. That body of rules covers yet another book!

I have learned as well, that not everyone can be at home in a form of Christianity so burdened with law and distinctions. Those laws and their accompanying subtleties can be an unsupportable burden for some kinds of people who have come to be Roman Catholics. One must take all of them with a grain of salt. One must learn to be subtle about all this. One must learn to bend the law. The whole history of the Society of Jesus has to do with learning complex ways of making such complexity liveable for ordinary people. Subtle reasoning is very close to the heart of the Jesuit Order. The early Jesuits knew very well that someone had to take this huge mass of accumulated law and custom which has grown up through the twenty centuries of the Christian Roman tradition, and cut through it for ordinary, and one presumes, less subtle people. That's what casuistry is all about . . . and it is very easy to get lost in that forest of distinctions to the point where the mother lode of love is forgotten.

The Jesuits, after all, as one of my scripture professors was fond of noting, himself a Jesuit, are the Pharisees of Christianity. I do know that there *are* reasons for law. Law embodies, we hope, the spirit of the U.S. Constitution. Law is meant to embody Jesus' command of love. All large systems have laws. Without traffic laws nobody would be able to drive to work in the snarl of cars that would shortly develop if one took down all the traffic lights, speed limit signs and such. Countries, cities, and universities are complex organizations. Without rules they would be chaotic, but there is a heart to all of it, whether secular or profane, and that heart is simple. Forget it and all law becomes trivia.

43. John 14:1
Do Not Let Your Hearts Be Troubled

The Passage

"Do not let your hearts be troubled. Believe in God; believe also in me."

Commentary

There are a number of times where this and the other gospels speak this message of the untroubled heart. It has warmed me over the years. Where does it say, "Learn of me, for I am meek and humble of heart, for my yoke is easy and my burden light?"

I see the truth here. It reminds me of a well known mystic of my generation, Jesuit Father Frank Ring. Frank once told me when I had come to visit him in at his parish down in a small town in Belize that his voices, both the interior one and the voice of his director, told him not to be in too much of a hurry, not to try so hard, not to always be looking for new ways to do penance, not to try to prove his generosity.[19]

"Do not let your hearts be troubled," the gospel says. That has to do with letting go. One of my cousins told me that a gifted advisor had given him the following advice: "When you have noticed yourself having this or that worthy cause between your teeth, when you are straining every muscle over some inconsequential bit of doing good, say to yourself, 'Mark, let go! Just let go.'" I think of a lovely song by John Lennon, written after he had left The Beatles for a quieter life, its title, *I Just Had to Let it Go.*" Wise words, these.

---

19.   Frank Ring, S.J. was a Jesuit priest and mystic whom I interviewed in Belize during the summer of 1999. He was an old friend of mine, going back five decades. He died two years after my visit.

44. John 14:1-4
The Dwelling Places in the Father's House

The Passage

"Do not let your hearts be troubled. Believe in God, believe also in me. In my father's house there are many dwelling places. If it were not so, would I have told you that I go prepare a place for you? And if I go and prepare a place for you, I will come again and take you to myself, so that where I am there you may be also. And I know the way to the place where I am going."

Commentary

I learned the "dwelling places" as "mansions" (in an older translation) and loved the grace of that word—"There were," Jesus said, "Some really good places at Dad's." All this a reflection on what we today call "heaven." There are all sorts of hints about it in the gospels, none of them strike me as fitting the description I learned by heart as a boy, taken from the *Baltimore Catechism*. This last in turn was taken from some Christian writers. We called heaven "the beatific vision," not a very arresting phrase. I think the general idea was that the beauty of God is such that you could just look at him (always a HIM!) forever and ever and never get bored. The idea of staying in one spot forever comes pretty close to a good description of hell for me. I don't stay in one place very long without getting the fidgets.

My favorite philosophy professor, no doubt reflecting the thought of Thomas Aquinas, used to say of heaven, "Ho, there'll be no resting there; there will be ceaseless intellectual activity!" On another occasion he told me that he thought of heaven as a place where there would always be someone to argue with . . . and I knew he dearly loved a good fight, matching his wits with some worthy adversary. What about me and my mansions? Well, I do hope that whenever I die, my place of residence will be *roomy*. *Woodsy* wouldn't be bad either. I'd want my favorite people there, as long as wishing seems to be part of this description. I'm not so sure about the Beatific Vision.

My godmother told me once when she was an old lady, knowing that she would die soon, that she really didn't know what would come to her at the time of her own death, maybe something, maybe nothing at all. Whatever it was, she was tired of waiting for it and devoutly hoped to get on with things, so that she could find out. My own heaven is mostly one of hopes. I do believe that my dear Lord loves me, so I'm not "deathly" afraid of death. I think there have been some informed "hot guesses" about future life, but they seem to me to be just that, hot guesses, some hotter than others. There's heaven; there's hell. For Catholics there is mention of half-way houses on the journey toward heaven where one can become purified before standing in God's presence. The operant term is Purgatory.

Many religions seem to think that there should be some sort of shining up period—whether zipping off to Purgatory or getting recycled until you get smart enough to be ready for the big show, life "in the mansion".

By way of conclusion in this matter of *mansions,* I do think that you and I should make a friend of death. Our society's image of everybody as beautiful and young doesn't help much. Madison Avenue does not let you admit that you're getting old, and hence closer to death. The ad men say that women are supposed to have gorgeous, long legs, good hips, firm tits, and good teeth . . . all their lives! Jesus! And we who are men (males) have been ordered to have flat stomachs, piercing eyes, chins with no fat on them, our bodies tall and tanned . . . We are to look like a Marlboro cowboy, jeans on our slim legs and muscles under our t-shirts. That is perhaps a little better than today's ghastly ideal for women, but both these visions are toughies for a nation of fat people as well as people who are inevitably approaching death via the aging process. It might be nice if those who decide these things featured guts and butts. I must admit, I wouldn't mind at all being a sort of perpetual Marlboro man for the duration of whatever heaven is. This worthy cowboy does, after all, spend a lot of time outside in the weather. It would be lovely if the company there were good too. Amen.

45. John 14-17
Lost in The Great Prayer

The Passage

(I am not going to print it out here; it is simply too long.)

Commentary

There is a very long passage there in John from the chapter thirteen right through chapter seventeen. All sorts of goings and comings. Threats and promises of peace. Forebodings like "They will put you out of the synagogues." It goes on and on. I've never been all that clear on what to make of this long passage called *The Great Prayer*. But I do know this: there are days in my life very much like these passages which today elude me, days that leave me small and confused, the long hard days, often in Winter, when my back aches and my spirit droops. The sun is more absent than present—and I feel dried out or cold. There *are* those.

When those days are with me I have little sense of direction and not much joy. What to make of them? People do say that they are a part of it all. They are the dark nights. It doesn't do to fight them too much. One *does* emerge from the winter times, usually, and in my life so far, always. Some day, as well, I may see clearly what the *Great Prayer* in John's gospel is about. In the meantime I think of long and confusing times as well as long and confusing scripture passages as opportunities to joke about things. It is well to have some other task to do, something simple, something I won't be tempted to rush, something I understand. I think it good as well to see the people I love, and to remember old and dear sayings, the mantras that have served me well over the years. It is important not to run away too fast, like a badly frightened soldier in a battle. To stay then, to face the wintery dragon, to keep a rhythm of work and rest, to see my dear ones, to know that my own ability to be compassionate to others is born of hard times. In dark times it helps me to remember the old slogan, "They can't chase you if you won't run." Somebody else is going to have to explain John's Long Prayer to you!

46. An Aside on my Family

N.B. It might well be a good idea to leave this passage out of a published form of these notes.

I have not said in these notes, not yet anyway, that I'm writing them as a small present for my sons Joe and Matt and for Matt's bride, Johanna. So you dear ones, I've been thinking of you in these mornings of the past months, months which have now stretched out to more than three years. I've been thinking how proud I am to be a father to two of you and an in-law father to the third.

I often think of your ages, and what I was doing when I was the same age. I was getting my first real taste of teaching at Rockhurst High School in Kansas City, Missouri. I taught first and second year Latin, and after classes were over each day I worked in the school gymnasium taking care of athletic equipment and being in charge of the student managers of the various sports we had at that school. There were five hundred boys in the school at that time. The teachers were mostly Jesuits, six or seven seminarians and a larger number of priests. There were three athletic coaches, two Math teachers, and a couple of English teachers who were lay people, but everyone else was a member of the Society of Jesus, the Jesuit Order. I'd been a Jesuit for seven years at that time, two years a novice, two years a junior studying languages, and three years a philosopher studying the philosophy of Thomas Aquinas.

Those seven years began for me in the fall of 1949 when my mom and dad drove me out to the Jesuit novitiate on the first of September. I was nineteen years old and bored to death with college. I'm not all that sure why I joined the Jesuits, except that I did want to help people somehow, didn't like college, and the Jesuits were a respectable alternative to working for my dad, which I did **not** want to do. He was much too large in my life for me to make my living working for him. There was just too much of him. I wanted to leave home too. So, there were the Jesuits. My dad's brother was an S.J. I had gone to school in Jesuit schools ever since starting high school—four years at St. Louis U. High, three semesters at Holy Cross College in Massachusetts and one semester at St. Louis University. One of my best friends at Holy Cross had joined the Jesuit Order a year before . . . and I had a Jesuit mentor named Father Bakewell Morrison, who gently steered me toward the Order. I remember throwing a half-smoked Chesterfield cigarette out the window my dad's car as we drove solemnly out to the Jesuit novitiate, ten miles or so from where my family lived.

The novitiate was only ten miles from home but it might as well have been a continent away. I didn't spend a single night at home for the next twenty years. I thought it a bit like joining the Marines. There was a war on in Korea. Some of my friends were in that. One of them got killed two weeks after he arrived in that country. Anyhow, at the age of twenty-six I was assigned to Rockhurst High School and was there for three years, the standard time in those days for what we called Regency. I was green as grass in the teaching business, never having taught anything except catechism to the grade school kids. I'd had a tough time studying St. Thomas—ugh! I had chronic headaches and got all Cs in my philosophy courses graduating from St. Louis University on the same day as my younger sister. She graduated *magna cum laude* with a major in philosophy and a specialization in creative writing. She was in the first graduating class of a part of the university called The Writer's Institute, a special program for aspiring writers.

So, these days I think of the three of you and wonder where you'll wind up and who your future companions will be. I wonder if you at your age have anything in common with me when I was your age, teaching high school. This summer I'll go to the 40th anniversary celebration of the graduation of the first class I taught at Rockhurst, the class of 1959. Forty years is a long time.

I think of you three as at some kind of turn in the road. Matt's band is probably going to lose their bass guitarist.[20] That guitarist has been very important to the band. That impending loss underlines the possibility of breakups, and how fragile young alliances are.

Joe seems to me to be looking off a precipice as well. Joe, we have talked lately about my mom's comment to me when I was younger than you are now. "Be grateful you're not a cabbage." I chuckle at that comment now and wonder if there have *ever* been any cabbages in my extended family. I can't think of any as I sit here on my heels in my prayer room writing. (By cabbages my mother was referring to people with little initiative and not much imagination.)

---

20. Both my sons are singers in Rock and Roll bands. Both write some of the songs they sing. Matt is married and lives next door to me and my wife. Joe is single and lives a few miles away.

Looking back to my late teens I remember how I felt alone in making a series of decisions which led me to the Jesuits. Neither my mom nor my dad provided much except their presence. I wasn't worried that they'd flip out if I did this or that, but I knew it was up to me when I left Holy Cross College in January of my second year there, and came home to St. Louis University. I was worried about my older sister . . . I wanted to help. She was at home having been pretty much dragged back from her escape to Greenwich Village in New York, where she had been living what was then called The Bohemian Life: lots of literary stuff, drinking, more sexual freedom, the American version of the Left Bank of Paris. Our parents did not approve of this life-style.

We two returnees from the East both enrolled at St. Louis University that January. My dad bought us a second hand, black Plymouth sedan that I promptly named *The Black Bastard.* Between the two of us that Winter and Spring we dented the hell out of the car's front end in a series of minor accidents. We parked it each night in the driveway at home in such a way that dad couldn't see the dents. He was not happy when he finally realized how much we banged up the old B.B. I went out for track at St. Louis U., running the mile and the two mile distances. I took English, Latin, Logic, Spanish and World History there at the university and did not do well. I was bored silly by all of it.

The following fall I entered the Jesuits and my older sister went off to a very expensive private mental hospital in Baltimore, where she stayed for most of a year. I had no idea what was wrong with her except that she was wild and didn't get along with my parents. My mom read her mail in an effort to keep track of her, and had a fit when she ran away to New York, changed her name and had an affair with one of our distant cousins. When I came back from Holy Cross, there she was at home in St. Louis on a pretty short leash, having been dragged back from New York by my parents, as I mentioned earlier. She and my mom were at loggerheads . . . and my Dad was, I think, protecting his twenty-year old daughter from all the bad guys, which pretty much included any male animal she chose to cultivate. So, you see, I was good and she was bad; it stayed that way from then on in the eyes of my family . . . and it is still that way after all these years. Wow! I escaped from all this mess, at least in body, when I entered the Jesuits, and I was glad to be gone.

My early training, called the novitiate, was fun—not so much study. I thought I was going to be a saint and was disgustingly pious, sincerely of course, but that made it all the more disgusting. My sister was back there in Baltimore trying to get her cool back. She came home after a year there and not long after all that became engaged to a charming, intelligent and somewhat feckless man with gobs of money and only occasional employment. The engagement didn't last. They broke up but have remained friends over the years right up to the present moment.

I'm not sure what she did in the next couple of years, stayed home, made her debut to St. Louis society and then married a newspaperman when I was studying philosophy in St. Louis. The marriage didn't last all that long, long enough for her to have her first child, whom you all know. Things were pretty crazy; I think she discovered a bit of her beloved Greenwich Village right in St Louis. A couple of years after the birth of her first child she moved to England and had another son, by writer. She didn't stay very long in London with him.. I never met hm. She moved back to St. Louis, never living far from my parents. She and my parents struggled over the rearing of those two boys and they lived as much at my parents' house as they did with their mother. I'm not sure when she met her third husband, but I do know that he was a part of the Bohemian scene in the Gaslight Square area of St. Louis. She married him, as you know, and had three more children by him.

All this time I was laboring away in the Jesuits—four years at Florissant, which was out in the country at that time, and not the large suburb of St. Louis that it is today. After four years my class and I went to St. Louis University for three years of Philosophical study, living right down town on the campus of St. Louis U. My younger sister and I were there at the same time. She was a great favorite with the Jesuits there and an excellent student, not as wild as her older sister. She married a local artist 1957, when I was teaching Latin at the Jesuit high school in Kansas City.

My purpose in writing this small sketch of those years is to let you know that none of the three of us born into my family had an easy time of it settling down. All of us were and are up and down people, subject to great enthusiasms and equally great periods of melancholy and desperation. In many ways all three of us have been vagabonds, living alternately in Europe or the United States, now here, now there, but somehow bound to our family with very strong ties, ties which often enough were very hard to see as anything but manacles. We all have a quality of fierce independence, even defiance in the face of the rules of church and the customs of family which have bound us together. I'm sure these notes on the gospels reflect some of that defiance, some of that intelligence, and some of the strange love that has bound each of us more closely than we'd like to the family and social class we have come from. So when I write a commentary on the gospels, it is as much an autobiography as it is thoughts on the message of Jesus.

47. John 18-19
The Passion

The Passage

I am not going to spell out the whole two chapters here. Better for you to take up your New Testament and read them for yourself.

Commentary

I have feared the Passion and loved it all these years. Over and over it has come back to me like an old magical robe, familiar with age, never worn out, always fresh, always fearsome. The cloth of this robe, strangely, is soft and usable. The Passion after all, is for Christianity what the four noble truths are for Buddhism.[21] It puts hard times right at the center of the Christian message. There he is, across the Kidron creek on a hill in the dark, outside among the olive trees, waiting. Judas comes with the soldiers. Peter takes a swing at Malchus with his sword, Malchus the high priest's servant. They take Him. He doesn't try to get away. This is how it is. Imagine facing all that with calm.

Off and on, all of your life, you get clobbered . . . from birth it's there like a shadow—wherever you go at whatever age. Jesus is no exception. He moves into it. He knows there is no escape. There is something focused about this. He doesn't speak here of resurrection. I think of Reinhold Niebuhr's prayer, "God, grant me the serenity to accept what I cannot change . . ." Why is the Passion a comfort? I think because it is honest and does not try to fool me . . . it is there . . . and my religion teaches me that I can go through it. This man who is my prophet, my hero, my Lord, He has been here, in the dark. He knows what it is. He does not make slick promises of easy deliverance. I see a Spring day's evening in Jerusalem, the stones, the trees, the friends, and the betrayer. This is a piece of everyone's life—the shadows there in the flickering summer night. It is long before dawn, the sun buried, the moon carrying blood in its pale rays. It's what we all dread and what we all know.

---

21. The four noble truths of Buddhism are: 1) All existence is suffering. 2) All existence is passing. 3)There is no permanent soul. 4) The path that leads to the cessation of suffering is the Buddhist path.

48. John 18:25-27
Peter

The Passage

N.B. This is after Jesus has been captured and taken away.

Now Simon Peter was standing and warming himself. They asked him, "You are not one of his disciples, are you?" He denied it and said, "I am not." One of the slaves of the high priest, a relative of the man whose ear Peter had cut off, asked, "Did I not see you in the garden with him?" Again Peter denied it, and at that moment the cock crowed.

Commentary

I think of this scene at night, in the shadows, not cold but crisp enough for Peter to want to warm himself by an open fire. It was a terrible and terrifying time. Everyone had run away, all Jesus's followers save a few women. The whole Jesus thing had happened very quickly, just a year or two, but here both direction and pace were even more bewildering. Where had it all gone? What was going on? The Great One taken with the brutal swiftness of those who have nearly absolute power.

I am reminded of my younger sister's suicide thirty years ago, so final, so swift, so total. True, she had lived with an emotional disease for a long time, perhaps a bi-polar disorder. Death was always there in the shadows of her affliction, but there had been hope that she would recover.[22] Then that phone call from my dad. I was driving a taxi cab in Ottawa, just beginning my doctoral work at the University of Ottawa, just married to my dear one, having left the Jesuits and the priesthood, when my father gave me the news of her death. Suddenly she was gone. Thirty-six years old, sole alone there in a London flat with the gas jets turned on and the room sealed. There in the silence as the flow of gas filled her room, swift, sure, deadly, no one to see its quiet and deadly passage. No second or third chances. She was gone.

---

22. Joan Gross Canepa took her own life by sealing up her London apartment very carefully so as to make it air tight, and then turning on the gas of her stove in the kitchen without lighting the incoming gas. She was thirty-six years old, mother of two young children, separated from her husband and children, living in London, England alone.

Peter then, at the fire, numb, frozen, and lost, he says those words of rejection about the man he loved, "I know not the man." And there was a lot of truth in that lie. He knew Jesus but he did not know that bound up in Jesus there was, inescapably, suffering. Peter is all of us; he is my sister Joan. I know that. In that cold comfort I know that I am not alone here. As the poet Hopkins said,

> "It is the blight man was born for
> It is Margaret you mourn for."

49. John 18:28-38
Jesus before Pilate

The Passage

Then they took Jesus from Caiaphas to Pilate's headquarters. It was early in the morning. They themselves did not enter the headquarters, so as to avoid ritual defilement and to be able to eat the Passover. So Pilate went out to them and said, "What accusation do you bring against this man? They answered. "If this man were not a criminal we would not have handed him over to you." Pilate said to them, "Take him yourselves and judge him according to your law." The Jews replied, "We are not permitted to put anyone to death." (This was to fulfill what Jesus had said when he indicated the kind of death he was to die.)

Then Pilate entered headquarters again, summoned Jesus, and asked him. "Are you the King of the Jews?" Jesus answered, "Do you ask this on your own, or did others tell you about me?" Pilate replied, "I am not a Jew, am I?" Your own nation and the chief priests have handed you over to me. What have you done? Jesus answered, "My kingdom is not from this world. If my kingdom were from this world, my followers would be fighting to keep me from being handed over to the Jews. But at it is, my kingdom is not from here." Pilate asked him, "So you are a king?" Jesus answered, "You say that I am a king. For this was I born, and for this I came into the world, to testify to the truth. Everyone who belongs to the truth listens to my voice." Pilate asked him, "What is truth?"

Commentary

When I was in my teens I had a black and white print of an etching of Jesus before Pilate. I brought it with me to the novitiate in the large leather-bound New Testament my mother gave me when I entered the Society of Jesus. Jesus in the picture is dressed in white, the garment of a fool. He is looking at Pilate who is seated perhaps a dozen feet away. There is a small tear in the long white garment Jesus wears. The tear is up at the top where the open neck lies upon his shoulders. He is looking directly at Pilate with his expression of anger and defiance. This is a *man* here.

I cherished that picture instinctively because the dignity and fierceness of Jesus. I don't think I'd ever seen anything, any picture, where he was so very obviously unafraid and defiant. So powerful, none of the sweetness of the traditional Sacred Heart pictures I'd known all my life, none of the despair of the scarecrow Christ on the cross. This was a man . . . I revered him like that with his head up, looking directly at the seated Pilate and his soldiers. His pride is what I'm thinking of. I kept that picture; I guarded it very privately for years. It disappeared the way anything you owned disappeared in the Jesuits. We traveled around a lot and we traveled light. We didn't carry much. I may have forgotten it was in that New Testament my mother gave me when we turned in all our possessions just prior to taking first vows. Eighteen years after those vows, when I left the Jesuits, I packed everything I owned in an old, olive-drab army footlocker, the same size as the one I'd come with to the novitiate. Jesuits aren't long on *stuff,* at least this one wasn't. At any rate the picture was no longer with me when I left, but the memory of it was strong then, as it is now.

So, that fierce pride of Jesus dressed in the white garment, those flashing eyes, they were my alpha and omega then. And in a way they still are—so bare and proud, so utterly unbent. This one wasn't just anybody's prophet, not then, not now.

50. John 19:25-28
The Crucifixion

The Passage

. . . standing near the cross of Jesus were his mother, and his mother's sister, Mary the wife of Clopas, and Mary Magdalene. When Jesus saw his mother and the disciple whom he loved standing beside her, he said to his mother, "Woman, here is your son." Then he said to the disciple, "Here is your mother." And from that hour the disciple took her into his own home.

After this, when Jesus knew that all was finished, he said (in order to fulfill the scripture), "I am thirsty." A jar full of sour wine was standing there. So they put a sponge full of wine on a branch of hyssop and held it to his mouth. When Jesus received the wine, he said, "It is finished." Then he bowed his head and gave up his spirit.

Commentary

At the cross are John and Jesus' mother, and some other women. The Passion, especially at the end, becomes more and more the province of women. The men ran away; the women stayed there, at the end. There is a deep imprint of women in Jesus's life in both John's gospel as well as Luke's narrative. I think of his mother Mary, the woman at the well, Lazarus' sisters, Mary Magdalene and various women at the scene of his death. Bernard Cooke, a young and intelligent Jesuit theologian, once addressed me and my fellow Jesuits in training on the subject of the relationship of Jesus with women. Cooke said Jesus' relationship with women was a scandal during his earthly life just as it is a scandal now. He voiced the comment of a mythical bystander, "These young rabbis are all alike." To say that Jesus was a ladies' man is not too strong, I think, anymore than to say that the very early Christian community was a ladies' church. That conviction has grown with me down the long years since I first read the gospels.

This conviction of mine is no thin piece of fashionable feminism. Through the seventy years of my own life I can look back on a real treasury of women friends. I have a memory of bathing with my mother as a very small boy in her own bath tub, one of my own earliest and dearest memories—her skin tone, her breasts, her calmness and delight there in her bathroom with green tiles on the walls. She had a trick of making a soap bubble by putting her thumbs and index fingers together, forming a triangular space filled with the thin and shining surface of a soap bubble.

I had two sisters, no brothers, and there were always two other women who worked for my mother living in the house during my entire childhood and youth, until I left home. I have had women as friends throughout my life. If you take them all together these women, older and younger, were a huge part of whatever in me was feminine and loving and romantic. I think of everyone of these women often.

And so I have been glad that Jesus was very close to so many women, even here at his death. Odd perhaps for me to feel this way, I who spent twenty years leading a celibate life. They have made a long chain leading to Toni, my dark lady, with whom I have spent the last thirty years, following two decades as a Jesuit. Toni, my wife with whom my life has been so tied and entwined in every thing I have done and felt and thought these past three decades.

I am grateful that my prophet Jesus' own short life was so clearly marked at key times by the women who loved him and the women he himself loved in turn. I do enjoy knowing this in the face of another old strand of Christianity which has sought to cover with real embarrassment the women in Jesus' life and the women in the lives of those who came after him, that the pious managers in black have wished down the ages that these very close ones had not besmirched the pure gospel message with their love, their bodies, and their very clear mark, engraved indelibly on his life and the early shocking years of those who came after Him.

51. John 20:1-18
Resurrection

The Passage

Early on the first day of the week, while it was still dark, Mary Magdalene came to the tomb and saw the stone had been removed from the tomb. So she ran and went to Simon Peter and the other disciple, the one whom Jesus loved, and said to them "They have taken the Lord out of the tomb, and we do not know where they have laid him." Then Peter and the other disciple set out and went toward the tomb. The two were running together, but the other disciple outran Peter and reached the tomb first, He bent down to look in and saw the linen wrappings lying there, but he did not go in. Then Simon Peter came, following him, and went into the tomb. He saw the linen wrappings lying there, and the cloth that had been on Jesus' head, not lying with the linen wrappings but rolled up in a place by itself. Then the other disciple, who raced the tomb first also went, and he saw and believed; for as yet they did not understand the scripture, that he must rise from the dead. Then the disciples returned to their homes.

But Mary stood weeping outside the tomb. As she wept, she bent over to look into the tomb; and she saw two angels in white, sitting where the body of Jesus had been lying, one at the head and the other at the feet. They said to her, "Woman, why are you weeping? She said to them, "They have take away my Lord, and I do not know where they have laid him." When she had said this, she turned around and saw Jesus standing there, but she did not know that it was Jesus. Jesus said to her, "Woman, why are you weeping? Whom are you looking for? Supposing him to be the gardener, she said to him, "Sir, if you have carried him away, tell me where you have laid him, and I will take him away." Jesus said to her, "Mary!" She turned and said to him in Hebrew, "Rabbouni!" (which means teacher). Jesus said to her, "Do not hold on to me, because I have not yet ascended to the Father. But go to my brothers and say to them, 'I am ascending to my Father and your Father, to my God and your God.'" Mary Magdalene went and announced to the disciples, "I have seen the Lord"; and she told them that he had said these things to her.

Commentary

He is gone; He is Not gone. There is much running about and confusion among the men. What's going on? Mary Magdalene is at the heart of it. I am reminded that when we celebrated the resurrection of Jesus on Easter in the Jesuit novitiate where I began my training, there were purple cloths of mourning which entirely covered the many marble statues in the chapel, a large, Romanesque church with a barrel-arched ceiling rising fifty feet above the floor and pews. Those purple wrappings had covered the statues for the forty days of Lent symbolizing that penitential season. They were well fastened with pins around each life-sized statue for the whole forty days which preceded the Easter celebration. At the ringing of the bell for the Gloria at Mass on Easter Sunday these large purple draperies suddenly disappeared. They were drawn very quickly through a hole in the vaulted ceiling above us, each having been pulled by a very fine and nearly invisible cord. One of the Jesuit brothers lay on the other side of that hole in the space between the church roof and the ceiling and pulled those cloths with great dexterity, seemingly miraculously up into the heavens above. There was no noise at all, nor was any explanation forthcoming later. Only the choir singing the Gloria, and the organ, which had been silent for the forty days of Lent was blasting away full born in accompaniment to the choir. Magic!

He was alive! Magic indeed, that event so much at the heart of the Christian message. In the past two decades I have come to understand that all the magical stories of the resurrection in the gospels are about the first Christian community's experience of the empowering presence of Jesus with his people after his death rather than an historical account of his bodily exit from the tomb. That has been a wonderful insight for me. In all honesty though, I who loved Santa Claus as a child, am somewhat bereft at the loss of the literal meaning of the resurrection of Jesus and the stories in which it is told.

His words to Magdalene, "Do not touch me, I am not yet ascended to my Father" indicate that He is present but not the same as before. I think of the story of the two disciples on the road to Emmaus, not told here in John's gospel, those two disciples who walked with the risen Jesus, not knowing it was he, and then later "recognized him in the breaking of the bread." They are wondrous stories, filled with the truth of the presence of Jesus among his people in the days, the weeks, the months and years following his crucifixion and death.

Easter is a morning feast, the old Latin from the Easter Mass, "Valde mane Sabbatorum" still rings in my ears.[23] I associate Easter with dew and flowers, new life, echoing the shadows and light in the cave of Christmas where his life began. I am reminded, as I have noted earlier, of the trees in New York's Central Park during the waning weeks of Winter. They become so blackened with soot, so carbonized that they seem quite literally to be dead. The walks in the park at that time of year are covered with sodden leaves and colored scraps of paper, pieces of plastic all packed together into a dense rug, bound by the muck of the ground. There are patches of dirty snow and dark footprints which seem to be the prints of death himself.

And yet, when Easter comes, each year those dead trees bloom and leaf out in the chilly air of Spring. The breaking through, the swelling tendrils, moving ever so slowly and surely in the silence, the return of birds from the South, the rainbow, all these are a part of it. Death is so very palpable in the Winter's black and brown, so heavy and damp, so cold. In this connection I used to write a letter to a favorite former student of mine every Easter time. She had married, her husband having died after only a few years of union. She had only her baby to live for . . . and Spring's slow and magical movement. Easter's resurgence of life meant much to her, as it has meant much to me. Winter grinds me down. In later years I've associated back packing during the Spring holiday break at my university with Easter. I have gone each year at the beginning of March to the Smoky Mountains in Tennessee with a close friend to walk through the days of early Spring with hope once again alive in my cramped soul and body. I experience in those days a rebirth, a dawn.

The new fire ceremony of my church is a part of it as well, the lighting of the Easter candle, symbol of a resurgent life. The death of winter is so very deep. As I get older it lodges in my bones, a very real ache in my fingers and toes, in my shoulders, the dullness of it, the numbing darkness. It is this slow magic of new life that comes by inches and seconds that is Easter for me. It lies next to despair in the tomb.

------

23. Translated "Very early on the morning of the Sabbath." It refers to the women who came to the grave to anoint the body of Jesus, only to find the tomb empty, the Saviour risen from the dead.

I associate it with that huge Easter candle I mentioned above, used in many Christian churches, lit for the first time in the dark hours before dawn on Easter Sunday. It is a great and lively salute, a sacred erection, shockingly stiff right there for all to see in the church. I find a delicious scandal in that fat candle. And I am reminded of all those roadside lingam shrines I once saw in the mountains of India.[24] I saw them in the late mountain spring almost twenty years ago, and I still hear my niece Priya Helweg's amused explanation to me concerning the significance of those smooth and upright stones gracing so many roadside shrines. Priya said, "Uncle Frank, those are what guys have." Our Easter candle is not so different from those Indian lingams. It is a bold and unvarnished sign of life and creativity. It means that Jesus is alive and among us still. He is risen indeed. Alleluia!

---

24. The phallus of the Hindu god Shiva or its emblematic representation.

52. John 21:1-14
At the Charcoal Fire

The Passage

After these things Jesus showed himself again to the disciples by he Sea of Tiberias; and he showed himself in this way. Gathered there together were Simon Peter, Thomas called the Twin, Nathanael of Cana in Galilee, the sons of Zebedee, and two others of his disciples. Simon Peter said to them, "I am going fishing." They said to him, "We will go with you." They went out and got into the boat, but that night they caught nothing.

Just after daybreak, Jesus stood on the beach; but the disciples did not know that it was Jesus. Jesus said to them, "Children, you have no fish, have you?" They answered him, "No." He said to them, "Cast the net to the right side of the boat, and you will find some." So they cast it, and now they were not able to haul it in because there were so many fish. That disciple whom Jesus loved said to Peter, "It is the Lord!" When Simon Peter heard that it was the Lord, he put on some clothes, for he was naked, and jumped into the sea. But the other disciples came in the boat, dragging the net full of fish for they were not far from the land, only about a hundred yards off.

When they had gone ashore. They saw a charcoal fire there, with fish on it, and some bread. Jesus said to them, "bring some of the fish that you have just caught." So Simon Peter went aboard and hauled the net ashore, full of large fish, a hundred fifty three of them; and though there were so many, the net was not torn. Jesus said to them, "Come and have breakfast." Now none of the disciples dared to ask him, "Who are you?" because they knew it was the Lord. Jesus came and took the bread and gave it to them, and did the same with the fish. This was now the third time that Jesus appeared to the disciples afer he was raised from the dead.

Commentary

"Just after daybreak, Jesus stood on the shore." I see the mists on the lake. He is here on the beach with the fire burning next to him. What then? Like most of the passages on which I have written, this one goes very far back for me, fifty years at least. It is that feel of the morning chill, the sunlight. He is never "the old Jesus" in these Easter comings. He is here now, suddenly, when they don't expect Him. It is that aura which touches me, that freshness. A new chapter has begun. He is no longer just a companion. Now he comes and goes. They don't always know who it is at first. Something is going on. Indeed, all the earlier miracles on water, the "nature" miracles in all four gospels have only to do with the closest ones, the twelve, now the eleven. All have a common edge to them. "Without me you can do nothing." Dominic Crossan's phrases for the Easter appearances are "his empowering presence" and "Easter took a long time." How wonderful to make note of that continued presence after his death by telling a story. For a long time now the stories about Jesus have spoken more clearly to me than the centuries of philosophy about his continued presence after his death. Words like "hypostatic union" and "the substance of Jesus is present in the consecrated bread and cup under the accidents of bread and wine."

How much better to use as a guide the way small groups of Jews read from the book of Exodus at Passover time, at the Seder meal. The event of the Exodus is told again and experienced again by this or that small knot of Jews down three millennia in all sorts of remote parts of the world. I recall that just inside the entrance door of Sephardic synagogues the world over is a small rectangular sand box filled with sand.[25] An old Sephardic synagogue I once saw in the Virgin Islands had such a sand box, perhaps seven feet by four or five. One could not gain entrance to the building without walking through that sand. It represents of course the sand of the Sinai peninsula through which and over which Moses and his fledgling Jews walked those forty years in days long gone by. When you go in that building you walk those old steps again, just as you walk them again at Seder. This is not just a story. It is the very long journey which one still walks in the footsteps of Moses and the very first Jewish people. It is the ancestors present, the deed done again.

So, Easter is, I think, the deed done again. So is the presence of Jesus in the bread and wine. It is real, or as the Beloved Apostle said in that fishing boat in the passage I'm writing about, "It is the Lord." He

---

25. The Sephardic Jews are the branch of the Jewish People who spread outside Palestine to North Africa and Spain. When they were expelled from Spain in 1492, they scattered to the New World in many places, including the Virgin Islands

was there then, just as he is here now when you read the Easter stories. When I sing that old sweet song of love called the gospel, "Were you there?", I can say, "Yyes I was; Yes, I am; I am there now. He is here now. He really is.

Part Three

The Gospel According to Matthew

53. Matthew 1:1-17
The "Begats"

The Passage

An account of the genealogy of Jesus the Messiah, the son of David, the son of Abraham.

Abraham was the father of Isaac, and Isaac the father of Jacob, and Jacob the father of Judah and his brothers, and Judah the father of Perez, Zerah, and Tamar, and Perez the father of Hezron, and Hezron the father of Aram, and Aram the father of Aminadab, and Aminadab the father of Nahshon, and Nahshon the father of Salmon, and Salmon the father of Boaz by Rahab, and Boaz the father of Obed by Ruth, and Obed the father of Jesse, and Jesse the father of King David.

And David was the father of Solomon by the wife of Uriah, and Solomon the father of Rehoboam, and Rehoboam the father of Abijah, and Abijah the father of Asaph, and Asaph the father of Jehoshaphat, and Jehoshaphat the father of Joram, and Joram the father of Uzziah, and Uzziah the father of Jotham, and Jotham the father of Ahaz, and Ahaz the father of Hezekiah, and Hezekiah the father of Manasseh, and Manasseh the father of Amos, And Amos the father of Josiah, and Josiah the father of Jechoniah and his brother, at the time of the deportation to Babylon.

And after the deportation to Babylon: Jechoniah was the father of Zerubbabel, and Zerubbabel the father of Abiud, and Abiud the father of Eiliakim, and Eliakim the father of Azor, and Azor the fathgr of Zadok, and Zadok the father of Achim, and Achim the father of Eleazar, and Eleazar the father of Matthan, and Matthan the father of Jacob, and Jacob the father of Joseph the husband of Mary, of whom Jesus was born who is called the Messiah.

So all the generations from Abraham to David are fourteen generations; and from David to the deportation of Babylon, fourteen generations; and from the deportation to Babylon to the Messiah, fourteen generations.

Commentary

When I was a young man we called this list of Jesus' ancestors "the begats" because an earlier translation translated "was the father of" as "begat". It's a long list of names not all that familiar to contemporary people. Whatever else it is, it's not history. There are too many omissions. I think of Homer's list of ships. I think of today's obsession with genealogies.

I've a friend who has traced her family line back in time to pre-Revolutionary War days and have found myself wondering why that was so important to her, that long list of names. I think she wants to know who she is, and to savor the fact that there really are some interesting people in her background and that she herself has worth. She doesn't want to be a cipher herself. So she reaches back in time and finds comfort in interesting people in her bloodline. Those people make her proud of herself, and justly so. She *is* somebody.

Erik Erikson describes the crisis of old age as one of Integrity versus Despair. I think that lists of ancestors have to do with integrity and pride in one's own legitimacy versus the despair that is integrity's counter-player. Despair being the knowledge that one doesn't amount to much, as well as the knowledge that there will be no second chances, or precious few of them once most of one's life has been lived. You have to stand for what your past has brought you, because the past is most of what you now have, the future being of not long duration.

So Matthew composes this litany of ancestors taking Jesus back first to David, the first of the line of Hebrew kings after Saul, and then to Abraham, the shadowy ancestor of all the Jews. Matthew makes it very clear that Jesus is Jewish with respectable ancestors, going all the way back to the father of all believers, Abraham. I ask myself, "Is this like The Daughters of the American Revolution?" Those famous snobs who trace their lineage back to those who fought in the American Revolutionary War. I remember that some members of the D.A.R. tried to prevent Marian Anderson from singing in Washington, D.C. in a large public venue, because Ms. Anderson was black and the daughters didn't want any tar-brush singing in a respectable place in the cradle of the republic.

Do you suppose Matthew is just a snob? His efforts at making his Messiah are very thin history, after all. Maybe he wanted a Messiah with a first-rate background in order to make respectable this peasant from a backwater town named Nazareth. You could look at it that way and not be entirely wrong. I think it depends on the stature of the person you are trying to legitimate. The fact is that Jesus was and is a paradox. He is more famous precisely as one who came of Endsville (read Nazareth) in a backwater area (read Galilee) in a very unimportant small province of the Roman Empire (read Palestine). I think Matthew wants to remind his readers that his Man was Jewish, a Jew's Jew. And it is perfectly true that if one pushes one's ancestors back far enough in any given people, you'll find *somebody* who is famous by the very mathematics of it all. Matthew is pointing proudly to the history of his own people as the ancestors of Jesus. A country fellow might put it this way: "This here Jesus is a Jew boy; no ifs, ands or buts." And so he is.

54. Matthew 1:18-25
Joseph's Dilemma

The Passage

Now the birth of Jesus the Messiah took place in this way. "When his mother Mary had been engaged to Joseph, but before they lived together, she was found to be with child from the Holy Spirit. He husband Joseph, being a righteous man and unwilling to expose her to public disgrace, planned to dismiss her quietly. But just when he had resolved to do this, an angel of the Lord appeared to him a dream and said, "Joseph, son of David, do not be afraid to take Mary as your wife, for the child conceived in her is from the Holy Spirit. She will bear a son, and you are to name him Jesus, for he will save his people from their sins." All this took place to fulfill what had been spoken by the Lord through the prophet:

> "Look the virgin shall conceive
> And bear a son,
> and they shall name him
> Emmanuel,"

which means, "God is with us." When Joseph awoke from his sleep, he did as the angel of the Lord commanded him; he took her as his wife, but had no marital relations with her until she had borne a son; and he named him Jesus.

Commentary

And so, the famous story of his miraculous conception and birth. I ask myself, "What does it mean?" I know there have been other miraculous births in the Bible. Abraham's Sarah conceived a son miraculously, whose name was Isaac.[1] You will recall that The Lord was having lunch with Abraham and mentioned that he and Sarah would have a son. Sarah was listening in on the conversation and laughed because she and Abraham were old people; she was no longer having her period. So she laughed at the Lord's promise. Isaac, you will recall, is the Hebrew word for laughter. Isaac, after Abraham is the one from whom the Hebrew people are

---

1. Genesis 18:1-15.

all descended. And then there was Samson's birth, and the birth of Samuel.[2] Both of these men were great champions of the Jewish people. The account of their births tells us that from the start the hand of God was on each of them.

So, Mary's conception of Jesus had forebears with Sarah, the mother of Isaac, with the unnamed mother of Samson, with Hannah, the mother of Samuel. In the Bible the birth of a baby with no human father points out that this one is from God. I think it is quite clear that in Jesus' day and before, it was commonly thought that a father placed a tiny germ of a person in the mother. She was the receptacle in which the child grew, nothing more. We were a while getting to know about sperms and eggs in the reproductive process. The child then, when born would be a kind of clone of the father, whether human or divine.

So much for the biology of the ancient world. I'm not here going to presume what the actual biology of these births was. I want to see only what the accounts mean for all these famous Jewish men of God. It means that this one is destined for greatness. The hand of God is in a special way upon this person, as well as his mother. Something wonderful is occurring here and from its very conception this one will be different from the others.

I know that Matthew's gospel was written for Jews rather than Gentiles and that they would be familiar with the stories of the births of Isaac, Samson and Samuel. I'm not sure what to do with Joseph's dilemma, except to note that his enlightenment about the whole situation occurred in a dream! Dreams are important in the Bible; and Biblical people put more stock in them then modern people have done, up until recently. Freud's insistence on the importance of dreams was a discovery with antecedents! I wonder myself if I had had a dream about some important choice in my life, would I have paid attention? Suppose I'd had a dream in which an angel advised me not to go to graduate school. I think I'd have gone anyway.

What is the importance of Joseph's dream then? I think it is a powerful indicator that God's voice to us is almost always a hidden voice rather than a direct one. The divine voice is not like the voice one hears on the radio or on TV or on the phone. It requires a real sensitivity, an openness, and kind of alertness to the voice of another world. A kind of

2. Judges 13:1-24 the account of Samson's birth. I Samuel 1:1-29 the account of Samuel's birth.

willingness to hear the divine will as it appears indirectly in the circumstances of our lives. A modern psychologist might say that one must be in touch with one's interior voices if one is to live life fully. I think of Joseph as such a person, a man sensitive to the voice of God as it appears in the ordinary and extraordinary events that are a part of anybody's life.

I note, in closing, that there is nothing in Matthew's account which indicates that Joseph and Mary refrained from sex after the birth of Jesus. Nor is there anything in the text precluding later brothers and sisters of the Lord. I'm not sure I want to be holier than the Biblical account here. There is a Christian tradition that Mary was forever a virgin, but it strikes me as very thin, considering the lack of evidence in the gospels. May I respectfully ask, "What's so great about married people refraining from sex?" I wonder whose idea *that* was!

55. Matthew 2:1-12
The Visit of the Wise Men

The Passage

In the time of King Herod, after Jesus was born in Bethlehem of Judea, wise men from the East came to Jerusalem, asking, "Where is the child who has been born king of the Jews? For we come to pay him homage." When King Herod heard this, he was frightened, and all Jerusalem with him and calling together all the chief priests and scribes of the people, he inquired of them where the Messiah was to be born. They told him, "In Bethlehem of Judea; for so it has been written by the prophet:

> 'And you, Bethlehem, in the land
> of Judah,
> are by no means least among
> the rulers of Judah;
> for from you shall come a ruler
> who is to shepherd my
> people Israel.'"

Then Herod secretly called for the wise men and learned from them the exact time when the star had appeared. Then he sent them to Bethlehem, saying, "Go and search diligently for the child; and when you have found him, pay him homage." When they had heard the king, they set out; and there, ahead of them went the star that they had seen at its rising, until it stopped over the place where the child was. When they saw that it had stopped, they were overwhelmed with joy. On entering the house they saw the child with Mary his mother; and they knelt down and paid him homage. Then opening their treasure chests, they offered him gifts of gold, frankincense, and myrrh. And having been warned in a dream not to return to Herod, they left for their own country by another road.

Commentary

Who has not followed a star? I have, and you have too. People all over the world consult the signs of the zodiac. You don't follow a star the way you would follow someone in a car. If the stars were that close, earth would be burned to a cinder. Granted, the planets move, but I wouldn't want to try to follow their track from way down here. So, I wonder, what did these Magi, the wise ones, do? Who were they? And above all, what does their journey mean?

There is nothing about number in the account. We don't know how many there were. It's clear that they were not Jewish. They simply "came from the East." They bore princely gifts. They consulted Herod the Great, a satrap king appointed by the Romans, a toady to Roman power. He is known to have been ruthless. And he is portrayed as such by Matthew. Herod is an historical character. Nobody knows whether or not the wise ones were merely symbolic or whether they were real people. Contemporary Biblical scholars, most of them, see the Magi as symbolic. What do they symbolize? They symbolize the world outside Jewry. They are the earliest patron saints of the Gentile world. That's you and me. Their feast, that of Epiphany, is a very old one, older than Christmas. Matthew, somewhat surprisingly, is telling his Jewish audience right from the start that the message of Jesus, if primarily delivered to the Jewish people, is directed to those outside Jewry as well. It is a celebration of the wideness of the Christian message, a message for all people and all nations. Christianity, like Buddhism and Islam is a missionary religion; its followers bring its message to others. We moderns know that a message meant for everyone can be beautiful, but it can also be destructive. The wideness of God's mercy is the beauty; the tendency on the part of those who spread the gospel has often been one which discounted the religions of other people and their cultures. That's the beast.

I know a story of a Dutch, Christian missionary in Africa who lived a small group of native people there;he baptized no one. He merely lived with the people in their village. He told them that in perhaps a generation or two, when the people really knew what his religion was about, perhaps then, and only then, would there be, could there be, a real local branch of Christianity and not an ersatz Western form of religion imposed on a people to the extinction of their own very legitimate culture and religious beliefs.

I know as well, of Jesuit missionaries in China and Paraguay who came to different cultures with great respect for the religious wisdom and culture of the people. The most famous of them, Matteo Ricci, is still honored in China; his tomb is in Beijing. His respect for Chinese ancestor worship, his interest in Chinese painting, architecture, and Mandarin prose got him into trouble with his more narrow minded superiors in far away Rome. His wisdom was condemned, his work nearly forgotten until modern times, when he has emerged as a great seminal figure in the history of ecumenism and the movement among believers in various religious traditions to respect each other's religious messages and insights.

So, the wise men cast a long shadow on Christianity. There is nothing in their story which indicates that they abandoned their own culture or religious beliefs in their paying homage to the one born king of the Jews. That this different kind of a king would make the likes of Herod nervous is not hard to understand.

56. Matthew 2:13-13-23
A Massacre and a Journey to Egypt

The Passage

Now after they had left, an angel of the Lord appeared to Joseph in a dream and said, "Get up, take the child and his mother, and flee to Egypt, and remain there until I tell you; for Herod is about to search for the child, to destroy him." Then Joseph got up, took the child and his mother by night and went to Egypt, and remained there until the death of Herod. This was to fulfill what had been spoke by the Lord through the prophet "Out of Egypt I have called my son."

When Herod saw that he had been tricked by the wise men, he was infuriated, and he sent and killed all the children in and around Bethlehem who were two years old or under, according the time that he had learned from the wise men. Then was fulfilled what had been spoke through the prophet Jeremiah:

> "A voice was heard in Ramah,
>   wailing and loud lamentation,
> Rachel weeping for her children;
>   she refused to be consoled,
>   because they are no more."

When Herod died, an angel of the Lord suddenly appeared in a dream to Joseph in Egypt and said, "Get up, take the child and his mother, and go to the land of Israel, for those who were seeking the child's life are dead." Then Joseph got up, took the child and his mother, and went to the land of Israel. But when he heard that Archelaus was ruling over Judea in place of his father Herod, he was afraid to go there. And after being warned in a dream, he went away to the district of Galilee. There he made his home in a town called Nazareth, so that what had been spoken through the prophets might be fulfilled, "He will be called an Nazorean."

Commentary

The gospels are not without blood. That has always frightened me. The story of Herod's massacre of "The Innocents" is a gruesome tale, and I must ask myself, "What does it mean?" It could be that it is just what happened, something recorded by Matthew for us to shudder at and wonder that such violent means would be taken to eliminate a possible rival to Herod's throne, or whatever king might come after Herod. Far more likely, it is a heavily symbolic tale. There is no record anywhere of such a massacre, for one thing. For another, we have seen that these infancy narratives in Matthew are well within the forms of Semitic literature of the time as commentaries and reflections on the significance of Jesus as Messiah rather than mere historical recountings.

I find it useful to prescind from the question of the historicity of this account, and ask the question which is so central to this book, "What does it mean?" I recall that Matthew's gospel is directed to a Hebrew audience, people who were familiar with what we call *The Old Testament*. Matthew is presenting Jesus as a part of a sacred Jewish tradition. So he links his story with the story of Joseph from the book of Genesis, Joseph the dreamer, the son of Jacob, who journeyed to Egypt, became powerful in the court of the Pharaoh, and eventually brought all his brothers and their families to live there, where they stayed until Moses led them away from Egypt and back to the land of Canaan, the Promised Land.

Matthew links his Joseph to the great Joseph of centuries gone by, both having acted under messages from God received in dreams. Matthew is tying Jesus to the history of his people as Messiah. You will recall that Moses led his people out of Egypt to freedom. The return of Joseph, Mary, and the Child echoes this earlier journey of liberation. Matthew wants us to see Jesus as the new Moses.

We have a rich weaving here. Don't try to read it the way you'd read a tightly organized and linear piece of prose, rigorous in its logic. Read it the way you'd listen to a song or a poem, rich in insight and allusion. Read it with your intuitive hat on rather than your logical hat. If you do that, you won't require Matthew's accounts of the birth and childhood of Jesus to be exact historical accounts. You can see them instead as a rich tying of Jesus to the tradition of his people, an account of his early days written in the light of what he did later and pointing to the significance of his life in the tradition of his people. Matthew's infancy narratives are more song than tract, more poetry than prose.

57. Matthew 3:1-12
Again, John the Baptist

In those days John the Baptist appeared in the wilderness of Judea, proclaiming, "Repent, for the kingdom of heaven has come near." This is the one of whom the prophet Isaiah spoke when he said,

> "The voice of one crying out in
> the wilderness:
> 'Prepare the way of the Lord,
> Make his paths straight.'"

Now John wore clothing of camel's hair with a leather belt around his waist, and his food was locusts and wild honey. Then the people of Jerusalem and all Judea were going out to him, and all the region along the Jordan, and they were baptized by him in the river Jordan, confessing their sins.

But when he saw many Pharisees and Sadducees coming for baptism he said to them, "You brood of vipers! Who warned you to flee from the wrath to come? Bear fruit worthy of repentance. Do not presume to say to yourselves, 'We have Abraham as our ancestor'; for I tell you, God is able from these stones to raise up children to Abraham. Even now the ax is lying at the root of the trees; every tree therefore that does not bear good fruit is cut down and thrown into the fire."

"I baptize you with water for repentance, but one who is more powerful than I is coming after me; I am not worthy to carry his sandals. He will baptize you with the Holy Spirit and fire. His winnowing fork is in his hand, and he will clear his threshing floor and will gather his wheat into the granary; but the chaff he will burn with unquenchable fire."

Commentary

You have seen The Baptizer before, in both Mark and John the Evangelist, John the cousin of the bridegroom, John the Wildman, the prophet who doesn't mince words.[3] Years ago I read a passage in one of John

---

3. If I have not noted this before, Jesus is sometimes referred to as the bridegroom, the special one, whose bride is his chosen people.

Steinbeck's later books, called *Travels with Charlie in Search of America*. It's a kind of journal that Steinbeck kept while traveling across the United States in a pickup truck with his dog Charlie. One Sunday, acting on impulse, Steinbeck walked into services in a church in a small town. The sermon was all hell-fire and brimstone. The preacher was forceful and uncompromising. Good was good and bad was bad. That was that! Steinbeck, to his own surprise, was delighted. He had heard too many mealy-mouthed preachers of a feel-good message in which honest guilt was the prime evil and what passed as a moral code was a license to do whatever you felt good about.

I'm with Steinbeck. I know, yes I do know, that life is complex and that ethical decisions are often difficult to make. I know that most of the time questions of ethics involve situations that are ambiguous. So a mother asks herself, on a daily basis, "Do I side with my husband or my child? My husband has a hot temper and likely to overdo his anger at my teen-aged son, but on the other hand somebody has to take that mouthy kid in hand." Real life's moral decisions are never easy.

And yet, who has not loved the fiery prophets who speak when others are silent? The brave ones who don't care about the consequences of telling the truth, who are not intimidated by the great ones of the world? I love those men, and John was one of them. I love those words, "You brood of vipers! Who warned you to flee from the wrath to come? . . . Even now the ax is lying at the root of the trees; every tree therefore that does not bear good fruit is cut down and thrown into the fire." John the Baptist was a stand-up guy. And yes, I know, I've spoken of him before. He's worth repeating.

58. Matthew 4:1-11
Tempted in the Desert

The Passage

Jesus was led by the Spirit into the wilderness to be tempted by the devil. He fasted forty days and forty nights, and afterwards he was famished. The tempter came and said to him, If you are the son of God, command these stones to become loaves of bread." But he answered, "It is written,

> 'One does not live by bread alone,
> > But by every word that comes
> > > from the mouth of God.'"

Then the devil took him up to the holy city and placed him on the pinnacle of the temple, saying to him, "If you are the Son of God, throw yourself down; for it is written,

> 'He will command his angels
> > Concerning you,'
> And 'On their hands they will
> > Bear you up,
> So that you will not dash your
> > Foot against a stone.'"

Jesus said to him, "Again it is written, 'Do not put the Lord your God to the test.'"

Again the devil took him to a very high mountain and showed him all the kingdoms of the world and their splendor; and he said to him, "All these I will give you, if you will fall down and worship me." Jesus said to him, "Away with you, Satan! for it is written,

> 'Worship the Lord your God,
> > And serve only him.'"

Then the devil left him, and suddenly angels came and waited on him.

Commentary

Denys Arcand's film *Jesus of Montreal*, depicts this scene in a modern day venue. The devil is a lawyer who takes the Jesus character to the top floor of a skyscraper in the city of Montreal. There the two of them look out over the city of Montreal through the great plate-glass windows which provide a bird's eye view of the city. It is night; you can see the lights of the city down below, the shadows, the vast expanse of buildings of the city sometimes called the Paris of the West. And the lawyer tells the Jesus character, "You could have all this; it could be yours; the world could be at your feet if you copyright your story and get it to the right publishers, if you appear on the talk shows, if you let me handle the business end of your career. You could be the most talked about person in the world if you'll let me handle the publicity."

It is not hard for me to imagine the devil as a lawyer-advertising expert. The devil, after all is basically not one, but legion. Normally the devil does not wear red tights and carry a pitchfork. He is primarily a smooth prophet, a slippery one, who lives right on my block, at home and where I work. He offers me success and esteem at a bargain price. He's good at sales.

59. Matthew 5:1-11
The Beatitudes

The Passage

When Jesus saw the crowds he went up the mountain; and after he sat down, his disciples came to him. Then he began to speak, and taught them, saying:

> "Blessed are the poor in spirit, for
> theirs is the kingdom of heaven.
> "Blessed are those who mourn, for
> they will be comforted.
> "Blessed are the meek, for they will
> inherit the earth.
> "Blessed are those who hunger
> and thirst for righteousness, for they will be
> filled.
> "Blessed are the merciful, for they
> will receive mercy.
> "Blessed are the pure in heart, for
> they will see God.
> "Blessed are the peacemakers, for
> they will be called the children of God.
> "Blessed are those who are persecuted
> for righteousness sake, for theirs is
> the kingdom of heaven.
> "Blessed are you when people revile you
> And persecute you and utter all kinds of evil against
> you falsely on my account. Rejoice and be glad, for your
> reward is great in heaven, for in the same way they persecuted
> the prophets who were before you."

Commentary

I have sweated over these famous words down the years. Sometimes I wonder, "Do the beatitudes mean that if you have hard times, it's okay, because later you'll be rewarded in heaven? That sounds an awful lot like, "There will be pie in the sky when you die!" And that is what a wagish American Socialist once said is the Christianity in which rich people preach these words to poor people in order to keep themselves rich and the poor ones poor. The pie comes later, not now. I cannot think the gospel means that. You can't get out of the plain message, however, that these people: the poor in spirit, the mourners, the meek, those who thirst for righteousness, the merciful ones, the pure in heart, the peacemakers, those who are unjustly persecuted, for them there is a reward.

But what? Heaven is a long way off for most of us. Nobody has ever come back to tell us what it is like. None of us have ever been there . . . if there is such a thing as "there" in that place of reward. I think myself that the promised kingdom, the comfort to come, the inherited earth, the being filled or fulfilled, the mercy to come, the vision of God, the state of being children of God, the very kingdom itself is more here than there, more now than then, more a state of mind than a place. The word *serenity* comes to mind. Can I even imagine being serene in the face of all the hard times of which the beatitudes speak? Can there be such a reward?

I don't know for certain. I have only intimations. I have met people who dealt with hardship with serenity. True, I've never met anyone who was serene all the time, despite bad times. I know too that people who seem to have it made are often not serene at all. Richard Cory after all, "Went home and put a bullet through his head."[4] What is this reward? I'll try to imagine it. I know that acceptance has to do with serenity, as the famous prayer says, "God, grant me the serenity to accept the things I cannot change." I know too from other passages in the gospels that the kingdom Jesus spoke of so often seems clearly to be made up of the people who precisely do not have it made, the nuisances and the nobodies.

I think the kingdom is the state of mind which generous people often have. I think of it as a balance . . . a quality of not being overcome by poverty or loneliness. And I think of it as being amazingly simple rather than amazingly complex. The rewards Jesus speaks of are, I believe, basically inner rewards rather than outer ones.

If I could bottle this condition and sell it, I'd be a millionaire. I think it is a journey, a passage; rather than some sort of immutable essence

---

4. Confer E.A. Robinson's poem entitled *Richard Cory*. There is a musical version of this by Simon and Garfunkel.

that you have or don't have. It is here but not here; it is already but not yet. It certainly does not exclude suffering and hardship. I think I have gotten glimpses of it in other people, and glimpses of it in myself. And I can't say much more than this, not even after seventy years.

60. Matthew 5:38-42
Turning the Other Cheek

The Passage

"You have heard it said, 'An eye for an eye and a tooth for a tooth.' But I say to you, Do not resist an evildoer. But if anyone strikes you on the right cheek, turn the other also; and if anyone wants to sue you and take your coat, give your cloak as well. And if anyone forces you to go one mile, go also the second mile. Give to anyone who begs from you, and do not refuse anyone who wants to borrow from you."

Commentary

Well, that tears it. Oh my! He wants a lot, this Jesus. I'm old enough to know that turning the other cheek is a clear statement prohibiting violence. And I know as well that nobody ever gets there, to that blessed nonviolent state. I think it was G.K. Chesterton who said, "Christianity hasn't failed; it's never been tried." Amen, Gilbert. I might add that Jesus' attitude toward cloaks and clothing doesn't seem to fit the capitalism of my country very well either. I do understand the idea of utopia, where everyone is generous and given to sharing; and no one uses violence to settle either personal or corporate hatreds. What is much more difficult to say is, "Well, then, dammit, how about the real world?" . . . where violence is as common as rain and where conspicuous consumption at the cost of the world outside the world of America is just how we do things here in the land of the free and the home of the brave.

There is some value in framing the question, I think. There is also some value in locating the field of action . . . here and now, not there and then. Frankly, I see the turning of the other cheek and the sharing of what one has as practical mostly in the micro-world of the day to day existence. I have grown tired of "big picture morality," mostly because I don't have all that much to do with it. The everyday comes, as they say, every day. It is made up of small things. I have known too many thinkers of global morality who disdained the ground beneath their feet. And I know that honesty about the law of love always flirts with despair.

There's no escaping daily violence and daily possessiveness. It is here, in me, now, at breakfast, at work, when I sleep and when I am awake. What is available to me each day, I'm going to do badly; I know that. That's why I will always love the publican in the back of the temple who says, "Lord, be merciful to me, a sinner." And then I can get on with small kindness, small generosity, and trying to love the people I know. Mostly, that's what I have, and what you have too. In brief, the call to peacefulness and sharing is not a division of people into two opposed groups. It is something that all of us struggle for, cursed with violence and selfishness as we are, no matter how far away such a state may be. As Gandhi once said, "Nonviolence is meaningless unless it begins at home."

61. Matthew 6:1-13
Showing Off Your Goodness

The Passage

"Beware of practicing your piety before others in order to be seen by them; for then you have no reward from your Father in heaven.

"So whenever you give alms, do not sound a trumpet before you, as the hypocrites do in the synagogues and in the streets, so that they may be praised by others. Truly I tell you, they have received their reward. When you give alms, do not let your left hand know what your right hand is doing, so that your alms may be done in secret; and your Father who sees in secret will reward you.

"And whenever you pray, do not be like the hypocrites; for they love to stand and pray in the synagogues and at the street corners, so that they may be seen by others. Truly I tell you, they have received their reward. But whenever you pray, go into your room and shut the door and pray to your Father who is in secret; and your Father who sees in secret will reward you.

"When you are praying, do not heap up empty phrases as the Gentiles do; for they think that they will be heard because of their many words. Do not be like them, for you Father knows what you need before you ask him.

"Pray then in this way:
Our Father in heaven.
    hallowed be your name.
Your kingdom come,
Your will be done
    on earth as it is in heaven.
Give us this day our daily
    bread.
And forgive us our debts,
    as we also have forgiven
        our debtors.
And do not bring us to the
        time of trial,
But rescue us from the
        evil one."

Commentary

A few years back, about forty of them, to be precise, I had a somewhat tyrannical old Irish-American as Spiritual Father during my humanistic studies of language, literature, and history in the portion of Jesuit training called The Juniorate. His name was Father Patrick Regan, S.J. We called him "Paddy" behind his back. He was in charge of our fledgling prayer lives. We each went to see him once a month for an assessment of how our prayer lives were going. One of the things he asked us to do was to write out a sample of our daily hour of meditation. If you wrote a few sentences, that was good. If you had one sentence, that was better. If you wrote only a word or two, "That," said Paddy, "Was what prayer was all about." It is interesting to me to find words of similar advice from Jesus in this portion of Matthew's gospel.

Jesuits, then and now, have a veritable phobia against visible piety. They are quite secular holy people, those of them who are holy. I've often wondered about that. Why should you go to such great lengths to avoid any smallest show of being pious? I might add, that after the first year or two, we almost never shared our spiritual lives with each other. One might think such an exchange of ideas would be most normal, the way baseball players give each other tips on batting. No sir, we did not do that. Do you suppose it was because we had taken to heart Jesus' words about going to the Father in secret? "Well, maybe," says I. You can see for yourself that Jesus was not sympathetic to those who wore their religion on their sleeves. He was clearly more concerned with inner attitudes of prayerfulness than outer shows of piety. Is that what Jesuit piety is about? I'm not going to let the Jesuits off the hook.

There was a famous old member of the Order in the generation of S.J.'s before mine, who was quoted as saying, "We are just bachelors, Father, that's all we are." Another wise old man, a colleague of mine at Western Michigan University, and an expert in Oriental history once told me, "The Jesuits went to all those far off places in the sixteenth century, to India, to China, Japan and they learned to fit in very well. Some of them fitted in so well that they forgot why they came!" Indeed. One can become so adept at hiding one's piety, so versed in the art of camouflage that one can forget entirely what it is one is concealing. That's true too!

I might add here that Jesus was quite aware that the one he called "Abba" is aware of our needs before we ask him. He knew we do not tell

God anything new in our requests. When we request things in prayer, our petitions are like good manners. A child at table is taught to politely ask for another serving of this or that. It's not so much that the small one might go hungry, should she not ask for food. Her mom and dad will see to that. It's more of an acknowledgment of her dependence on her parents, a kind of "Thank you, mom and dad, for taking care of me." So, when we say the prayer Jesus suggested "Give us this day our daily bread" it's not asking God to come up with some kind of special intervention. Nor is it an attempt to get out of earning our keep. It is a recognition that all creation comes from God. We need to say that; it reminds us who we are and who God is.

62. Matthew 6:25-34
Worry & Beauty

The Passage

"Therefore I tell you, do not worry about your life, what you will eat or what you will drink, or about your body, what you will wear. Is not life more than food, and the body more than clothing? Look at the birds of the air; they neither sow nor reap nor gather into barns, and yet your heavenly Father feeds them. Are you not of more value than they? And can any of you by worrying add a single hour to your span of life? And why do you worry about clothing? Consider the lilies of the field, how they grow; they neither toil nor spin, yet I tell you, even Solomon in all his glory was not clothed like one of these. But if God so clothes the grass of the field, which is alive today and tomorrow is thrown into the oven, will he not much more clothe you—you of little faith? Therefore do not worry, saying, 'What will we eat? Or 'What will we drink?' or 'what will we wear?' For it is the Gentiles who strive for all these things; and indeed your heavenly Father knows that you need all these things. But strive first for the kingdom of God and his righteousness, and all these things will be given to you as well.

"So do not worry about tomorrow, for tomorrow will bring worries of its own. Today's trouble is enough for today."

Commentary

I am reminded that these verses are not part of a philosophical thesis. If they were, one could object that if you don't work, you'll starve. If you don't dress properly, you'll get fired from your job, embarrass your friends, and most likely put an end to whatever chances for romance you may have. Most girls do not fall for slobs. I find myself thinking that the Jewish people of France, Germany and Poland were not saved from the ovens of the Nazis by avoiding worrying about it, and for that matter, not saved by prayer or a good life either.

I don't think Jesus is talking about lack of responsibility here. I think he's talking more about going with the flow of life. I think he's talking about not being in love with yourself, about being so tightly wound that there is no joy left, no freedom, no lightness. Transactional analysis speaks of a game people play called "Ain't it awful." In such a game my partner and I focus so exclusively on disasters, both near and far, that we cannot see the beauty of good conversation between friends or the joy of drinking a glass of beer. As Alice Walker once put it, "If you should walk through a field of purple and not notice it, God would be pissed off!"

There is some beauty in everyone's life, including your life and also mine. It's vital to notice it; there are real troubles enough without making more new ones. I recall an impish aunt of mine speaking to her husband about his reticence about kissing her, "It won't make you sick, George, you might even learn to like it!"

63. Matthew 7:1-5
Not Seeing the Log in your Eye

The Passage

"Do not judge, so that you may not be judged. For with the judgment you make you will be judged, and the measure you give will be the measure you get. Why do you see the speck in your neighbor's eye, but do not notice the log in your own eye? Or how can you say to your neighbor, "Let me take the speck out of your eye,' while the log is in your own eye? You hypocrite, first take the log out of your own eye, and then you will see clearly to take the speck out of your neighbor's eye."

Commentary

The bit of not seeing the log in one's eye is old bit of wisdom; we've all heard it. Psychologists call it projection. You find some quality within yourself that you know is bad. Then you transfer that quality to some-body else and hate it there. The trick, of course, is that you don't realize you are doing this. It's especially common, this finding the speck in your neighbor's eye, if you yourself are an idealist, if you have high standards of moral behavior.

Where's the damage? If seeing the proverbial speck in your sister's eye doesn't hurt anyone, it's not a big deal, except that your judgment might draw some snickers from those who know you. I think the real damage of perpetually seeing other people's faults is that it is often the mark of a bore. People get tired of diatribes.

Down deep I think the real problem with this stuff is that you don't get to know yourself and that you bore other people. Usually people who gossip don't do much harm, especially if all the gossips know that they are gossiping. I had a professor friend who told me over lunch during a very long winter's semester, that he had an entire class of student-idiots whom he was trying to teach. I knew that it was unlikely that forty mo-rons had been assembled in one classroom. I also knew that my friend was having a rough time in his own life. That was why he had lost his touch in the classroom and no longer knew the students for what they were. He was the one who was dumb, not them. I find myself thinking of Paul Simon's Song, *You're the One*. It's about blaming your lover for what you yourself are. Do you know that song? Jesus knew it in spades.

64. Matthew 7:21-23
Saying, "Lord, Lord."

The Passage

"Not everyone who says to me, 'Lord, Lord,' will enter the kingdom of heaven, but only the one who does the will of my Father in heaven. On that day many will say to me, 'Lord, Lord, did we not prophesy in your name, and cast out demons in your name, and do many deeds of power in your name?' Then I will declare to them, 'I never knew you; go away from me, you evildoers.'"

The Commentary

Jesus does have a sharp tongue, does he not? Who are the bad guys who say, "Lord, Lord?" Not me, of course, not you either. Oh no, not us! Well, maybe us, but just once in a while. It's not easy to notice when you try to catch yourself with your own hand in the cookie jar, i.e., saying the words, "Lord, Lord!". I think Jesus is talking about the people who do all the right things, who step on all the bases. They do all the good stuff, like giving to United Way and going to church on Sundays, the ones who always show up for work on time, the ones who work overtime without being told to. Whatever the rules are, they keep the rules, and more. However it's what's underneath all these good deeds and fine words that counts. What is in your mind and heart that is the Lord's concern. You can hate all those bastards you serve so diligently. Loving people is harder than keeping the rules. It takes a lifetime to learn to love. Saying, "Lord, Lord" is okay, but it's the easy part.

65. Matthew 8:5-13
Healing the Centurions's Servant

The Passage

When he entered Capernaum, a centurion came to him, appealing to him and saying, "Lord, my servant is lying at home paralyzed, in terrible distress." And he said to him, "I will come and cure him." The centurion answered, "Lord I am not worthy to have you come under my roof; but only speak the word and my servant will be healed. For I also am a man under authority, with soldiers under me; and I say to one, 'Go,' and he goes, and to another, 'Come,' and he comes, and to my slave, 'Do this,' and the slave does it. When Jesus heard him, he was amazed and said to those who followed him, "Truly I tell you, in no one in Israel have I found such faith, I tell you, many will come from the east and the west and will eat with Abraham and Isaac and Jacob in the kingdom of heaven, while the heirs of the kingdom will be thrown into the outer darkness, where there will be weeping and gnashing of teeth." And to the centurion Jesus said, "Go; let it be done for you according to your faith." And the servant was healed in that hour.

Commentary

A centurion, I'm sure you know, is a Roman soldier, an officer in command of a hundred foot soldiers. Centurions were not Jews. This particular centurion knew the power of Jesus.

"You are in charge, Jesus, a word from you is enough." Those were his words; that was his thought;. What's the point here? I think the point is that Jesus knows that it is what is in your heart that counts, and not whether you are Jewish or a Roman soldier or some kind of big deal. Belonging to the right club, in this case being Jewish, is not enough. Jesus clearly is himself a practicing Jew. He's not against Jews, he simply says that what is in your heart counts more than being merely a member of the Chosen People. The history of the world is filled with groups of people who have considered themselves to be the chosen ones. And who am I to say that they have not been chosen? The problem lies in thinking that nobody else is chosen or in thinking that being one of the chosen people is enough to be one of the good guys.

I recall C. S. Lewis saying in his book on the psalms of the Bible that it is very easy to confuse your own enemies with God's enemies. The psalms, if you give them a good reading, contain a lot of invective. I'm thinking of psalm twenty-three, the Shepherd Psalm, the one about the Lord being your shepherd, the one where it says that even if you should walk in a dark and dangerous place, you will fear no evil, for you know the divine shepherd is with you. This sounds like a remarkably consoling and peaceful psalm. If you read on a bit, however, you hear the psalmist say, "You prepare a table before me in the presence of my enemies." The psalmist has this lovely dream of getting even with his enemies by eating a nice meal in their presence, the meal having been prepared by the Lord and the enemies of the psalmist those who must look on without being at the table. The presumption is that my enemies are also the Lord's enemies. It's an easy mistake to make if you are, or think you are, one of the chosen people.

Nobody expected Jesus to heal the servant of a centurion. The Jews hated the soldiers of Rome. Besides being Gentiles they were the business end of Rome's empire. They were the ones who held the Jewish people and their land as conquered people in their own beloved Promised Land. Who'd have thought a good Jewish boy would dirty his hands with the likes of these goy soldiers? He surprised them; he said that it's faith that counts. Without it, it doesn't matter at all what your affiliation is. And furthermore, at the great feast of the future kingdom there are going to be a lot of people like the centurion there eating with the great ones of history: Abraham, Isaac, and Jacob. Some of the heirs of the kingdom, some of the Hebrew people, would be on the outside looking in. This is no condemnation of being Jewish; it is merely an underlining that one's inner attitude counts more than belonging to the right church.

66. Matthew 8:14-17
Peter's Mother-in-law: Healers and Moms

When Jesus entered Peter's house, he saw his mother-in-law lying in bed with a fever; he touched her hand, and the fever left her, and she got up and began to serve him. That evening they brought to him many who were possessed with demons; and he cast out the spirits with a word, and cured all who were sick. This was to fulfill what had been spoken through the prophet Isaiah, "He took our infirmities and bore our diseases."

The Passage

There's a lot here. I won't belabor the fact that if Peter had a mother-in-law, he must have had a wife too, he, who was to be the prince of the apostles. Such a naughty boy to have been a married man. Tch, tch! Here, and in many places in the gospels, Jesus is presented as a healer. I have asked myself many times, "What would a healer be like in the times we live in?" I remember that my own mother, years before she became a serious Christian, took me to a healer as a young boy of perhaps eight years. The healer's name was Father Samatoski; he was a Catholic priest. My mom brought me to him because I suffered from asthma and bronchitis as a child and was extremely thin, too thin for my mom's liking anyhow. Here's what I remember. Father Samatoski was a nice man; He had me take off my shirt and lie on my back on the kind of table doctors have in their offices. He bent my knees pushing them up to my chest, first one, then the other. He asked me what I liked to eat and I told him. He said I should eat those things I liked. He may have said a little prayer over me, but I don't remember it. Then we went home, my mom and I.

All the rest of the times when I was sick or ailing, I was sent to the family doctor. Dr. Goodrich was our main family healer. For the most part we didn't visit the likes of Father Samatoski, although I never heard anyone say anything derogatory about him.

I forgot something. We *didn't* go to the family doctor most of the time. Most of the time we went to my mother, who had all the power of our family doctor and Father Samatoski wrapped into one. She said things to me like, "Brave soldier!" if I had a cut knee or a banged up finger. She knew about iodine and Merthiolate. She knew about band-aids. She took our temperatures to see if we really were sick and not just faking it to get out of going to school. Usually she was the one who took us to the doctor. She read to us and tried to get us to eat. If you didn't have a bowel movement in the morning you first got a suppository, and if that didn't work, an enema. Besides being a pretty good amateur physician, she had a plentiful supply of what the most effective healers always have; she had a mother's love.

Medicine and healing in our family really were the province of two people then, my mom and Dr. Goodrich. Without giving it much thought, we knew the power of TLC. My mom had a confident and sympathetic manner. I usually trusted her too. So, basically we had a mother's touch and a doctor's science. The mother's touch was what Jesus had in abundance. He took sick people seriously; he brought them in; he received them and listened to them. Some sicknesses, then as now, make the sick person an outcast unless some special person takes the sick one in, brings her back into the family, holds her, touches her. I think the bringing back, the acceptance, and the love are just as important as the scientific stuff. Don't you?

Norman Cousins, a well known writer for *The New Yorker* weekly magazine, once wrote a lovely and amusing book about his own recovery from what was understood by his medical advisers to be a terminal illness. His cure lay in the choice of a physician he utterly trusted and watching a great many very funny movies. He actually did recover. Jesus would have understood that recovery. Healers are merciful people. There's more to it than science.

67. Matthew 10:25-33
No Fear—Hell, and a Father's Love

The Passage

So if they have called the master of the house Beelzebul, how much more will they malign those of his household!

So have no fear of them;[5] for nothing is covered up that will not be uncovered, and nothing secret that will not become known. What I say to you in the dark, tell in the light; and what your hear whispered, proclaim from the housetops. Do not fear those who kill the body but cannot kill the soul; rather fear him who can destroy both soul and body in hell. Are not two sparrows sold for a penny? Yet not one of them will fall to the ground apart from your Father. And even the hairs of your head are all counted. So do not be afraid; you are of more value than many sparrows.

Everyone therefore who acknowledges me before others, I also will acknowledge before my Father in heaven; but whoever denies me before others, I also will deny before my Father in heaven.

Commentary

Jesus is speaking about being scared here, scared of people who might not like hearing his message. And I find this a hard passage for a number of reasons. Here's a hard line from this passage: ". . . rather fear him who can destroy both soul and body in hell." We all learned what hell was about as kids. It never ended; it was hot; you didn't want to go there. And if you were bad and died being bad, that's where you went. That was that.

Well? How about it? There are a large number of words in the New Testament Greek about a place of punishment and most of them are translated into English as "Hell". The one used here indicated the city dump outside Jerusalem, associated with pagan fire rites. In this regard I am reminded of another controversy regarding the end of things, the time of reward or punishment after death. When I was an undergraduate

---

5. He is referring to those who reviled the early Christians. It was against the law to be a Christian in the Roman Empire for the first three centuries of its existence. Christians, as we all know were sometimes fed to lions in the Roman Colosseum, their religion being against the law.

at Holy Cross College, there was a learned Jesuit named Leonard Feeney thirty miles away at Harvard University. He was the Catholic chaplain there and he made it quite clear to all who would listen that Harvard was the Scarlet Woman, The Whore of Babylon, and that anybody who went to school there was flirting with going to hell. Father Feeney added that, with no ifs ands or buts, anyone who was not a Roman Catholic could not be saved. As far as I know there have been only two public excommunications from the Catholic church in these United States and Father Feeney was one of them. Pope Pius XII bounced him for saying "Extra Ecclesiam, nulla salus."[6] I'm grateful for that. And it reminds me of something I've mentioned before in these notes, that different religions are prone to think of themselves as the only righteous ones, that if they are the People of God, then nobody else can claim this title . . . a brassy and self-centered belief if there ever was one.

I am aware as well that to say that those who don't toe the line for this or that religious message are often threatened with all sorts of horrible things. It does strike me as strange that the one who hung out with drunks and prostitutes has been presented to us as one who preached everlasting punishment for bad people. This passage simply does not say that. I think that the hell I learned about as a child, the one that never ends, the one that you cannot escape from, ever, is more the product of medieval scholastic theology than it is firmly rooted in the New Testament. You and I (and Jesus!!) worship an all-loving God who loves all different kinds of humans and all different kinds of religious persuasions. If the Pope of Rome once bounced a priest from membership in his church for saying that only Roman Catholics could be saved, that condemnation was only a stone's throw from a condemnation of believing in an eternal and inescapable punishment for people who have done bad things.

In the New Testament Jesus speaks trenchantly of punishment and suffering; that's true. And that squares with the life experience of anyone who has been alive very long. I can recall giving a retreat years ago to a group of Illinois farmers. When it came time for a treatment of hell, I said to them, "Of course there is a hell, and all of us have been there." "Life," as someone has said, "is brutal and short." Nobody escapes terrible times, sometimes richly merited, sometimes not. "The rain," as Jesus said once, "Falls on the just and the unjust alike."

---

6. The Latin for "Outside the Church there is no salvation."

I have nothing against the descriptions of deserved human suffering in the mouth of Jesus. I resent the way some preachers and some Christian churches twist the biblical metaphors for hell and make them part and parcel of a punishment which is not only everlasting but inescapable for those who go there. The New Testament words of punishment don't say that. Such a place is contradictory to the notion that God is Love. When Jesus tells us not to fear, because we are worth many sparrows, when he tells us only to fear those who can destroy our spirits rather than our bodies, this is meant to be a message of hope rather than a threat of much more than life imprisonment. I'm counting on the Father that knows the number of hairs on my head, however few, and I'm not about to be seduced into thinking that this same Father will put me away forever for my sinfulness. I get enough hell right here. Perhaps you do too.

68. Matthew 11:25-30
The Easy Burden

The Passage

At that time Jesus said, "I thank you, Father, Lord of heaven and earth because you have hidden these things from the wise and the intelligent and have revealed them to infants; yes, Father, for such was your gracious will. All things have been handed over to me by my Father; and no one knows the Son except the Father, and no one knows the Father except the Son and anyone to whom the Son chooses to reveal him.

"Come to me all you that are weary and are carrying heavy burdens, and I will give you rest. Take my yoke upon you, and learn from me; for I am gentle and humble in heart, and you will find rest for your souls. For my yoke is easy, and my burden is light."

Commentary

So, you have hidden these things from the wise and intelligent and have revealed them to infants! Oh, that has to be one of the dearest things he ever said . . . especially for those who have felt stupid or inadequate or not too fond of their own gifts. There is a place of privilege for yo-yos, indeed one of honor! Again, I think that the wise and intelligent ones are a part of us all—and the infants and babes are another part. As if both these qualities exist in all of us. I do believe that. You have your wise part, all those things you know, all the tricks you have acquired over however many years you have lived. You have as well your own private infant, your child self who knows very little and is aware of that. This the part the Father speaks to.

Jesus says a few lines down in this passage:

> Come to me all you who are weary and carrying heavy burdens, and I will refresh you, for my burden is easy and my yoke is light. Take my yoke upon you and learn from me, for I am gentle and humble in heart, and you will find rest for your souls, for my yoke is easy and my burden light.

When he says those amazingly gentle words, this man so capable of fire and anger, when he says those words he is talking to the infant in you and me, not the guileful part. The burden, after all, for each of us, is to be only what we are, not what we *would be* or even should be, but what we are. Such a very mild request! Such a light burden compared to the load of all those things we want to be or could be or desperately wish we were. If I am content with that, I will be his brother and I will hear the voice of the one who sent him.

69. Matthew 12:15-21
The Servant (Jesus Our Father)

The Passage

When Jesus became aware of this, he departed.[7] Many crowds followed him, and he cured all of them, and he ordered them not to make him known. This was to fulfill what had been spoken through the prophet Isaiah:

> "Here is my servant, whom I
>   have chosen,
>   my beloved, with whom my
>   soul is well pleased.
> I will put my Spirit upon him
>   and he will proclaim justice
>   to the Gentiles.
> He will not wrangle or cry aloud,
>   nor will anyone hear his voice
>   in the streets.
> He will not break a bruised reed
>   or quench a smoldering wick
> until he brings justice to victory.
>   And in his name the Gentiles
>   will hope."

Commentary

This is one of the most astounding things about Jesus, the Messiah, the Anointed One, the One whom the Chosen People awaited. They were expecting a king, like David or Solomon. And what they got was a lowly and humble Servant, echoing the famous Songs of the Servant in the prophet Isaiah.[8]

I am reminded of the statues (bultos) of Christ Our Father, so central to the Christianity of the Penitente movement in New Mexico. I have one

---

7. Jesus was aware that there was a conspiracy on the part of a number of people to have him put to death.

8. Isaiah 42:1-4; 49:1-6; 50:4-9; 52:13-15–53:1-12.

of them in my prayer room. Jesus is tall, wearing a plain black gown, his hands tied in front of him. He stands, feet together, blood on his very Spanish face. His beard and the hair on his skull are black, the latter pulled back like the hair of a bull fighter. His expression one of unutterable sadness. He is not the Christ of the resurrection. He is the one who has suffered and still suffers. He is the servant of all, the lowly one, who does not raise his voice, the one who bears the iniquities of us all. There is spittle in his beard. Somehow he carries the sins of the world within him. What a surprise that he is the Father's Chosen One, this man of compassion and sadness.

I have come back to him many times, forgotten him many times, until hardship or tragedy comes my way, yet again. Then I remember him once more and I take comfort in him; he touches my aching heart, my old bones, my tissues of sadness, for I know that he knows my sorrows, my losses, my times of emptiness; and I take refuge in him.

If you have never read the Isaiah's Songs of the Servant, read them now. There are four of them, as I have indicated in the footnote. You will come back to them. They may well become a will become a treasure for you, just as they are for me.

70. Matthew 13:1-9, 18-23
The Parable of the Sower

The Passage

That same day Jesus went out of the house and sat beside the sea. Such great crowds gathered around him that he got into a boat and sat there, while the whole crowd stood on the beach. And he told them many things in parables, saying: "Listen! A sower went out to sow. And as he sowed, some seeds fell on the path, and the birds came and ate them up. Other seeds fell upon rocky ground, where they did not have much soil, and they sprang up quickly, since they had no depth of soil. But when the sun rose, they were scorched; and since they had no root, they withered away. Other seeds fell among thorns, and the thorns grew up and choked them. Other seeds fell on good soil and brought forth grain, some a hundred fold, some sixty, some thirty. Let anyone with ears listen!"

* * *

"Hear then the parable of the sower. When anyone hears the word of the Kingdom and does not understand it, the evil one comes and snatches away what is sown in the heart; this is what was sown on the path. As for what was sown on rocky ground, this is the one who hears the word and immediately receives it with joy; yet such a person has no root, but endures only for a while, and when trouble or persecution arises on account of the word, that person immediately falls away. As for what was sown among thorns this is the one who hears the word, but the cares of the world and the lure of wealth choke the word, and it yields nothing. But as for what was sown on good soil, this is the one who hears the word and understands it, who indeed bears fruit and yields, in one case a hundredfold, in another sixty, and in another thirty

Commentary

Eons ago, or so it seems, when I was a Jesuit novice, all wrapped up in a black serge cassock and even more wrapped up in the joy and insularity of my two year introduction to prayer and the spiritual life, I recall our using the expression "The hundredfold" as though we fledglings were clearly the chosen ones. After a good day, we'd say, "Part of the hundredfold!" We were the seed that had been sown on good soil, and that was that! We had either arrived or were on the door step of perfection—eager, passionate, and naive. Good kids, most of us but numbingly narrow. I recall one of our teachers telling us, "I'm not saying you men don't have any virtue, but I am telling you that it's never been tried." That was putting it nicely.[9]

Today, I wonder, "Who are the receptive ones? Which of us is the good ground Jesus spoke of, where the Word fell and flourished. I just wonder that . . . and I don't think I know. What I really think is that most of us are a mixture of path, rocky ground, and good soil. And I do know that receptivity has much more to do with patience and waiting than setting forth every morning in the gray dawn, sword in hand to slay dragons or to ferociously cultivate the seeds sown by the divine sower. The ground is a place of nourishment rather than a field of battle. I think Jesus would have been delighted at the Buddha's suspicion of great deeds.[10] I am reminded of the gospel theme of Servant, treated in my essay just before this one. The image of the Servant goes well with the image of good ground, for both of them have to do with silence and waiting as a part of hearing what Jesus called The Word. Roots, after all, take time to grow, and of course, they are not easy to see. They are hidden; they lie beneath the ground, and they grow by millimeters rather than by feet or yards or miles. All this business of hearing takes time. Jesuit novices don't know that.

---

9. I can't help but note that, perhaps tragically, priests in our country do not differ from the ordinary populace as much as one might think. The recent torrent of accusations concerning sexual abuse of children and adolescents is evidence of this.

10. Chögyam Trungpa, the Tibetan Buddhist teacher, speaks masterfully of the deceptive shallowness of great deeds in his *Cutting Through Spiritual Materialism*. Boston: Shambala, 1987, p. 83-84. Trungpa notes that even heroes, the doers of great deeds, must eventually come home and face themselves. This is the hardest and most difficult challenge in anyone's life.

71. Matthew 13:54-58
Rejection at Home

The Passage

He came to his hometown and began to teach the people in their synagogue, so that they were astounded and said, "Where did this man get this wisdom and these deeds of power? Is not this the carpenter's son? Is not his mother called Mary? And are not his brothers James and Joseph and Simon and Judas? And are not all his sisters with us? Where then did this man get all this?" And they took offense at him. But Jesus said to them, "Prophets are not without honor except in their own country and in their own house." And he did not do many deeds of power there, because of their unbelief.

Commentary

You know this story already. You know it when your mother looks at you . . . and right away you are seven years old again. Sometimes you know it when you meet your old high school friends, the ones that knew you when you were "Matty" or "Jo Jo." You know it when you sense that condescension in this or that old friend or neighbor. You want to say, "Hey, wait a minute! I'm doing all right. I've done some good stuff. I'm making my mark. I've had a shot of redemption. I've had some photo opportunities. You don't really know me; you just think you do."

It's paralyzing. I experience it when I go back and visit my old Jesuit friends and they look knowingly at me and call me by an old nickname. They call me "Yogi" and they have taken my measure, oh so carefully. And I want to *explain* to them. With most people I don't need to explain. I'm just who I am. That's it, but oh when I go back to see my old homeys; then it's a different story. I wonder sometimes, "Why do I go back? Why did Jesus go back? It sounds like he didn't do much better than I do. He was all thumbs in Nazareth."

72. Matthew 15:21-28
The Canaanite Woman

The Passage

Jesus left that place and went away to the district of Tyre and Sidon. Just then a Canaanite woman from that region came out and started shouting, "Have mercy on me, Lord, Son of David; my daughter is tormented by a demon." But he did not answer her at all. And his disciples came and urged him, saying, "Send her away, for she keeps shouting after us." He answered, "I was sent only to the lost sheep of the house of Israel." But she came and knelt before him, sing, "Lord, help me." He answered, "It is not fair to take the children's food and throw it to the dogs." She said, "Yes, Lord, yet even the dogs eat the crumbs that fall from their masters' table." Then Jesus answered her, "Woman, great is your faith! Let it be done for you as you wish." And her daughter was healed instantly.

Commentary

What is it that attracts me to this story? Is it the fact that the woman from Canaan is noisy? She yells. She makes a nuisance of herself. Is it her persistence? She won't take no for an answer. And Jesus is more than blunt with her at first, implying that she is a dog! A pushy woman here, fighting for her daughter. She is an outsider by both gender and religion . . . and he tests her. She's like a young man wanting to join a Zen monastery in Japan today. He must spend three days sitting on the door-step of the monastery. Each time he asks to come in, he is rebuffed, the door slammed in his face. Finally, they let him in. Jesus says it is her faith that lets him hear her; it seems to me it is her persistence too, her very quality of being a pest. And so I am reminded that the kingdom is one of nuisances and nobodies. She is both.[11]

---

11. If you want to read more about the kingdom being made up of nuisances and nobodies, read, *Jesus, a Revolutionary Biography* by John Dominic Crossan, New York: HarperCollins, 1987, p. 54-74.

73. Matthew 16:13-20
Peter the Rock and the Pope

The Passage

Now when Jesus came into the district of Caesarea Philippi, he asked his disciples, "Who do people say that the Son of Man is?" And they said, "Some say John the Baptist, but others Elijah, and still others Jeremiah or one of the prophets." He said to them, "But who do you say that I am?" Simon Peter answered, "You are the Messiah, the Son of the living God." And Jesus answered him, "Blessed are you, Simon son of Jonah! For flesh and blood has not revealed this to you, but my Father in heaven. And I tell you, you are Peter, and on this rock I will build my church, and the gates of Hades will not prevail against it. I will give you the keys of the kingdom of heaven, and whatever you bind on earth will be bound in heaven, and whatever you loose on earth will be loosed in heaven." Then he sternly ordered the disciples not to tell anyone that he was the Messiah.

Commentary

This is an important passage to me. Like most of the other parts of scripture I like, it goes way back, to my childhood. In this case it goes back to grade school and the Baltimore Catechism, one or another version of which I studied in school all the way through the primary grades. The catechism saw this passage was a sort of summary of all things Catholic. When Jesus said to Peter, "You are Peter, and on this rock I will build my church, and the gates of Hell (sic) will not prevail against it," and so on and so forth, well, that was it! Peter was the first pope of my church, the Roman Catholic Church. There it was in bold print, right in the gospel. Furthermore the gates of hell, not to mention any other adversaries, would just not cut the mustard when it came to rivaling the Catholics. The stuff about binding and loosing nailed down the pope's authority. If he bound you, you were bound by God. If he let you loose, then you were loose. Period.

We got the whole papacy out of this passage on the place of Peter in the church that was to be. How fascinating to me that I was middle aged before it occurred to me, no doubt prompted by some heretic or other, that this passage, whatever else it meant said not one thing about Rome, the papacy or any kind of central church authority which might come after Peter. It is quite clear that Jesus singled out Peter the Rock to be an important person, possessing the keys to the kingdom was surely an honor, but says not one thing about Peter's administrative function among the followers of Jesus, his successors, about Rome, or the institution of the papacy, not to mention bishops or priests.

And I wonder why I never noticed that. I really do wonder. Maybe it was because I didn't know anybody who really spelled out the limitations of this piece of Matthew's gospel. My church was pretty much turned in on itself in the days of my childhood. We were, for the most part, a people apart when it came to religion and religious controversy. We just didn't hear it much. I heard vaguely about people who went off to "non-Catholic" colleges like Yale and Harvard and "lost their faith". My Protestant mother and her family were a bit of a problem, but my mom's allegiance to the Episcopal church was very vague, and she went to church with my dad and us kids at the right church, the Catholic one.

I do hope I never forget how easy it is not to think of the gospels with a critical eye, especially in the face of words which don't say what we were taught they did say. I hope I don't forget how very easy it is to think words mean whatever my people say they mean. When the flavor is just plain vanilla and that's all you know, well then, there just aren't any other flavors. It's amazingly easy to be fooled when nobody disagrees with the foolishness. I do keep trying to remember that and I hope you do too.

74. Matthew 17:1-13
The Transfiguration (again)

The Passage

Six days later, Jesus took with Peter and James and his brother John and led them up a high mountain, by themselves. And he was transfigured before them, and his face shone like the sun, and his clothes became dazzling white. Suddenly there appeared to them Moses and Elijah, talking with him. The Peter said to Jesus, "Lord it is good for us to be here; if you wish, I will make three dwellings here, one for you, one for Moses, and one for Elijah." While he was still speaking, suddenly a bright cloud overshadowed them, and from the cloud a voice said, "This is my Son, the beloved; with him I am well pleased; listen to him!" When the disciples heard this, they fell to the ground and were overcome by fear. But Jesus came and touched them, saying, "Get up and do not be afraid." And when they looked up, they saw no one except Jesus himself alone.

As they were coming down the mountain, Jesus ordered them, "Tell no one about the vision until after the Son of Man has been raised from the dead." And the disciples asked him, "Why then, do the scribes say that Elijah must come first?" He replied, "Elijah is indeed coming and will restore all things; but I tell you that Elijah has already come, and they did not recognize him, but they did to him whatever they pleased. So also the Son of Man is about to suffer at their hands." Then the disciples understood that he was speaking to them about John the Baptist.

Commentary

We have seen the Transfiguration before. I know that. I think it's a gospel story that needs repeating for a number of reasons. One of those reasons is that the particular brand of Christianity which is my home placed an overwhelming emphasis on the sufferings of Jesus. I've wondered sometimes what it would be like were I to bring someone who knew nothing about Christianity into a Catholic church for them to look around. Very central in most Catholic churches even today, is image of Jesus on the cross, naked except for a rag around his waist, covering the pubic area of his body. His body is torn, sometimes lifeless, sometimes writhing in agony. On his head the crown of thorns. He is nailed to the cross, the nails going right through his hands and feet. A visitor might say, "Who is the dead guy up on the cross? He sure is featured in this church. Look at all those pictures on the walls of the building of him carrying that cross and the actual nailing shown in graphic detail. The suffering Jesus is everywhere! Is this the point of your religion? Is that where it all ends?"

I think I'd have a rough time trying to explain to such a one that suffering is only half the story . . . that Jesus rose gloriously after all that bloody torture and death. "Where are the pictures of that?" my friend might say. "If I read the body language in the sacred images of your place of worship, I don't see much evidence of the joyful side of it all."

And I'd be stumped. I might wonder myself, "Where's the Easter part? Where's the triumph? Where's the joy? How come there are no pictures of the Transfiguration or the rising itself? Where are the pictures of his risen life with his people?" I might wonder, "Do my people come to church every Sunday to see this man in agony, whipped, scourged, carrying his cross, wearing that dreadful crown of thorns? Ridiculed before the Roman governor, made a fool of before the satrap king Herod?" There is a fascination with evil and suffering for most people; I know that. *The National Enquirer* is the largest selling newspaper in this country and its stock in trade, along with the sex lives of movie stars, is tragedy, predictions of the end of the world, murders of prominent people. O.J. Simpson got more publicity for the murder of his wife in this and other more respectable publications than he ever did as a football player. We see the current tragedies of the Kennedy family nearly weekly . . . and there are a lot of them!

"Well," says my imagined visitor, "Is that what your church is about? A kind of morbid fascination with the demise of its founder, scene by scene, blow by blow, thorn by thorn?" I might reply weakly, "Well, we're changing all that," or "Wait a minute, I can explain everything!" I don't really know why a history of nearly exclusive emphasis on the sufferings of the savior seems so much part of my own part of Western Christianity. Perhaps it is because carnage has always had more readers than joy. I don't know. Maybe it is because throughout human history we have wars, famines, disease, and death as a major part of anyone person's lifetime. As the poet says:

> It is the blight man was born for.
> It is Margaret you morn for.

This, if for no other reason, is why I want you to see the Transfiguration again. And remind myself and you that the Transfiguration of Jesus is a prefiguring of the resurrection, a preview of the joy of Christianity, so often left to the side. And I note too, that after this marvelous experience of joy on top of the mountain, as they walk down, Jesus reminds his friends that he must die. To quote, his words were, "So also the Son of Man is about to suffer at their hands." He said that. Christianity is not a religion that pretends that hard times do not exist, as I have noted above, but the Transfiguration reminds me that it is also a religion of joy.

75. Matthew 18:21-35
Forgiveness—Karma

The Passage

Then Peter came and said to him, "Lord, if another member of the church sins against me, how often should I forgive? As many as seven times?" Jesus said to him, "Not seven times, but, I tell you, seventy-seven times.

"For this reason the kingdom of heaven may be compared to a king who wished to settle accounts with his slaves. When he began the reckoning, one who owed him then thousand talents was brought to him; and, as he could not pay, his lord ordered him to be sold, together with his wife and children and all his possessions, and payment to be made. So the slave fell on his knees before him, saying. 'Have patience with me, and I will pay you everything.' And out of pity for him, the lord of that slave released him and forgave him the debt. But that same slave, as he went out came upon one of his fellow slaves who owed him a hundred denarii; and seized him by the throat, he said, 'Pay what you owe.' Then his fellow slave fell down and pleaded with him, 'Have patience with me, and I will pay you.' But he refused; then he went and threw him into prison until he would pay the debt. When his fellow slaves saw what had happened, they were greatly distressed, and they went and reported to their lord all that had taken place. Then his lord summoned him and said to him, 'You wicked slave! I forgave you all that debt because you pleaded with me. Should you not have had mercy on your fellow slave, as I had mercy on you?' And in anger his lord handed him over to be tortured until he would pay his entire debt. So my heavenly Father will also do to every one of you, if you do not forgive your brother or sister from your heart."

Commentary

This is another tough passage of the gospel. He doesn't let up . . . seven times is a lot of times to forgive, or so Peter thought. Seventy-seven is a whole lot more. We both get the picture. And then he tells a perplexing parable. The slave who would not forgive his fellow slave after having been forgiven himself. I do wonder about the fate of the bad guy slave. It seems there is a limit to the patience of both the king and the heavenly Father. What do you do with that? I can conjure up a scene with fire and devils in the next life, and wonder again about God as a loving Father.

Doesn't it seem that the Father too should forgive seventy-seven times? I can't help but wonder about that.

I've found some help in the Hindu notion of *karma*. Put briefly the idea of karma tells us that any transgression or sin carries with it its own punishment; as every act of love carries also with it its own reward. This way of looking at things cuts through the metaphors of punishment as something separate from wrong-doing. Likewise being a good person is like being a snowball. Snowballs get larger as they roll along. And so too for his malice, lies, and thievery, the thief or liar is degraded in the karmic way of looking at things by the deed itself. "Virtue," my mother used to say, "Is its own reward." I see nothing in this way of looking at things that contradicts the Father's punishment; it just puts the punishment where I think it ought to be, right here and right now, part and parcel of the deed, and not a matter of the Father's vengeance or His lack of patience.

Instead of seeing a vengeful God, the notion of karma sees that being mean demeans the doer himself as well as hurting the victim. I don't think that karma rules out need for the police or courts of law or jails, to name some of the common results of evil-doing outside the deed itself. It just means that the very nature of things carries reward and punishment. Understanding that helps me and makes sense to me. Maybe it will for you too. And yet we both know very well that on the surface of things at least, some people get away with murder. I didn't say I had an answer to all this, just some help. Karma is some help to me.

76. Matthew 19:16-30
The Rich Young Man—Poverty

The Passage

Then someone came to him and said, "Teacher, what good deed must I do to have eternal life?" And he said to him, "Why do you ask me about what is good? There is only one who is good. If you wish to enter into life, keep the commandments." He said to him, "Which ones?" And Jesus said, "You shall not murder; You shall not commit adultery; You shall not steal; you shall not bear false witness; Honor your father and mother; also, You shall love your neighbor as yourself," The young man said to him, "I have kept all these; what do I still lack? Jesus said to him, "If you wish to be perfect, go, sell your possessions, and give the money to the poor; and then come, follow me." When the young man heard this word, he went away grieving, for he had many possessions.

Then Jesus said to his disciples; "Truly I tell you, it will be hard for a rich person to enter the kingdom of heaven. Again I tell you, it is easier for a camel to go through the eye of the a needle than for someone who is rich to enter the kingdom of God." When the disciples heard this, they were greatly astounded and said, "Then who can be saved?" But Jesus looked at them and said, "For mortals it is impossible, but for God all things are possible."

Then Peter said in reply, "Look, we have left everything and followed you. What then will we have?" Jesus said to them, "Truly I tell you, at the renewal of all things, when the Son of Man is seated on the throne of his glory, you who have followed me will also sit on twelve thrones, judging the twelve tribes of Israel. And everyone who has left houses or children or fields, for my name's sake, will receive a hundredfold, and will inherit eternal life. But many who are first will be last and the last will be first."

Commentary

I want to let this story and Jesus' explanation of it stand. I don't want to make any sophisticated arguments to soften its bare message. There it is, "If you would be perfect, go, sell your possessions, give the money to the poor, and then come, follow me." The meaning for the rich young man is obvious. Jesus was right there to follow, and his prospective follower had to get rid of most of his worldly belongings if he wanted to follow Jesus. What does the story mean now, when the presence of the Lord with his people is not so visible as it was to the rich young man? The "sell what you have" is clear enough even now. So is, "Give to the poor." How about "Come, follow me?" I want to know what he has in mind in getting rid of your "stuff."

It's a hard one. Perhaps my own story can show you what I mean. When I was nineteen years old, I walked away from my Dad and Mother's money and joined a religious order called the Jesuits, as I have told you before. I thought I knew exactly what Jesus meant. I dumped my stuff and gave myself to a group of men whose aim was to follow Jesus. That was that! Twenty years later I realized that the members of most religious orders of men, including my own Jesuit people, live middle class bachelor lives in the service of God. They don't own anything personally, but they are well provided for. They have clothes, good food, places to sleep, and a position of honor in the larger community around them. Do they differ radically from the people around them? Mind you, they are good people, but so are most people. It is not clear to me today that nuns and priests, or for that matter mullahs or practitioners of Zen, Buddhist lamas, or Hindu holy men and women differ as sharply from their more secular counterparts as I once thought. It is not easy to walk away from your possessions; they have a way of catching up with you. My standard of living today is not so very different from that of my old Jesuit friends. We are all quite comfortable. Some of us are good people and some of us are not.

The state of perfection is both very simple or very complicated. Poverty is about the simple part. What in the world does it mean, though? Clearly it means living simply. Clearly it means not having your life dominated by clothes, cars, housing, and food. I don't think Jesus ever said that it was bad to eat or wear decent clothes, or to get enough sleep. He looked for generous people, not crazy ascetics. I can only go back to the law of love, and repeat what he said was the bottom line in all this living business, "Love your God; love your neighbor as yourself." Everything else rests on that, including whether you have great possessions or few.

I don't think it's a bad idea to know that if you do have a lot of the goods of this world, then you will not, very likely be one the favored ones in the kingdom. So, you're not number one in this rather strange order of things called Christianity. Maybe it's good to know that. Then you won't take yourself too seriously. Maybe then you will get on with being who you are where you are, that being the hand you have been dealt. So, what if you won't be seated on a throne judging the twelve tribes of Israel on that Great Gettin' Up Morning? Perhaps you will be reminded of something else that Jesus said in the context of the Rich Young Man story. He mentioned that it was as hard for a rich person to be saved as it was for a camel to go through the eye of a needle. He really did say that. And then he said, "For mortals it is impossible, but for God all things are possible." God can save us rich guys; we just won't have front row seats in whatever comes after death. That, I think, is that. And if you reply that you're going to give away all your stuff to follow Jesus, I might grin and say, "It's easier to say that than it is to do it. If you succeed in doing that," I say, "My hat is off to you."

77. Matthew 20:1-16
The Laborers in the Vineyard

The Passage

"For the kingdom of heaven is like a landowner who went out early in the morning to hire laborers for his vineyard. After agreeing with the laborers for the usual daily wage, he sent them into his vineyard. When he went out at about nine o'clock, he saw others standing idle in the marketplace; and he said to them, 'You also go into the vineyard, and I will pay you whatever is right.' So they went. When he went out again at about noon and about three o'clock, he did the same. And about five o'clock he went out and found others standing around and he said to them, 'Why are you standing here idle all day?' They said to him, 'Because no one has hired us.' He said to them, 'You also go into the vineyard.' When evening came, the owner of the vineyard said to his manager, 'Call the laborers and give them their pay, beginning with the last and then going to the first.' When those hired about five o'clock came, each of them received the usual daily wage. Now when the first came, they thought they would receive more; but each of them also received the usual daily wage. And when they received it, they grumbled against the landowner, saying, 'These last worked only one hour, and you have made them equal to us who have borne the burden of the day and the scorching heat.' But he replied to one of them, 'Friend, I am doing you no wrong; did you not agree with me for the usual daily wage? Take what belongs to you and go; I choose to give to this last the same as I give to you. Am I not allowed to do what I choose with what belongs to me? Or are you envious because I am generous? So the last will be first and the first will be last.'"

Commentary

The note in *The HarperCollins Study Bible* remarks simply of this passage, "Status reversal characterizes the kingdom." Ain't it the damn truth? Who hasn't felt for the guys who worked all day and got the same as those who worked for as little as an hour? Do the good guys, the ones who worked all day, get the short end of the stick in Jesus' kingdom? Is that what this story means? If you the reader expect me to cut right through this seeming unfairness with a neat little statement that will clarify the whole business and leave you thinking, "Why didn't I think of that?", I'm afraid I can't do that. I know I'd be one of the envious ones.

Here's what I can do. I can remember that right here in my own vineyard, life is not fair. The damnedest people get the goodies. Good people, hard working people are often not the ones blessed with the good things of life. You know this and I know it too. I can't even imagine living in Bosnia, Serbia, Iraq or Afghanistan, Israel or Palestine; where death is so sudden, so soon, and life for ordinary people does not include enough to eat or the protection of a system of law. A favorite author of mine once said of her own religion, "Being Jewish can get you killed!" Being Black or Hispanic can get your car pulled over and searched for drugs by the police, while drivers of lighter complexion rarely get such a hassle from the keepers of the law.

I am one of the lucky ones; maybe you are too. Through no fault or virtue of my own, I am comfortable. I don't spend a lot of time lamenting my blessings. I do try to do my bit for those not so fortunate; I give a lot to charities and try to look out for my neighbors who don't have much. Such a good guy I am! You might say that I got a full day's wage for working only an hour. And if you think I'm being too modest, then think of your own examples; there are lots of other fortunate people, who have no particular claim on their good fortune.

How very interesting that the gospel stands the normal world on it's head. The folks who have hard times are the ones favored in the kingdom . . . and of course we lucky ones don't like that. I still wonder what this kingdom is, this place Jesus talks of so often. For the life of me I can't see the blessings of being murdered or maimed or hungry or out of work. Jesus says there are some such blessings. I do wonder what. I've talked to you about the hypocrisy so often associated with putting the kingdom in the next life. "Pie in the sky when you die" is cold comfort. That leaves us here, now, today. Where is the blessing here? I know some poor people have remarkable dignity. I know that some of them have cleaner consciences than those better off than they are. I also know that some poor folk are liars and cheats and just all round jerks, just as bad as some of the more fortunate ones.

Jesus had great compassion for the poor ones; he found something special there. He did know, and I do understand this, that poor people are not necessarily bad people; much of the time they have had, as the song says, "Just bad luck." What is there for me to do in all this? Only this, to have compassion on the people who don't have much and to know that much poverty and misery are the luck of the draw rather than something one has merited by hard work or a good attitude. That's all I can do with this haunting tale of the vineyard, to try to be generous, like my Lord, and to know that in many ways I am not generous at all.

78. Matthew 22:15-22. 23:23-27
A Question of Taxes

The Passage

Then the Pharisees went and plotted to entrap him in what he said. So they sent their disciples to him, along with the Herodians, saying, "Teacher, we know that you are sincere, and teach the way of God in accordance with truth, and show deference to no one; for you do not regard people with partiality. Tell us, then, what you think. Is it lawful to pay taxes to the emperor, or not?" But Jesus, aware of their malice, said, "Why are you putting me to the test, you hypocrites? Show me the coin used for the tax." And they brought him a denarius. Then he said to them, "Whose head is this, and whose title?" They answered, "The emperor's" Then he said to them, "Give therefore to the emperor the things that are the emperor's and to God the things that are God's." When they heard this, they were amazed; and they left him and went away.

* * *

"Woe to you, scribes and Pharisees, hypocrites! For you tithe mint, dill, and cummin, and have neglected the weightier matters of the law: justice and mercy and faith. It is these you ought to have practiced without neglecting the others. You blind guides! You strain out a gnat but swallow a camel!

Woe to you, scribes and Pharisees, hypocrites! For you clean the outside of the cup and of the plate, but inside they are full of greed and self-indulgence. You blind Pharisee! First clean the inside of the cup, so that the outside also may become clean.

Woe to you, scribes and Pharisees, hypocrites! For you are like whitewashed tombs which on the outside look beautiful, but inside they are full of the bones of the dead and all kinds of filth. So you also on the outside look righteous to others, but inside you are full of hypocrisy and lawlessness."

Commentary

I am surprised at his mildness, here, given the fact that the story is told as one where his enemies were trying to trick him into opposing the tax and therefore of guilty of disloyalty to Rome. Getting in trouble with Rome was putting your neck into the noose. Given all that, his response is mild. He doesn't tell them to be tax resisters, paying only that part of the tax that is not spent on armament, as a number of modern day American Christians do. Neither here nor elsewhere does he condemn slavery, except in so far as the slaves were among those most powerless and therefore deserving places of honor in the kingdom. His doesn't talk about paying a living wage either, except in so far as he does rail against the officials of Jewry for putting taxes on certain herbs and seasonings which poor people could ill afford to pay, while they themselves lived in luxury. He does not talk about pacifism except on a one to one basis. Despite the nervousness of the Romans about his being a possible revolutionary, he says nothing to the Jews about throwing off the yoke of Rome, however unjust that was. "Give to Caesar the things that are Caesar's and to God the things that are God's." That is the translation I learned as a boy.

What to make of that? I think that Jesus knew that government was a part of the human equation. He was not an anarchist. He knew that all governments are to some degree unjust too. He did not want to start his own movement with changing the structures around him, but within the human heart. Gandhi once said that militant nonviolence meant nothing if it did not begin in the individual person, in the home, in the family and neighborhood, the places closest to a person's heart. I think the Christian message has profound political implications and implications for the work place as well, but it has its origin within each one of us, in our own hearts. One must begin at the beginning. That's what I think. Social justice flows from individual justice. If it does not have the human heart as its base, it is meaningless. Give to God the things that are God's and then decide just which things are Caesar's and which things are not Caesar's. That's the nub of it. And if Pontius Pilate, the governor, did indeed have suspicions that the message of Jesus in its roots was a revolutionary one which would quite soon bring Rome and the Christian community into conflict, then Pilate was a perceptive man.

And if you still doubt that Jesus was a man who sometimes breathed fire, the latter of these two passages should lay that to rest!

79. Matthew 25:14-30
The Parable of the Talents

The Passage

"For it is as if a man, going on a journey summoned his slaves and entrusted his property to them; to one he gave five talents, to another two, to another one, to each according to his ability. Then he went away. The one who had received the five talents went off at once and traded with them, and made five more talents. In the same way the one who had the two talents made two more talents. But the one who had received the one talent went off and dug a hole in the ground and hid his master's money. After a long time the master of those slaves came and settled accounts with them. Then the one who had received the five talents came forward, bringing five more talents, saying, 'Master, you have handed over to me five talents; see, I have made five more talents.' His master said to him, 'Well done, good and trustworthy slave, you have been trustworthy in a few things. I will put you in charge of many things; enter into the joy of your master.' And the one with the two talents also came forward, saying, 'Master, you handed over to me two talents; see, I have made two more talents.' His master said to him, 'Well done, good and trustworthy slave; you have been trustworthy in a few things, I will put you in charge of many things; enter into the joy of your master.' Then the one who had received the one talent also came forward, saying, 'Master, I knew that you were a harsh man, reaping where you did not sow, and gathering where you did not scatter seed; so I was afraid, and I went and hid your talent in the ground. Here you have what is yours.' But his master replied, 'You wicked and lazy slave! You knew, did you, that I reap where I did not sow, and gather where I did not scatter? Then you ought to have invested my money with the bankers, and on my return I would have received what was my own with interest. So take the talent from him, and give it to the one with the ten talents. For to all those who have, more will be given, and they will have an abundance; but from those who have nothing, even what they have will be taken ways. And for this worthless slave, throw him into outer darkness, where there will be weeping and gnashing of teeth.'"

Commentary

There are moments as I write this commentary, when I shudder at the bluntness of the gospel. There are times when I wonder, "Is this the Good News that Jesus brought us? It seems so very, very harsh sometimes. This story is no exception. Who would not shudder at the thought of being the slave who buried his talent in the ground? Being cast into outer darkness where there will be weeping and gnashing of teeth is a brutal image. I cannot escape that, even if I know very well that I myself have already experienced being cast into outer darkness, where I have sobbed and ground my teeth in my misery. Oh yes, I've been there; so have you. Who was it that coined the phrase, "Shit happens!"? Yes, it does.

Now, having said that, having refused to sweep the harshness of this story under the rug, I want to go on. In this parable I do find a silver lining. I think it has to do with the recognition that we have all been given different talents, some this; some that. Some more; some less. Jesus says that we are called to use what we have, not what we don't have. The slave who had been given but one talent was not condemned for having only one, but for not using what he had. If you have ever been plagued by what one might be called "the Messiah Complex" you will understand what I'm saying here, and what I think Jesus was saying as well. Have you ever imagined yourself doing great things? Have you ever tried to be Superman when you as a matter of fact were only man? Have you tried to be Wonder-Woman when you were just woman? If you have, you know that it doesn't work.

I know, by the way, that I have sometimes been told that my only limitations are the limitations of my courage and imagination. I have sometimes believed that too. It's all part of positive thinking. Frankly, I think a lot of this kind of thinking is bullshit, to use a blunt phrase of my own. You find out, gradually that what you can do and what you'd like to do don't always coincide. I can remember being six feet tall, weighing one hundred and thirty pounds, being slow of foot and awkward in my movements and at the same time desperately wanting to be a football player on my school's team. After years of lusting to be a football player, I arrived at the startling insight that there was no way I could make the squad of my high school team. The talent just wasn't there. One does not live by desires alone, you might say.

Only slowly, very, very slowly have I come to the realization that I am not required to be somebody else and that the only talent I need to develop is my own. It's not how much I have, it's what I do with what is there. One of the very few times in my life when I've heard a voice I felt was divine one, that voice said to me, "All I want is you." You can look at the parable of the talents that way and not soften its message, the only talent God holds you to is the one you have. I'm grateful for that. The word "talent" by the way, means in this context, a very large amount of money. Just one talent is a whole lot. Get the picture?

80. Matthew 25:31-46
Sheep and Goats: the Social Gospel

The Passage

When the Son of Man comes in his glory, and all the angels with him, then he will sit on the throne of his glory. All the nations will be gathered before him, and he will separate people one from another as a shepherd separates the sheep from the goats, and he will put the sheep at his right hand and the goats at the left. Then the king will say to those at his right hand, 'Come, you that are blessed by my Father, inherit the kingdom prepared for you from the foundation of the world; for I was hungry and you gave me food, I was thirsty and you gave me something to drink, I was a stranger and you welcomed me, I was naked and you gave me clothing, I was sick and you took care of me, I was in prison and you visited me.' The righteous will answer him, 'Lord, when was it that we saw you a stranger and welcomed you, or naked and gave you clothing? And when was it that we saw you sick or in prison and visited you?' And the king will answer them, 'Truly I tell you, just as you did it to one of the least of these who are members of my family, you did it to me.' Then he will say to those at his left hand, 'You accursed, depart from me into eternal fire prepared for the devil and his angels; for I was hungry and you gave me no food, I was thirsty and you gave me nothing to drink, I was a stranger and you did not welcome me, naked and you did not give me clothing, sick and in prison and you did not visit me.' Then they also will answer, 'Lord, when was it we saw you hungry or thirsty or a stranger or naked or sick or in prison, and did not take care of you?' Then he will answer them. 'Truly I tell you, just as you did not do it to one of the least of these, you did not do it to me.' And these will go away into eternal punishment, but the righteous into eternal life."

Commentary

This is another of what I have learned to call the "Oh my!" passages in the gospel. It is so stark, so clear, so majestic and fearful, yet at the same time so very beautifully horizontal. Those who take care of others take care of Jesus; that's it. If I speak of the punishment of hell or heed it, and I sometimes do, I think of hell primarily as a self-made, standing alone and lonely, cut off from other people. I recall a Jewish housewife once telling me, "If I take care of keeping a kosher kitchen, everything else follows." Who was it who said, "Food is love."? Jesus has spoken so many times of the primacy of love. The commandments reduce to one; take care of that and everything else follows; neglect it, and you are alone. That, it seems, is the difference between the sheep and the goats.

There is something added here, as well, when he says, "If you have cared for one of these least ones, you have taken care of me." Strong medicine that. When I was a novice in the Jesuits, we practiced giving short sermons, always in the form of stories, I remember a dear friend and fellow novice speaking about a derelict standing under street light, the dark of a summer night around him. A passerby slipped a dollar bill into his hand and disappeared into the evening gloom. The last line of the story went like this, "Then Jesus smiled, hitched up his ill fitting old trousers, took another drag on his cigarette and shuffled off into the night, his worn out shoes making a slapping noise on the pavement as he moved off." That was it; no explanations, no tortured logic, no frills. Take it or leave it. That's all there is; there isn't any more.

81. Matthew 26:31-35
Deserters—Almost All

The Passage

Then (after the Last Supper) Jesus said to them, "You will all become deserters because of me this night; for it is written:

'I will strike the shepherd,
and the sheep of the flock will
be scattered.'

But after I am raised up, I will go ahead of you to Galilee." Peter said to him, "Though all become deserters because of you, I will never desert you." Jesus said to him, "Truly I tell you, this very night before the cock crows, you will deny me three times." Peter said to him, "Even though I must die with you, I will not deny you." And so said all the disciples.

Commentary

If, as the saying goes, "The brave one dies but once, the coward a thousand times," then put me down with the cowards . . . me, Francis, the writer here commenting. Yes, I know, this is so. 'Well?" You say, "So? Are you sure you're not a courageous fellow who is humble?" "Yes, I'm sure." "Well," you say, "How do you know?" "I know because I have already died at least five hundred of my allotted thousand and am showing no signs of avoiding a death or two today."

"And?" You say, "And I have a feel for those disciples, even Peter the braggart, the loud mouth. For all the ferocity of the gospel message, there still seems room for those who panic. These, after all are the same ones who first preached the gospel. He didn't kick them out. And of course there were some exceptions. Some did not run away. Did you know that? Those who stood at the cross, those who walked the walk up Golgotha, those who went to anoint his dead body, were all women, every one of them. How very strange.

82. Matthew 26:36-46
Agony in the Garden

The Passage

Jesus then went with them to a place called Gethsemane; and he said to his disciples, "Sit here while I go over there and pray." He took with him Peter and the two sons of Zebedee, and began to be grieved and agitated. Then he said to them, "I am deeply grieved even to death; remain here, and stay awake with me." And going a little farther, he threw himself on the ground and prayed "My Father if it is possible, let this cup pass from me; yet not what I want but what you want." Then he came to the disciples and found them sleeping; and he said to Peter, "So could you not stay awake with me one hour? Stay awake and pray that you may not come into the time of trial; the spirit indeed is willing, but the flesh is weak." Again he went away for the second time and prayed, "My Father, if this cannot pass unless I drink it, your will be done." Again he came and found them sleeping, for their eyes were heavy. So leaving them again, he went away and prayed a third time, saying the same words. Then he came to the disciples and said to them, "Are you still sleeping and taking your rest? See, the hour is at hand, and the Son of Man is betrayed into the hands of sinners. Get up, let us be going. See, my betrayer is at hand."

Commentary

Why am I always surprised that He wanted to escape from of all this trouble and treachery? When I remember my mother once telling me that Lord Nelson, the English admiral at the battle of Trafalgar, the one who bested Napoleon at sea, is said to have told someone that he had never known fear; what's more he didn't even know what fear was. On another occasion, the same Lord Nelson is said to have been warned of some disaster approaching his fleet of ships. When called upon to look at the approaching danger, he put his spy glass to his blind eye, saying at the same time that he saw nothing to be afraid of. Jesus wasn't like that.

Jesus uses a good semitic figure of speech when he says, "Father, let this cup pass from me." The cup from which he did not want to drink was the agony ahead, the cross, the desertion, the death. I don't think you have to invoke the divine mind in Jesus for him to have known what was coming. He knew very well as a human being, that things were coming to a head. He knew his enemy and he knew his friends; he knew who would prevail. Brutal punishment for even minor dissenters from Roman hegemony was the trademark of the Roman overlords. Nobody was going to save him from all this and he knew it. Yet he did wish to escape it; he wanted to be free of it, and he asked for that from his Abba, his father. That helps.

83. Matthew 27:44-56
The Crucifixion: The Ground Beneath Their Feet

The Passage

The bandits who were crucified with him also taunted him in the same way.

From noon on, darkness came over the whole land until three in the afternoon. And about three o'clock Jesus cried with a loud voice, "Eli, Eli, lema sabachthani?" That is, "My God, my God, why have you forsaken me?" When some of the bystanders heard it, they said, "This man is calling for Elijah." At once one of them ran and got a sponge, filled it with sour wine put it on a stick, and gave it to him to drink. But the others said, "Wait, let us see whether Elijah will come to save him." Then Jesus cried again with a loud voice and breathed his last. At that moment the curtain of the temple was torn in two, from the top to bottom. The earth shook, and the rocks were split. The tombs also were opened, and many bodies of the saints who had fallen asleep were raised. After his resurrection they came out of the tombs and entered the holy city and appeared to many. Now when the centurion and those with him , who were keeping watch over Jesus, saw the earthquake and what took place, they were terrified and said, "Truly this man was God's Son!"

Many women were also there, looking on from a distance; they had followed Jesus from Galilee and had provided for him. Among them were Mary Magdalene, and Mary the mother of James and Joseph, and the mother of the sons of Zebedee.

Commentary

And so we have it, at the stark heart of Christianity is Messiah nailed to a cross. His words of seeming despair, "My God, My God, why have you forsaken me?" In another place I have reminded you the reader that his words are a quote from Psalm 22. I'm going to show you that psalm again right here:

> My God, my God, why have you
> forsaken me?
> Why are you so far from
> helping me, from the
> Words of my groaning?

O my God, I cry by day, but you
                    do not answer;
              and by night, but find no rest.

Yet you are holy,
              Enthroned on the praise of
                    Israel
In you our ancestors trusted;
              they trusted and you delivered
                    them.

* * *

Deliver my soul from the sword,
              my life from the power of
                    the dog!
Save me from the mouth of the
              lion!

From the horns of the wild oxen
              you have rescued me.
I will tell of your name to my
                    brothers and sisters;
              In the midst of the
                    congregation I will
                    praise you;[12]

* * *

There is both despair and hope in this psalm and in Jesus who quotes
it. How often the two go together in real life. Despair and hope are
indeed sisters; only seldom do they appear apart from each other. So it is
here with the dying Christ. I do not wish to mitigate either end of the
terrible balance between the two. They are the words of desperation, of

---

12. Psalm 22:1-4, 19-23. This is a long and rich psalm. I quote only this
much of it to show both the despair and hope of the psalmist and Jesus who
quotes its opening lines.

a man dying during torture, dying unfairly. We have a word for it in English. That word is *lynching*. It is a part of our history in these United States . . . the grim execution of a person without trial whether or not he is guilty. It is almost always part of a mob scene with only a few, fraudulent trappings of justice. No wonder to me that Jesus is sometimes portrayed by American artists as a Black man.

Matthew tells us further that at the moment Jesus breathed his last breath that "The earth shook, and the rocks were split." I am reminded of Salmon Rushdie's novel, *The Ground Beneath her Feet*. In that novel there are earthquakes accompanying the death of the book's heroine, a rock star, Vina Aspara. In Rushdie's story she was a woman who had stood out in protest during a time of great international turmoil, warfare and unrest, the nineteen sixties of our own times, her music a sound of protest and hope. As Rushdie has one of his characters put it, a man who promoted Rock and Roll music:

> He wants to say—his eyes are gleaming now, and the energy pours from him with redoubled, frightening force—that what the war has turned him on to is its consequent music because in this dark time it's the rock music that represents the country's most profound artistic engagement with the death of its children, not the music of peace and psycho-tropic drugs, but the music of rage and sorrow and despair. Also of youth, youth surviving in spite of everything, in spite of the children's crusade that's blowing it apart. (A mine, a sniper, a knife in the night: childhood's bitter end.)[13]

I am using this quote for a number of reasons, one of them being that I do regard much of the music of Rock and Roll much as Rushdie's character sees it, music which is one of the prime artistic attempts of our own time to protest the manifold injustices of our own time . . . racism, consumerism, prudery, and the power of great corporations to do almost anything to make a profit: from selling arms to warring nations to enslaving third world countries in the process of making more and more of the stuff of luxury for Americans and Europeans.

That Rushdie should imagine the ground as breaking, the planet shaking at the death of one of the prophets whose music protests much of the ills of the world does not surprise me. That Matthew's gospel should

---

13. *The Ground Beneath Her Feet* by Salmon Rushdie, p. 265.

picture an earthquake in concert with the death of the Messiah surprises me even less. Matthew wants the reader to see that the ground beneath our feet is shaken by the death of this man. He goes on to say that the tombs of dead people opened in response to Jesus' death, and that these people who had died, arose and walked about mysteriously in the streets of Jerusalem. He adds that the great veil in the temple of all Jewry was at this moment torn in two, from top to bottom and that in the midst of all this the soldiers keeping guard over this execution were terrified by these strange reverberations of nature at the death of this man.

The earth, I suggest, is always affected by human tragedy and the passing of those who protest against tragedy. Global warming and pollution being good evidence that both Matthew's gospel and Rushdie's novel are keen enough to know that tragedy is never private and that evil inevitably leaves its mark on the planet we live on. If there is a silver lining in Matthew's grim account it is that the dead one's unexpected rising heralds a resurrection, a renewal of life and hope, accompanying his gruesome death. And as you know the earth can rejoice as well as be sad, the great stone said to have sealed the grave of Jesus will be seen rolling away as a very different kind of earthquake from its predecessor of three days before.

84. Matthew 28:1-10
The Resurrection of Jesus

The Passage

After the sabbath, as the first day of the week was dawning, Mary Magdalene and the other Mary went to see the tomb. And suddenly there was a great earthquake; for an angel of the Lord, descending from heaven, came and rolled back the stone and sat on it. His appearance was like lightning, and his clothing white as snow. For fear of him the guards shook and became like dead men. But the angel said to the women looking for Jesus who was crucified. "Do not be afraid. I know that you are looking for Jesus who was crucified. He is not here; for he has been raised, as he said. Come, see the place where he lay. Then go quickly and tell his disciples, 'He has been raised from the dead, and indeed he is going ahead of you to Galilee; there you will see him.' This is my message for you." So they left the tomb quickly with fear and great joy, and ran to tell his disciples. Suddenly Jesus met them and said, "Greetings!" And they came to him, took hold of his feet, and worshiped him. Then Jesus said to them, "Do not be afraid; go and tell my brothers to go to Galilee; there they will see me."

Commentary

And so, we see, the earth shakes again, this time in joy and wonder. The women are still in their place of primacy, the first ones going to the tomb. Perhaps you know that the word "angel" in Greek simply means "messenger", you don't have to imagine a seven foot tall hermaphrodite with wings, the way angels are often seen in pictures today. Only a resplendent and powerful person whose garments and mien remind one of the Transfiguration, so recently described as a portent of Easter. Most of the Easter accounts, including this one have people moving quickly, things happening suddenly, a huge rock pushed aside as though it were a pebble. The messenger tells them briefly that Jesus is risen, and then, "Go quickly and tell his disciples." The angel disappears. We are in another dimension. Jesus suddenly appears; his message is brief, "Do not be afraid." It echoes the words of the angel Then he says "Tell my brothers to go to Galilee; there they will see me." With these words he is gone.

I think that it's very important to understand that we are in a sort of time warp here. There is speed, fear, joy, confusion. Jesus is certainly not the same as before, not the tortured dead man, not even the companion of their travels. He is different. He comes and goes on the instant. He is here and not here. He is mysterious. I want to remind you to put on your imaginative hat. I want to remind you that the clear meaning of Easter is the presence of Jesus with his people. He has returned to them, but he is not the same. He is clearly not bound by time or space. Whatever you may think of the Resurrection of Jesus, whether you want to take it literally, or as I take it, a story making it clear that Jesus is present in his church in a way different from the old days when he walked the dusty roads with them, grew tired with them, was exasperated with them, was angry and tender by terms, this Jesus is well above the normal trivia of human living. I find this story and the other resurrection stories as fitting the way Semitic people described and underlined great events. You will remember the stories around his birth, their purpose is not so much a factual and historical account as is the underlining of the Messiah's birth. It makes clear that his trademark is poverty, openness to all, and one following the lines of the great Messiahs of the past: Moses and David, Samson and Samuel, Abraham and Isaac, the great heroes of the Hebrew people. The Resurrection stories are like the infancy stories. They are beautiful accounts trying to probe the mystery that the Christian community has felt down the ages, that somehow, someway He is still with them, alive, influential, active, visible above all in The Breaking of the Bread, which today we call the Eucharist.

I would add that it is legitimate to remember that Jesus himself heaped scorn on those who insisted on amazing works, miracles, healings, and tricks. It makes sense to me that he would have some chagrin if the great sign of his continued presence with his people was made merely into the biggest magic trick of all, the event of the resurrection. The real wonder is his continued presence with his people. No matter where you stand on the historical truth of the resurrection, this much is clear, its meaning is that Jesus remains present to those who follow him. The early Christians experienced this just as Christians today experience it. It is the mysterious vital heart of the Christian life.

85. Matthew 28:16-20
He Sends Them into the World

The Passage

Now the eleven disciples went to Galilee, to the mountain to which Jesus had directed them. When they saw him, they worshiped him; but some doubted. And Jesus came and said to them, "All authority in heaven and on earth has been given to me. Go therefore and make disciples of all nations, baptizing them in the name of the Father and of the Son and of the Holy Spirit, and teaching them to obey everything that I have commanded you. And remember, I am with you always, to the end of the age."

Commentary

These are the last verses of Matthew's gospel. I quote them here, because I want you to see some of the trademarks of this particular gospel. His message is for all peoples, quite clearly stated. It goes beyond the boundaries of Jesus' own Judaism. His followers are to teach his message, summarized in the great commandment of love. And finally, he will be with them always, the key to the meaning of the Resurrection. That the eleven are still confused at this climax of Christianity's beginnings, what does that mean? I think it means that we, like them, are never without doubt, even though we worship Him. Doubt being one of the less savory but ever present qualities of those who have followed him from that day to this. [14]

---

14. I am in debt to both Dr. Bernard Cooke and Dr. John Dominic Crossan's works for my remarks on the Resurrection of Jesus, but I hold neither one responsible for my remarks on this subject.

Part Four

The Gospel According to Luke

86. Luke 1:26-38
The Birth of Jesus Foretold

The Passage

In the sixth month the angel Gabriel was sent by God to a town in Galilee called Nazareth, to a virgin engaged to a man whose name was Joseph of the house of David. The virgin's name was Mary. And he came to her and said, "Greetings, favored one! The Lord is with you." But she was much perplexed by his words and pondered what sort of greeting this might be. The angel said to her, "Do not be afraid, Mary, for you have found favor with God. And now, you will conceive in your womb and bear a son, and you will name him Jesus. He will be great, and will be called the Son of the Most High and the Lord God will give to him the throne of his ancestor David. He will reign over the house of Jacob forever, and his kingdom there will be no end." Mary said the angel "How can this be, since I am a virgin?" The angel said to her, "The Holy Spirit will come upon you, and the power of the Most High will overshadow you; therefore the child to be born will be holy; he will be called the Son of God." Then Mary said, "Here am I, the servant of the Lord; let it be with me according to your word." Then the angel departed from her.

Commentary

Who has not heard this story in one version or another, in one way or another. In all the nearly endless reams of commentaries given to interpreting this amazing story, one thing has remained with me. I have it etched in my heart what Matthias Scheeben said, writing nearly a century ago, "When God became man; man became God." Scheeben knew that the coming of the Messiah marked an amazing and divine compliment to the human race. For it meant that the Holy One come to us is not just a spirit, a will o' the wisp, but a real human being with a real human mind and body. As if in the history of religious peoples here was one big exclamation point on the holiness of the human body in particular and the holiness of all material things in general.[1]

Lots of religious traditions, not just the ones which have their origins in the Jewish people, have felt that one's body is somehow a block to one's spirituality. Some of them have taught that the real world is the unseen world, the spiritual world, and that access to this higher world would come only in so far as a person could separate her- or himself from physical form. The body and all material things are often seen by religious people as a kind of trailer or wagon that one must put up with, the wagon being impossible to detach from the spirit short of death. Christianity has been plagued almost from its beginnings with a suspicion of bodily pleasure and joy, despite the fact of the divine visitation par excellence, when He took on our flesh, our materiality. "So what?" you may say. Here's what I think.

I think at its very root Christianity places a special emphasis on the holiness of the material world. It puts great emphasis on bodies and bodily pleasure, precisely because Jesus, like us, was an embodied person. Sexuality, gusto in eating and drinking, bodily health and beauty are all underlined by the coming of the Most High upon a young Jewish girl in Galilee two thousand years ago. I do wonder, and perhaps you have wondered too, why in the world Christianity has been so marked off and on throughout its history with a series of movements that hold the human body in contempt. There is a long chain of isms: Manicheeism, Puritanism, Jansenism are but a few names of movements within the Christian tradition which regard sexuality, health, and bodily joys of all kinds as things which drag one away from the basic spirit of the Christian tradition.

---

1. I might add that Indian religion has dozens of cases of gods becoming human. One might say that Hindus find no problem with Christianity's hall mark of the God-become-human. Their problem with Christianity is that in Christian belief this has happened only once!

I don't know how to account for this. Maybe it is the philosophy of Plato with its emphasis on immaterial forms, as it has become ingrained in Christianity. Perhaps it is the sufferings of women as they have conceived and born children down the ages. Maybe it has been the very real danger of addiction to sexual pleasure or addiction to drink or food. I don't know. All I offer you here in the story of Gabriel's appearance to the virgin in Galilee is the suggestion that all bodily things, including health and pleasure would seem of necessity to have become in a special way divine with the conception of the Messiah in the womb of a young woman.

87. Luke 1:46-56
Mary Visits her Cousin Elizabeth
The Magnificat

N.B. Rather than repeat a long text here introducing this event, I will merely note that after Mary became pregnant she traveled to the home of her kinswoman, Elizabeth, who had also conceived a child in a most unusual way, for Elizabeth was older than Mary and no longer having her menstrual period. This son, the cousin of Jesus, is to become John the Baptist, the rough wildman who introduced Jesus to his public life years later on the banks of the Jordan River. Elizabeth greets her kinswoman with words indicating that she knew of the greatness of the one to be born of Mary. In response to this recognition of the Messiah within her by her cousin, Mary said these words:

The Passage

And Mary said,

> "My soul magnifies the Lord,
>   and my spirit rejoices in God
>   my Savior,
> for he has looked with favor on
>   the lowliness of his servant.
>   Surely, from now on all
>   generations will call
>   me blessed;
> for the mighty One has done
>   great things for me,
>   and holy is his name.
> His mercy is for those who
>   fear him
>   from generation to generation.
> He has shown strength with
>   his arm;
>   he has scattered the proud in
>   the thoughts of their
>   hearts.

He has brought down the
> powerful from their
> thrones,
and lifted up the lowly;
he has filled the hungry with
> good things,
and sent the rich away empty.
He has helped his servant Israel,
> in remembrance of his mercy,
according to the promise he
> made to our ancestors,
to Abraham and to his
> descendants forever."

And Mary remained with her about three months and then returned to her home.

Commentary*

When I was sixteen years old and a junior in high school I somehow found myself driving to a nearby Church for Mass each morning during the forty days of Lent, that season of Penance which is traditional in a number of Christian traditions, in preparation for the Easter celebration of the Passion and Resurrection of Jesus. A number of young people went to that service, prior to heading off to school. The priests in the parish were young men; it was a new congregation, the church not yet built, and services held in a building which would later become a gym for the parish. There was an incredibly attractive young Filipino priest there. There was as well a young Irish-American priest with wavy hair and an impish sense of humor. My sister and the other high school girls who went to daily Mass there were all in love with these young clerics, besides being pious . . . and seeing no problem with the mixture of piety and infatuation. I remember that Lent as a wonderful forty days. It was the joy of being somehow holy on our own; nobody's parents had anything to do with our devotion or the fact that we shared it in the company of other teenagers and charming young priests, there in the Spring days of 1946. I carry that ambience with me to this day.

The Mass was most ordinary, no sermon, no singing, just the standard Latin rite, with one exception. It was customary in that church, at the end of Mass for everyone to recite the words of The Magnificat in English, priest and people, in unison, the Magnificat being the name we had for the passage from St. Luke I have just quoted above. I learned to love Mary's poem of acceptance and joy at being a most ordinary young woman chosen for a most extraordinary role in the history of salvation. What struck me then, as it does now, is theme of lowliness, the preference of God in Mary's prayer for those who have little in the way of the goods of this world. I might remind you that I was a very self-conscious high school boy, anything but a big deal, lost in the awkwardness of my newly acquired six foot body, skinny as a rail. I was filled with warmth as I gradually learned the words of that great soliloquy. There was a place for nobodies in my religion. The mother of the Messiah was one of those, and she knew there would be others down the years, me and others like me. And I still thrill at the words of this old song.

* *I am aware of the awful and rending scandal presently continuing to surface in the American Catholic Church. I can only offer here a memory that has nothing of sexual abuse involved in it, the more poignant because this is the kind of occasion in which there have been, as we know now, tragic episodes of priests taking advantage of young people. F.G.*

88. Luke 2:1-20
The Birth of Jesus

The Passage

In those days a decree went out from Emperor Augustus that all the world should be registered. This was the first registration and was taken while Quirinius was governor of Syria. All went to their own towns to be registered. Joseph also went from the town of Nazareth in Galilee to Judea, to the city of David called Bethlehem, because he was descended from the house and family of David. He went to be registered with Mary to whom he was engaged and who was expecting a child. While they were there, the time came for her to deliver her child. And she gave birth to her firstborn son and wrapped him in bands of cloth, and laid him in a manger, because there was no place for them in the inn.

In that region there were shepherds living in the fields, keeping watch over their flock by night. Then an angel of the Lord stood before them, and the glory of the Lord shone around them, and they were terrified. But the angel said to them, "Do not be afraid; for see—I am bringing you good news of great joy for all the people: to you is born this day in the city of David a Savior, who is the Messiah, the Lord. This will be a sign for you: you will find a child wrapped in bands of cloth and lying in a manger." And suddenly there was with the angel a multitude of the heavenly host, praising God and saying,

> "Glory to God in the highest
>   heaven,
>   and on earth peace among
>   those whom he favors!"

When the angels had left them and gone into heaven, the shepherds said to one another, "Let us go now to Bethlehem and see this thing that has taken place, which the Lord has made known to us." So they went with haste and found Mary and Joseph, and the child lying in the manger. When they saw this, they made known what had been told them about this child; and all who heard it were amazed at the what the shepherds told them. But Mary treasured all these words and pondered them in her heart. The shepherds returned, glorifying and praising God for all they had heard and seen, as it had been told them.

Commentary

Perhaps this passage from Luke describing the birth of the Divine Child is the most familiar one, the most fraught with personal memories, of all the scripture passages of the New Testament. My mother was so struck by the spirit of Christmas that she collected creches, small replications of the scene in the manger. We had little clay figures of Joseph and Mary, the shepherds and the infant made by my sisters when they were little girls, as a part of Christmas morning. They were placed on the seat of a wicker chair with a sheet over it just to the left of our Christmas tree, the sheet to give the appearance of snow. And there were lots of others, acquired singly through the years.

And I remember, years after my childhood, cutting silhouettes of the scene in the stable from black paper and mounting them in front of a plastic backdrop with a floodlight behind them, so that they stood out, black on white in their A-frame cave which two of us seminarians had erected in front of Rockhurst High School in Kansas City, Missouri. Rockhurst High was my very first teaching job as a member of the Jesuit Order. I remember too not knowing where to get some hay for our scene and slipping out to the zoo in Swope Park, scaling a woven wire fence at the zoo, grabbing two bales of hay and flipping them over the fence to a couple of surprised students from school, the surprise being, I suppose, that we were stealing the hay and that there was supposed to be a leopard somewhere in that enclosure where lay those tempting bales. We got away with it and our creche won some sort of prize that year and was written up in the *Kansas City Star*, contraband hay and all. We didn't tell the reporter from *The Star* where we got the hay.

I remember giving my first Christmas sermon as a priest, and suggesting strongly to my captive audience in a suburban Kansas City Church, that if Jesus were born on that day in 1962 in Kansas City that he would have been a child of color, black or brown, and that he would have been born in the slums of the Kansas City bottoms near the Missouri River rather than out in the suburbs where the comfortable people were, ourselves included.

Some years later I remember reading a poem by Lawrence Ferlinghetti at Mass on Christmas in the Jesuit church attached to St. Louis University where I taught religion to the undergraduates. I'm going to quote the poem here. You'll get the message.

Christ climbed down
from His bare Tree
this year
and ran away to where
there were no rootless Christmas trees
hung with candycanes and breakable stars

Christ climbed down
from His bare Tree
this year and ran away to where
there were no gilded Christmas trees
and no tinsel Christmas trees
and no tinfoil Christmas trees
and no pink plastic Christmas trees
and no gold Christmas trees and
no black Christmas trees
and no powderblue Christmas trees
hung with electric candles
and encircled by tin electric trains
and clever cornball relatives

Christ climbed down
from His bare Tree
this year
and ran away to where
no intrepid Bible salesmen
covered the territory
in two-tone Cadillacs
and where no Sears Roebuck creches
complete with plastic babe in manger
arrived by parcel post
the babe by special delivery
and where no televised Wise Men
praised the Lord Calvert Whiskey

Christ climbed down
from His bare Tree
this year
and ran away to where

no fat handshaking stranger
in a red flannel suit
and a fake white beard
went around passing himself off
as some sort of North Pole saint
crossing the desert to Bethlehem
Pennsylvania in a Volkswagon sled
drawn by rollicking Adirondack reindeer
with German names
and bearing sacks of Humble Gifts
from Saks Fifth Avenue
for everybody's imagined Christ child

Christ climbed down
from His bare Tree
this year and ran away to where
no Bing Crosby carollers
groaned of a tight Christmas
and where no Radio City angels
iceskated wingless
thru a winter wonderland
into a jinglebell heaven
daily at 8:30
with Midnight Mass matinees

Christ climbed down
from His bare Tree
this year
and softly stole away into
some anonymous Mary's womb again
where in the darkest night
of everybody's anonymous soul
He awaits again
an unimaginable
and impossibly

Immaculate Reconception
the very craziest
of Second Comings[2]

Those were the sixties and this is a very sixties Christmas poem.

And I remember some years later buying a Christmas tree for a dollar in the city of Ottawa in Canada and decorating it with the woman who shortly afterwards would become my wife. There were not a lot of ornaments on that tree. I was a doctoral student in religious studies at the University of Ottawa having very recently left the priesthood and the Jesuits to marry a brave young former nun who is my wife today and the mother of Joe and Matt, our sons.

That was more than thirty years ago and there have been more than thirty Christmases since that time, each one featuring the manger scene and shepherds from Luke's gospel. On one occasion when my son Joe was eight years old and his brother Matt six, we dramatized the scene at the inn. I was a donkey, Joe was Joseph, Toni was Mary. I clambered up the stairs of the house with Toni on my back accompanied by Joe and into Joe's bedroom where Matt the innkeeper awaited us. We all sat down on Joe's bed—Joe, Toni, and I the donkey. Matt had his lines to say and a little sense of drama of his own. With a flourish he announced, "No room on the end!"[3] and shoved all three of us off the end of the bed onto the hardwood floor. That was that!

So, we have, and you most likely have, a lot of memories of the first Christmas as told by Luke the evangelist. The memories match the times. If I have one enduring memory in all these ghosts of Christmas past, it is the knowledge that Jesus was born poor, that the first witnesses to his birth were sheep herders, not fancy folk, and that Luke wants firmly to establish the child as born of David's line, David the former shepherd himself, the greatest of the kings of Israel, from whose line his people expected another great king and priest, the Messiah. What they got was a shock, not the kind of King or Christ they were expecting. Celebrating his birth is still a surprise. He is very different sort of King than most.

---

2. "Christ Climbed Down" in *A Coney Island of the Mind* by Lawrence Ferlinghetti.

3. Matt's lines, of course, were supposed to read, "No room in the inn."

89. Luke 2:21-40
Jesus Is Named and Presented in the Temple:
Anna, Simeon, Growth

The Passage

After eight days had passed, it was time to circumcise the child; and he was called Jesus, the name given by the angel before he was conceived in the womb.

When the time came for their purification according to the law of Moses, they brought him up to Jerusalem to present him to the Lord (as it is written in the law of the Lord, "Every firstborn male shall be designated as holy to the Lord"), and they offered a sacrifice according to what is stated in the law of the Lord, "a pair of turtledoves or two young pigeons."

Now there was a man in Jerusalem whose name was Simeon; this man was righteous and devout, looking forward to the consolation of Israel, and the Holy Spirit rested on him. It had been revealed to him by the Holy Spirit that he would not see death before he had seen the Lord's Messiah. Guided by the Spirit, Simeon came into the temple; and when the parents brought in the child Jesus, to do for him what was customary under the law, Simeon took him in his arms and praised God, saying

> "Master, now you are dismissing
>   your servant in peace,
>   according to your word;
> for my eyes have seen your
>   salvation
>   which you have prepared in the
>   presence of all peoples,
> a light for the revelation to the
>   Gentiles
>   and for glory to your people
>   Israel."

And the child's father and mother were amazed at what was being said about him. Then Simeon blessed them and said to his mother Mary, "This child is destined for the falling and the rising of many in Israel, and to be a sign that will be opposed so that the inner thoughts of many will be revealed—and a sword will pierce your own soul too."

There was also a prophet, Anna the daughter of Phanuel, of the tribe of Asher. She was of great age, having lived with her husband seven years after her marriage, then as a widow to the age of eighty-four. She never left the temple but worshiped there with fasting and prayer night and day. At that moment she came and began to praise God and to speak about the child to all who were looking for the redemption of Jerusalem.

When they had finished everything required by the law of the Lord, they returned to Galilee, to their own town of Nazareth. The child grew and became strong, filled with wisdom; and the favor of God was upon him.

Commentary

They kept the law, these people; they were Jews. They didn't have much; that's why they offered a sacrifice of doves rather than a lamb, which was more costly. The child was circumcised. A year or so ago I went to a circumcision ceremony for the male child of a Jewish colleague at my university. I stood there while the moil cut off the fold of skin from the tip of the baby's penis. What ran through my mind was something like this, "These people know what suffering is about! That little surgical nip is quite different from Baptism. Here blood is drawn; there is pain. Babies don't take kindly to this; they howl!" I was awed. I thought right there that I had an understanding of Judaism I had never known before. In my heart I thought, "This is a no-shit religion! These people play for keeps. This is no puny gesture, this initial welcoming of a boy child into the faith of his mommas and poppas. Spilling blood is a part of Jewish history and they underline it right here at the beginning of a baby's welcoming rite."

Jesus was born into these people. His blood was drawn, his penis nipped just like any other Jewish boy. Pain is and has always been at the heart of being Jewish, from the get go. As for Simeon, he is the one who sees, the one who underlines the magic of the child. He announces the significance of this boy child; he tells us that this is no ordinary child. He tells us that Jesus is important to us outsiders as well as his own people, we who are the Gentiles. He warns his mother that a sword will pierce her heart. In Luke's gospel, Simeon is another person in who sets the stage for what will come later.

Anna? An old lady; we would call her a crone today, a wise old witch. She also knew that this was no ordinary child. She is not the only wise woman we will see in Luke's gospel. Both Luke's and John's gospels are rightly called "the gospels of women." Women, as we have seen, are a surprising and vital heart at the center of the Christian movement. Throughout history men have been embarrassed by this, upset by this prominence of women at the heart of the Christian message, and they still are.

At the end of this passage, there is a note that the family returned to Nazareth and that the child "grew and became strong" and that "God's favor was upon him." Just a few words here, just a hint that this Messiah, this Christ, grew and developed. God's favor was upon him, but there is no hint that he possessed all wisdom from the start or that he did not have to grow up, as all children do. He was no exception. A little later in this same chapter, after another visit of this family to Jerusalem, Luke comments:

> Then he went down with them and came to Nazareth, and was obedient to them. His mother treasured all these things in her heart. And Jesus increased in wisdom and in years, and in divine and human favor.

How wonderful that he had to learn, that his wisdom was not static and full right away, that it came gradually, as does yours and mine. He is a brother to us. He gives our own path dignity; he gives our own journey in knowledge and learning a special aura and grace.

90. Luke 3:23-38
His Ancestors, Another Version, 30 Years Old

The Passage

Jesus was about thirty years old when he began his work. He was the son (as was thought) of Joseph son of Heli, son of Matthat, son of Levi, son of Melchi, son of Jannai, son of Joseph, son of Mattathias, son of Amos, son of Nahum, son of Esli, son of Naggai, son of Maath, son of Mattathias, son of Semein, son of Josech, son of Joda, son of Joanan, son of Rhesa, son of Zerubbabel, son of Shealtie, son of Neri, son of Melchi, son of Addi, son of Cosam, son of Elmadam, son of Er, son of Joshua, son of Eliezer, son of Jorim, son of Matthat, son of Levi, son of Simeon, son of Judah, son of Josep, son of Joanam, son of Eliakim, son of Melea, son of Menna, son of David, son of Jesse, son of Obed, son of Boaz, son of Sala, son of Nahshon, son of Amminadab, son of Admin, son of Arni son of Hezron, son of Peez, son of Judah, son of Jacob, son of Isaac, son of Abraham, son of Terah, son of Nahor, son of Serug, son of Reu, son of Peleg, son of Eber, son Shelah, son of Calinan, son of Arphaxad, son of Shem, son of Noah, son of Lamech, son of Methuselah, son of Enoch, son of Jared, son of Mahaleel, son of Cainan, son of Enos, son of Seth, son of Adam, son of God.

Commentary

And who *are* all these people these ancestors of Jesus? Commentators say that the list, from Joseph to David, are people not otherwise known! And when we get to David, from there we go all the way back to Adam! The list of Jesus' ancestors in Matthew's gospel traces Joseph's ancestors and stops at Abraham. It is a Jewish list; Matthew's gospel was written for Jewish Christians. On the other hand, Luke's list goes back all the way to Adam, tracing Jesus' ancestors to a time far earlier than the beginnings of the Jewish people. He hints then, that the Messiah is for all of us, going beyond the Jewish line into what you might call just regular people, going all the way back to the first one, in the beginning of things.

I note that Luke says Jesus was about thirty years old when he begins his public life, a part of his life which did not last very long, at most three years. What do you make of a Messiah that dies before he's thirty-five years old? The Buddha, by contrast lived to a ripe old age, honored and respected for his accumulated wisdom. Muhammad did not live as long as the Buddha, but still lived twice as long as Jesus. Jesus died when he was a very young man! Christianity has no old sage or crone for a founder. Don't you wonder what Christianity would have been like, had Jesus lived to be an old man? Would he have stayed so fiery and outspoken? Would he have become a softer prophet? Would he have mellowed with the years?

There have been other great men in history and fiction who died young, from Shakespeare's Mercutio to Alexander the Great. I am aware as well, that the great ones of the world often do not fit the developmental paradigms of contemporary psychological theorists. I know as well that certain kinds of genius ripen early in the human life cycle: Mozart was a mature composer at twenty; Mathematicians are often most creative in their teens and twenties. Wisdom, on the other hand seems in most cultures to be reserved to the elders. Jesus never got to be an elder. How very intriguing!

There have been times in my own life when I have wished that Jesus had lived beyond his youth, times when his message has seemed so terribly stark and demanding that I wonder if he might have been more flexible in his demands had he lived longer. It has been the church's task down through the centuries to provide an old age for its founder . . . a collective and long tradition of wisdom at best. At worst, the quite literal application of the saying, "There is no fool like an old fool." We ourselves must learn to be old in the teachings of Jesus; he did not do this for us. I am quite aware of that at the age of seventy-two.

A modest footnote: I remind myself and the reader that Luke's stories of the conception, birth and childhood of Jesus belong to a Semitic literary form called midrash. They are theology rather than history for the most part. They are written to point to the importance and grace of the coming of the Messiah, the Christ. They are beautiful; they contain deep truths, but they are not a kind of ancient *CBS Was There*. They are profound fictions written to explain to the Christian community the importance of Jesus, his mother, and the heart of his message.

91. Luke 5:27-39
Fasting and the Bridegroom

The Passage

After this he went out and saw a tax collector named Levi, sitting at the tax booth; and he said to him, "Follow me." and he got up, left everything, and followed him.

Then Levi gave a great banquet for him in his house; and there was a large crowd of tax collectors and others sitting at the table with them. The Pharisees and their scribes were complaining to his disciples, saying, "Why do you eat and drink with tax collectors and sinners?" Jesus answered, "Those who are well have no need of a physician, but those who are sick; I have come to call not the righteous but sinners to repentance."

Then they said to him, "John's disciples, like the disciples of the Pharisees, frequently fast and pray, but your disciples eat and drink." Jesus said to them, "You cannot make wedding guests fast while the bridegroom is with them, can you? The days will come when the bridegroom will be taken away from them, and then they will fast in those days."

Commentary

The bridegroom is Jesus, of course. Christians down the centuries have taken this image of Jesus, which he originally picked for himself, and have found it a rich and lovely metaphor for him. The bridegroom, after all is a lover, but recently sworn in allegiance and joy to his bride. Mystics in the other religions of the book, i.e., Muslims and Jews, have taken this great figure of speech to their own hearts to describe their relationship to God. Christians have down the centuries haave used this title to describe their relationship with Christ. I think of an honored old hymn, better known to Protestants than to Catholics, entitled *In the Garden*. The words "and He walked with me and He talked with me" are bridal imagery. The poems of St. John of the Cross and the prose of St. Teresa of Avila use this imagery to describe the ecstasy of love they felt for the one they called *El Señor*.

Since Christianity contains so many images of Jesus on the cross or being scourged or crowned with thorns, it is refreshing to find that he also chooses the image of the bridegroom as a strong suggestion that his religion, although it does not sidestep suffering, is at heart a love affair and a message of joy. Amen! Levi, a.k.a. Matthew, threw one hell of a party for him;[4] Jesus chose that moment to tell us that he is the Bridegroom of his people. And so I say, "Thank you, Jesus!"

---

4. Matthew 9:5-16.

92. Luke 7:11-17
The Son of the Widow of Nain

The Passage

Soon afterwards he went to a town called Nain, and his disciples and a large crowd went with him. As he approached the gate of the town, a man who had died was being carried out. He was his mother's only son, and she was a widow; and with her was a large crowd from the town. When the Lord saw her, he had compassion for her and said to her, "Do not weep." Then he came forward and touched the bier, and the bearers stood still. And he said, "Young man, I say to you, rise!" The dead man sat up and began to speak, and Jesus gave him to his mother. Fear seized all of them; and they glorified God, saying, "A great prophet has risen among us!" and God has looked favorably on his people!" This word about him spread throughout Judea and all the surrounding country.

Commentary

You know, I am still wondering, even after all these years, "What was this man about?" I have just read the passage saying "He had compassion for her and said to her, 'Do not weep.'" What does that mean? He was a man with a large heart; I think that's it. When he saw people suffering, he wanted to do something about it. There's more to it than that, though, because when he felt this sorrow, he healed people; some of them he brought back to life when they were dead, like the son of the widow in this story. He was a healer then, like a doctor, like a mother. I've written about that earlier in this book. Still, I wonder, "What is a healer?" How do you get to be a healer? It's a gift; I know that, but I don't think it's a gift like a Christmas present, one that just comes to you out of the blue. It's not as if you wake up one morning and you're a healer all of a sudden, so then you get out of bed and take a walk and heal some sick people you see on the street or in their homes.

I wonder then, "How did he get that way?" How do other healers get that way. He wasn't, after all, the only healer who ever lived. Where does that capacity for compassion come from? I think, in my own experience, it comes from the healer having been hurt somehow, or crippled somehow, somehow wounded. I know that part of my ability as a teacher comes from having spent a number of years not being able to study much, so that for a period of years I got poor grades in college. I could only concentrate for short periods of time on my studies. I had headaches and other nervous afflictions all through my undergraduate and graduate years in this and that university. On the face of it, you'd think, "That's an odd way to become a professional teacher." It does seem logical to say that if you couldn't study much, you wouldn't learn much. You'd just be an ignoramus!

And yet, I know that there is some mysterious, volatile, and dangerous chemistry at work when you struggle painfully to do a job, like studying, and I know but it could really be almost any other skill or profession. Learning or performing any job may well be harder for you than for other people. You must learn to husband your time; you must learn to come to terms with your lack of talent or time or money or whatever it is that makes the learning process difficult.

In the process of laboriously learning a trade or a craft or an intellectual discipline under a severe limitation, something else can happen. For some people at least, this crucible, this painful process, can bring with it a sense of compassion for other people who have similar afflictions. If you haven't been there, you won't notice other people's troubles. If you do notice them without such an experience of your own, they will seem trivial somehow. You might think, "Why doesn't that one just snap out of it and do the work? She must be a lazybones. What that one needs is a good kick in the butt." In short, you could well be impatient with people who don't do as well as you do.

I simply cannot imagine a person who feels compassion for others without herself having experienced some real tough times. I'm sure of that. I wonder about the source of Jesus' compassion. We know next to nothing about his childhood and early manhood. How did he get that great sense of feeling with other people? Sometimes I think he must have been a cripple or abused as a child or blind . . . something like that. The pictures I've seen of Jesus, all of them, show a healthy and vibrant man, always handsome and built well, a man without blemish. That's how we imagine him, but I don't think that's how he was.

There had to have been some terrible blemish, some tragedy or failure in his background, for him to have been such a caring man. I could imagine Jesus with a bad leg, or blind in one eye, or a man whose skin color was different from most people. I know that tragedy does not always show up on a person's body, where others can see it, but it often does. Great healers are almost always disfigured somehow. When I think back in my own life about the people who have shown me kindness and understanding, if I really think about them, sure enough, there is some form of tragedy in their lives.

My godmother, who paid me the great compliment of encouraging me to continue to work as a writer was a painfully shy woman, well over six feet in height; she had raised her three children as a single mother, with little or no help from her erstwhile husband. The priest who helped me learn to study despite not being able to concentrate for long periods of time, was a brilliant man who had suffered a complete breakdown as a young university professor. When I knew him, he was suffering from a series of strokes which left one of his hands nearly useless. In my own life as a teacher it was a huge help to have had years when I wasn't a good student. I think the great healers and teachers of the world have all been people who were somehow savaged in childhood or adolescence.

I think Jesus, the man of compassion, the one who healed others, I think he must have had some awful experience in his earlier life. He wouldn't have paid much attention to the ordinary sight of a funeral procession had he not known sorrow himself. He would not have felt for sick people, for lame people, for people in the possession of some evil spirit, had he not had some experience to make him like them. It helps me to know that.

93. Luke 8:26-39
A Man Possessed by a Demon

The Passage

Then they arrived at the country of the Gerasenes, which is opposite Galilee. As he stepped out on land, a man of the city who had demons met him. For a long time he had worn no clothes, and he did not live in a house but in the tombs. When he saw Jesus, he fell down before him and shouted at the top of his voice, "What have you to do with me, Jesus, Son of the Most High God? I beg you, do not torment me"—for Jesus had commanded the unclean spirit to come out of the man. (For many times it had seized him; he was kept under guard and bound with chains and shackles, but he would break the bonds and be driven by the demon into the wilds.) So Jesus then asked him, "What is your name?" He said, "Legion"; for many demons had entered him. They begged him not to order them to go back into the abyss.

Now there on the hillside a large herd of swine was feeding; and the demons begged Jesus to let them enter these. So he gave them permission. Then the demons came out of the man and entered the swine, and the herd rushed down the steep bank into the lake and was drowned.

When the swineherds saw that wad happened, they ran off and told it in the city and in the country. Then people came out to see what had happened and when they came to Jesus, they found the man from whom the demons had gone sitting at the feet of Jesus, clothed and in his right mind. And they were afraid. Those who had seen it told them how the one who had been possessed by demons had been healed. Then all the people of the surrounding country of the Gerasenes asked Jesus to leave there; for they were seized with great fear. So he got into the boat and returned. The man from whom the demons had gone begged that he might be with him; but Jesus sent him away, saying, "Return to your home, and declare how much God has done for you." So he went away, proclaiming throughout the city how much Jesus had done for him.

Commentary

This is a story about a healing. For Jesus the healer, the key to the recovery of the possessed man lies in Jesus' knowing the name of the demons possessing him. Why would that make a difference? The name you are called goes deep into every person. I believe that. I can remember that when I was a kindergartner the other kids discovered that my first name was Francis. "That's a girl's name!" my playmates told me gleefully. I had a problem. I was a new kid, going to school for the first time, scared and vulnerable, and even my gender was doubtful. I knew that girls were human beings too, but I wasn't one of them. And I wanted to be at least a reasonably tough little guy, maybe not a big deal, but firmly classed with my fellow males. The name I was called had a lot to do with my life there in that kindergarten.

How did I solve the problem? I told them that my name was Bill, which worked like a charm until my mother found out and insisted over my objections that my name really was Francis, like it or not. So my old name came back to me and my troubles with it. Those who knew my name had power over me. Did they ever!

I remember too, that long ago Moses, the Biblical Moses, was confronted by a mysterious and powerful person who appeared to him in a burning bush.[5] Moses learned in this vision that the mysterious one, whose voice spoke from the burning bush was none other than the God of his ancestors, Abraham, Isaac, and Jacob. Moses was afraid. This was the Boss of Bosses here in front of him, ordering him to take off his sandals; the very ground he stood on was holy. Moses asked for God's name during this conversation, hoping that he would have some power over this mysterious person were he to know the person's name. In answer to his question, God replied, "Thus you shall say to the Israelites, 'I AM has sent me to you.'" "I AM" very likely is God's way of telling Moses that God will not reveal his name to Moses or anybody else and hence no mere human will ever have any power over him. God just said, "I am; that's enough for you, and that's all you're going to get!" This God is not a god to be pushed around; his people will never know his name.

Back to the man possessed. Jesus boldly asks the name of the demons possessing the man. The demons, knowing his power, have no choice but to tell him. Legion is their name. Legion being the name given in the Roman army for a force of 6,000 men. The afflicted man had a lot of devils. I have chosen this text to comment on because it involves the power attached to a person's name as well as the fear and fascination that together so often accompany the appearance of a divine

---

5. Exodus 3:1-16

person. I believe that the divine one, from that day to this, has brought out this two-fold reaction from people who experience his (or her) divine person.

The last paragraph in this fascinating story has Jesus send the spirits who had been in possession of the afflicted man, into a herd of pigs, who rushed down the slope of the hill where they were feeding and into the lake at the bottom of the hill where they drowned, one and all. And then, after this, people began to understand what had happened, informed by the awestruck swineherds that something amazing was going on.

> . . . when they came to Jesus, they found the man from whom the demons had gone sitting at the feet of Jesus, clothed and in his right mind.

There is a paradox of fear and peace in this story, which is surely a parable for all of us in our holy moments, knowing that fear, awe and peace are often in close proximity when we are aware of the divine dimension of the world we live in. It is as well a story in which the one who knows the name of his adversary has power over him.

94. Luke 8:43-48
A Woman Healed: Touch

The Passage

As he went, the crowds pressed in on him. Now there was a woman who had been suffering from hemorrhages for twelve years; and though she had spent all she had on physicians, no one could cure her. She came up behind him and touched the fringe of his clothes, and immediately her hemorrhage stopped. Then Jesus asked, "Who touched me?" When all denied it, Peter said, "Master the crowds surround you and press in on you." But Jesus said, "Someone touched me; for I noticed that power had gone out from me. When the woman saw the she could not remain hidden, she came trembling; and falling down before him, she declared in the presence of all the people why she had touched him, and how she had been immediately healed. He said to her, "Daughter, your faith has made you well; go in peace."

Commentary

I ask myself, "What is this story about?" A woman touches his clothes and is healed of her hemorrhage. What does that mean?" There are no words at all preceding the healing. Only the touch. And I think, "We talk about someone having just the right touch. We speak of someone being "touchy" as being sensitive to ridicule or imagined slights. We say after seeing a good movie or reading a good story, 'That really touched me!' We say when visiting a friend, 'I just wanted to touch base.'"

And I know very well that in my world today, there is a great emphasis on being careful whom you touch and how. Men need to know that they must be invited to touch a woman or they should keep their hands and arms to themselves. Touch is powerful medicine. We all know that. An embrace by a friend can mean more than a thousand words. A touch by someone you dislike or distrust is a strong affront.

So, she touched him; she put a hand on his clothing, just for an instant, thinking that in the press of the crowd no one would notice. And he did notice. He felt something go out of him. I can only underline here how deeply our bodies and spirits are entwine,. and say, as I have mentioned before, that there is a lot more to healing than biochemistry. There is acceptance and trust and caring. The woman in this story knew that and so did Jesus. He is no disembodied spirit, no godly ghost hiding under some kind of bodily appearance. He is a human being. He can be touched; there is power there. He notices; he is moved; he goes out to her.

95. Luke 9:46-48
Greatness: Children

The Passage

An argument arose among them as to which one of them was the greatest. But Jesus, aware of their inner thoughts, took a little child and put it by his side, and said to them, "Whoever welcomes this child in my name welcomes me, and whoever welcomes me welcomes the one who sent me; for the least among all of you is the greatest."

Commentary

A familiar theme in all the gospels is this one concerning who has the inside track in the kingdom. I have noted with Dominic Crossan that Jesus' kingdom is a kingdom of nuisances and nobodies. He has special regard for the "have-nots" rather than the "haves". This is still a hard doctrine for anyone with power or money or influence. I do not intend to hammer that hard lesson here, but I want to notice something else quite specifically. I want to point to what it is to be a child, children being specifically mentioned as favored in this particular passage.

I want to talk not so much of the vulnerability of children, how even today, kids are often merely chattel in the face of America's work ethic which demands that adults, men and women, be in the workplace rather than the home. I know that kids are increasingly left out of the formula of the American family. It is our own people who have coined the phrase "latch key kids." They are the ones who live lives strangely apart from their parents. When they go home, they must let themselves in the door or not get in. That's why they carry a key. They are among the strangers of contemporary society, unless one of them happens to shoot somebody or mows down his fellow students in some respectable Colorado suburb, his parents not having a clue of his desperate condition of loneliness right in the heart of a nice house in an affluent neighborhood. I'm not interested here in the primacy the gospel puts on the care of children, even though that primacy is clear.

Here I want to talk to you about another aspect of childhood and one with which Jesus was surely acquainted. Children in all societies play when they can. Play is a strange word in a society obsessed by work. Kids play games; they skip rope and play street ball. They imagine themselves part of other worlds and play their parts, endlessly taking on to themselves this role or that role. Childhood has a lot of theater in it. "You be the fairy princess. I'll be the prince. We'll meet at the well, led by a mysterious witch." There is a lot of Oz in the lives of children if they have the leisure to play.

There is a certain marvelous uselessness to play, even if I do know that much of children's play is practice in the skills they'll need when they grow up. Little girls wear their mother's shoes with delight, practicing for later days. There is a kind of frivolity in the games of children. I think of a cast of mind that is light and imaginative; it enables one to investigate any role in the world. It helps children see that there really are many things each one might become later in life.. Play is creative and bold; it can carry you anywhere and into any age. I'm not talking about the games grownups play, where winning is so often the be all and end all of the game. I'm talking about the joy of the game itself, where winning and losing are less important than they are to the grownups.

I think that Jesus was well aware of this quality of children: this lightness and imagination that makes children perpetually about the task of being in a play. I'm talking about the improv theater of childhood, the joy of it. I'm sure that when he told his mystified followers that the members of his kingdom are marked by an affinity for children that he meant that they should have some of the qualities of childhood itself, some of the awe children have, some of the mischief, some of the delight of play. I'm sure of that.

96. Luke 10:10-16
Unrepentant Towns

The Passage

N.B. Here the context is the instruction Jesus gives to his disciples as to how they should behave when he sends them out on their own to preach the kingdom.

"But whenever you enter a town and they do not welcome you go out, into its streets and say, 'Even the dust of your town that clings to our feet, we wipe off in protest against you. Yet know this: the kingdom of God has come near. I tell you, on that day it will be more tolerable for Sodom than for that town.

"Woe to you, Chorazin! Woe to you, Bethsaida! For if the deeds of power done in you had been done in Tyre and Sidon they would have repented long ago, sitting in sackcloth and ashes. But at the judgement it will be more tolerable for Tyre and Sidon than for you. And you, Capernaum,

> Will you be exalted to heaven?
> No, you will be brought down
> To Hades.

"Whoever listens to you listens to me, and whoever rejects you rejects me, and whoever rejects me rejects the one who sent me."

Commentary

I have talked with you before about Jesus' anger. He had plenty; he was a passionate man with a serious message. Attached to the anger of Jesus are the threats he made to those who did not hear his voice or those of his disciples. There is the same raw quality here as in his hot indignation. He threatens those that don't hear him in the person of his disciples with some sort of terrible punishment. "Hades" is the word here used. He compares the villages of Galilee which do not graciously receive his disciples with Tyre and Sidon, Phoenician seacoast towns which Jesus did not visit, they being Gentile cities.

Besides anger, here, it seems we have hatred and punishment. What in the world can one say about such a threat? I don't want to wish away this passage and others like it in the four gospels. They puzzle me to this day. Here's a partial explanation, and one that I have mentioned before in this commentary. It bears repeating. Both Hindus and Buddhists, in the context of good and evil deeds, explain retribution in terms of the deeds themselves, in terms of sinners themselves. The word for this is the Sanskrit term, "karma."[6] Deeds are seen as affecting both the doer and the one done to, right there, on the spot where one was hateful or murderous or mean. The bad one suffers by doing bad things. He or she is less a person, soiled and stinking from the act alone. A good deed carries the same kind of weight; the Good Samaritans of this world are themselves better for their compassionate deeds. Thus the result of evil or kindness remain in both the offender and the one offended. I see no contradiction between this way of looking at good and evil and Jesus' threats to the unrepentant cities of Galilee. The difference is in the language, in the telling.

I remind myself as well, as I have elsewhere in this book, that the gospel stories are as much the stories of the early Christian communities as they are of the life and deeds of Jesus. These stories reflect early Christian practice. They certainly often reflect the bitterness between the Christian Jewish community and the Jewish community still waiting for the Messiah. I might add that by their very nature the gospels were written at the very beginning of the Christian movement. Scholars tell us that all of them were completed much as we have them today by the year one hundred. If their central message was one of love, it is equally true that they are limited by the newness of the movement they preach. It takes years for any religious movement to see, if indeed its members ever do see, that there may be other chosen people besides themselves. Enthusiasm is like that, even enthusiasm for a message of love. The gospels, for all their beauty, are still records of a movement in its infancy, less aware than its founder was, that God has many chosen people, as is so eloquently clear in the next passage we study, that of the Good Samaritan.

---

6. Confer Part III, Matthew's Gospel, #75 for another mention of the term "karma."

97. Luke 10:25-37
The Good Samaritan

Just then a lawyer stood up to test Jesus. "Teacher," he said, "what must I do to inherit eternal life?" He said to him, "What is written in the law? What do you read there?" He answered, "You shall love the Lord your God with all your heart and with all your soul, and with all your strength, and with all your mind; and your neighbor as yourself." And he said to him, "You have given the right answer; do this. And you will live."

But wanting to justify himself, he asked Jesus, "And who is my neighbor?" Jesus replied, "A man was going down from Jerusalem to Jericho, and fell into the hands of robbers, who stripped him, beat him, and went away, leaving him half dead. Now by chance a priest was going down that road; and when he saw him, he passed by on the other side. So likewise a Levite, when he came to the place and saw him, passed on the other side. But a Samaritan while traveling came near him; and when he saw him, he was moved with pity. He went to him and bandaged his wounds, having poured oil and wine on them. Then he put him on his own animal, brought him to an inn, and took came of him. The next day he took out two denarii, gave them to the innkeeper, and said, 'Take care of him; and when I come back, I will repay you whatever more you spend.' Which of these three, do you think, was a neighbor to the man who fell into the hands of the robbers?" He said, "The one who showed him mercy." Jesus said to him, "Go and do likewise."

Commentary

This is perhaps the single most famous story that Jesus tells in the gospels. How interesting that "the good guy" was not one of the "good guys." How interesting as well that the story emphasizes deeds of love rather than correct thinking. Samaritans were regarded by Jews as neither Jewish nor Gentile. They were heretics, buying into only part of the law most Jews held to be holy. They did not worship at the temple. The story takes both Jewish professional religious classes as personifying a lack of concern for one's neighbor. I refer to the mention in the parable of Levites and priests. After all, one did not touch, without danger of incurring ritual impurity, the savaged or wounded body of another human being. Priests and Levites knew that kind of thing. The Samaritan, in his ignorance, did not. For Jesus compassion counted more than the small points of the law of Moses. There we have it. I will not make odious comparisons between priests and Levites of the days of old and the clergy of today, except to note that in the mind of Jesus being a priest or a member of the clergy was not the hallmark of holiness; being compassionate was. The current uproar within the Catholic church over the sexual abuse of children and adolescents by Catholic clergy is a case in point.

I find it of interest to note as well that the Samaritan did go about his business after helping the wounded man, leaving him in the care of the inn keeper until his return from whatever business drew him to take the road from Jerusalem to Jericho in the first place. He was generous with both his time and his money, but he did have business to pursue and didn't forget about it. To see the practicality of the Samaritan is useful to me. He did what he could; he did not remain indifferent to the man felled at the side of the road, but he had other fish to fry as well, other things to do. Romantics sometimes make the Samaritan into something he never was; he did not spend the rest of his life taking care of robbery victims. He simply helped with the means at hand. Can I say that people who give themselves totally to dramatic causes are prone to be meddlers and a peculiar form of self-righteousness which forgets the everyday of each life in favor of the spectacular and the unusual, the kind of rescue that gets you written up in the papers. In many ways the Samaritan was an ordinary person. I'm glad of that.

98. Luke 11:1-13
Ask and You Shall Receive: Prayer

The Passage

He was praying in a certain place, and after he had finished, one of his disciples said to him, "Lord, teach us to pray, as John taught his disciples." He said to them, "When you pray, say:

> Father, hallowed be your name.
> Your kingdom come.
> Give us each day our daily
> bread.
> And forgive us our sins,
> for we ourselves forgive
> everyone indebted to us.
> And do not bring us to the
> Time of trial.

And he said to them, "Suppose one of you has a friend, and you go to him at midnight and say to him, 'Friend, lend me three loaves of bread; for a friend of mine has arrived, and I have nothing to set before him.' And he answers from within, 'Do not bother me; the door has already been locked, and my children are with me in bed; I cannot get up and give you anything.' I tell you, even though he will not get up and give him anything because he is his friend, at least because of his persistence he will get up and give him whatever he needs.

"So I say to you, Ask, and it will be given you; search, and you will find; knock, and the door will be opened for you. For everyone who asks receives, and everyone who searches finds, and for everyone who knocks, the door will be opened. Is there anyone among you who, if your child asks for a fish, will give a snake instead of a fish? Or if the child asks for an egg, will give a scorpion? If you then, who are evil, know how to give good gifts to your children, how much more will the heavenly Father give the Holy Spirit to those who ask him!"

Commentary

After having read this passage, I find myself thinking, "Okay, how are you going to wiggle out of this one?" Here's my best answer. Mary

Doria Russell, writing about her own conversion to Judaism, says, "When you convert to Judaism in a post-Holocaust world, you know two things for sure: one is that being Jewish can get you killed; the other is that God won't rescue you." I might add, "It's not just the Jews of the post-holocaust world who have this insight, The Chosen People have had a rough time of it from the get go. I might add further from my own experience, "Being a Catholic doesn't get you out of anything either." Nobody gets out of tough times. As it says elsewhere in the gospels, "The rain falls on the just and the unjust alike."[7]

Alice Walker, who ought to know what trouble is, being both black and a woman, has helped me. Listen to her, speaking in the character of Shug in her novel, *The Color Purple:*

> Here's the thing, say Shug. The thing I believe. God is inside you and inside everybody else. You come into the world with God, but only them that search for it inside find it. And sometimes it just manifest itself if you not looking, or don't know what you looking for. Trouble do it for most folks, I think. Sorrow, lord. Feeling like shit.

I don't think I'd trust most people who would advise me that my prayers have been heard even when I have trouble or feel like shit, but I find Alice Walker a reliable witness. She and the characters she writes about know what trouble is, just as the Jewish people do. Alice Walker is black as well as being a woman. So, how about this "Seek and you shall find" stuff? You might say, "And how about Jesus himself? He didn't last too long, did he? And he got crucified for his pains. How about that? He, the very one who said, 'Knock and the door will be opened.' It sure does look as though when he asked for a fish, he got a snake instead."

I don't have an easy answer. I'm not certain it's an answer at all. Here's my thought. The whole Christian message is about deliverance through suffering. The chief symbol of Christianity is the cross. Whatever else Jesus meant, he wasn't telling people that they would get out of hard times if they prayed to the one he called The Father. You might ask, "What else would you ask of God, if not for happy endings and good times?" I think that if you are hoping for good times from your prayers, then you'd better get yourself another gospel and another religion. Chris-

---

7. See also my comments on Matthew 6:9-13.

tianity, of its essence doesn't offer that. Jesus didn't offer that. He offered something else, and I'm not sure what that something else is. What is it that he means when he says, "Seek and you shall find. Knock and the door will be opened"? I myself believe it's a cheap and shallow answer to say, "He offers heaven. Things will get better after you're dead." I don't think that answer will satisfy you either.

I think of Alice Walker's Shug saying, "Trouble do it for most folks, I think. Sorrow, lord. Feeling like shit." And I wonder, "What in the world can I get out of trouble?" I can think with of my own reaction, had I been told by a spiritual advisor at a time in my life when I was plagued by headaches and a bad stomach, "Francis, you'll be a better man for it. Just think of Jesus on the cross." I am grateful that no one else ever suggested such an answer to my troubles. What helped me then, in that desperate time of long ago? It was an old priest who taught me how to study in small units of time, so that my head didn't have time to hurt too much. Added to this was the kindness of that same old man who taught me how to practice that rather severe and disciplined way of study.

And, it's true too, that as one who has spent his working life as a teacher, as I have mentioned in another context in this book, I have some understanding of kids who have a tough time with studies. I've been there. If I had not, I'm not sure I'd understand. I know too that there are other people who have suffered from tension and depression as I have, or gone hungry or were poor or betrayed by a friend, I know that some of them become bitter and mean because of their hard times. Trouble, feeling like shit, hardens people sometimes, just as it can make them more understanding.

So, if I say the prayer Jesus suggested, "Give us this day our daily bread," at least I know that daily bread is sometimes the bread of trouble and sorrow. I know further that most of the compassionate people of my own acquaintance, Jesus among them, are that way in part because they have managed to survive days of very hard bread indeed, and have somehow brought something to the world because of it, something alive and flexible and joyous, something in fact divine.

99. What's Not in the Gospels

Commentary

It has occurred to me that it's just as important to know what is not in the gospel text as it is to know what's there. Two thousand years of tradition is a long time for messing with the text. Somebody once said that the great religious texts of the world, as long as they themselves were not tampered with, will always have great power, because from time to time someone looks at them freshly, for what they actually say or don't say, and realizes all over again that those words are the stuff of revolution and change, as well as the challenge of joy.

Well, what's not there? There is no mention anywhere in the four gospels of a Christian priesthood. There are references to both Jewish priests and the priests of other religions. Jesus himself is referred to in New Testament writings as a great priest, even if it is clear in the gospels themselves that he himself was never a priest or Levite, nor any kind of official, sacred person within his own Jewry. Other writings of the New Testament refer to the entire Christian people as a priestly people, but nowhere is there mention of an order of Christian priests.

Jesus, except in John's gospel does not refer to himself as God, ever. He calls himself the son of man and sometimes obliquely refers to himself as a king of a different kind of kingdom than a political kingdom or state in the secular sense.

Nowhere in the gospels does one see a separation of nature and grace or a division of human persons into body and soul. In both cases I am referring to a solid Semitic notion, shared by Jesus with his fellow Jews, that the world and human nature are basically one. A separation of the universe into sacred and profane simply isn't there. There are good and bad people regardless of citizenship, social class, or office in religion. The members of the kingdom, if anything, seem to be people apart from religious or social privilege. There is no two tiered world of nature and grace. There is simply one world and universe. God is a part of that world. There is no mention of special sacred Christian places or sacred vessels or buildings.

What's to be learned from all this oneness and simplicity? Does it mean that two thousand years of accretions to the Christian message are a collection of useless barnacles which must be removed in order to get at the essence of things Christian? I think to myself, "Yes and no."

I can see absolutely no reason for saying that the message of Jesus should take no social structure. Ideas, if they are to have an effect, always become embodied in some social structure or other. Christianity down the centuries has certainly done that, as have all religions. What seems important to me is that the structural forms of Christianity have and will continue to vary widely. They are legitimate in so far as they serve the message of Jesus. They can and will change; they are functional rather than sacred in themselves. One can make a case for the legitimacy of a church structure with priests, bishops, even a Pope, but it is important to remember that there can be other forms as well. Jesus simply didn't set up a structure. The forms of church government can be judged only by their quality as vehicles to reflect what Jesus did and said. Period. No structure has a corner or legitimacy.

As for the well entrenched church teaching dividing human beings into bodies and souls, well, that's an accretion we got from the Greeks. It has been a useful way of thinking about what it is to be human, that's true, but it has carried with it somehow, a long standing suspicion of material and bodily things within the Christian message that is just not there in the gospels. Jesus and his people made no such division. A human being was a unity to Jesus, not a duality. Matter and flesh, if you want to put it that way, was inseparable from spirit and soul, just as beautiful, just as sacred, just as Godly.

As for nature and grace, something in me says, "O my God, the complications that have been wrought on the Christian message by those who like to divide things up!" I can remember studying at some length just how long a person could be good and upright without God's special help, called actual grace in my tradition. Some wag in the class suggested about five minutes was about all he could handle. And then there was "sanctifying grace," which divided all the world into supernatural and natural. Jesus doesn't talk about that either. He does speak of new life, triumph over evil, and the reign of God, but he never speaks of two worlds, one natural and the other supernatural. I truly believe Jesus saw the world to be a holy place, flawed by evil, but holy. Holiness in his mind was a part of the world, not something that got dropped on top of it like a hat or smeared on like lipstick or pancake makeup. God's intervention in the world was the most natural thing in the world, a part of things, not apart from things. I believe that.

I might add in closing that I know full well that Christianity as well as other religious movements continue to develop as the days and years go by. The gospels are a privileged group of writings about a privileged time in history. They, along with the other sacred books of my tradition, have pride of place. They are our touchstones in the divine alchemy of the Christian movement. They keep us honest, or are meant to. It is well to know what is not in them as well as what is in them if we are to learn and adapt, if we are to grow and become strong, if we are to be filled with wisdom, and if the favor of God is to be upon us as it once was on Jesus himself in his years as a child in Nazareth.[8] If this small section of this book sounds like an outburst or an intemperate bit of prose, I can at least assure the reader that it is an outburst long in the making. I take some solace in having noted earlier that my dear Lord Jesus had a bit of a temper himself and was not always a person of measure.

---

8. This comment is an adaptation of the Luke's verses describing the child-hood of Jesus after he went home at the age of twelve years with his mother and father from the celebration of Passover in Jerusalem. Luke 2:52.

100. Luke 12:22-30
On Angst and Crazy People

The Passage

He said to his disciples, "Therefore I tell you, do not worry about your life, what you will eat, or about your body, what you will wear. For life is more than food, and the body more than clothing. Consider the ravens: they neither sow nor reap, they have neither storehouse nor barn, and yet God feeds them. Of how much more value are you than the birds! And can any of you by worrying add a single hour to your span of life? If then you are not able to do so small a thing as that, why do you worry about the rest? Consider the lilies, how they grow: they neither toil nor spin; yet I tell you, not even Solomon in all his glory was not clothed like one of these. But if God so clothes the grass of the field, which is alive today and tomorrow is thrown into the oven, how much more will he clothe you—you of little faith! And do not keep striving for what you are to eat and what you are to drink, and do not keep worrying. For it is the nations of the world that strive after all these things, and your Father knows that you need them. Instead, strive for his kingdom, and these things will be given to you as well.

"Do not be afraid, little flock, for it is your Father's good pleasure to give you the kingdom. Sell your possessions, and give alms. Make purses for yourselves that do not wear out, an unfailing treasure in heaven, where no thief comes near and no moth destroys. For where your treasure is, there your heart will be also.

Commentary

You know, I have the feeling that if this passage of Luke's gospel were to appear in a packet of sayings of the Buddha, the world would "oh" and "ah" over its wisdom, its freshness, its cutting through the sapwood of day to day existence, to the very heart of things. These words are not those of a sage in an affluent country like our own. I can see why you might be skeptical of their directness were it to appear in the sayings of George W. Bush, for example. Jesus lived in what today would be called a third world country. In his public life he was a nomad, having no fixed place where he lived. You can make a very good case for saying that he was born into the very bottom of the social world of Roman-occupied Palestine. He was a peasant who almost surely could neither read nor write. His family owned no land, but got by on the skills of Joseph his father, who is very inadequately described in English as a carpenter. Carpenters by and large are quite prosperous in our society. Joseph was more roustabout than carpenter.

So, then when he tells you not to worry about food or clothing, he knows whereof he speaks. His trust in the one he calls Father is not naive. He knows hardship, hunger, cold and the vagaries of weather. It is with this backdrop that he tells us that worry will not add a single day to our span of life.

A word on the one he calls Father. You know and I know, and Jesus knew, that the God of Jews and Christians is a spirit, having, to say the least, no gender. As Alice Walker's Shug once said, "God is a It!" So how can Jesus call this it "Father" . . . "Abba" in his own language, meaning something more intimate than our English "father". "Abba" was a pet name, the kind a child would use for its father, a very intimate name. The temptation to see this as rank sentimentality is strong, were we not to know the hardness of the life of Jesus of Nazareth and the bitter hardness of his death.

And so you and I wonder, "Whatever did he mean?" Intimacy for certain, but intimacy with what? Or who? I remember an old Jesuit priest once telling me that he once as a young man was giving a lecture to a Mayan peasant in Central America about the reasons for believing in God. The peasant first looked confused, then uncomfortable, and finally amused. He told the young priest, "You don't have to give me any lectures about God. God is in my cornfield, right under my feet. You are a silly white man for sure if you can't see that." It's the intimacy of bare feet on the ground and the physical connection with his corn plants that this Mayan peasant was talking about. He saw them as sacred. Guys with white faces and shoes on their feet didn't know things like that. They still don't.

So, if the peasant Jesus used an intimate family name for his God, you need not think him simple-minded or superstitious or looking for a Daddy in the sky to replace his human father. I think he was perceptive about the richness of the world, and knowing full well that human life is often brutal and always short, saw its goodness and beauty nonetheless. The author of that goodness and beauty he called "Abba."

There's more, and I may be out of suggestions here, let alone answers. At the end of the passage we are talking about he says, "Sell your possessions and give alms. Make purses for yourselves that do not wear out, an unfailing treasure in heaven, where no thief comes near and no moth destroys. For where your treasure is, there your heart will be also." That's tough. I think to myself, "Well, I give alms all right, but I am not about to sell my possessions. I wonder why he wants his people to do that. And, do I know *anybody* in real life who has done this, so I might at least get a handle on what Jesus is talking about? I'm going to look around in my life's acquaintances in hopes of getting a glimmer."

I do have a classmate in the Jesuits, a man who entered the Society of Jesus on the same day I did. He was from a farming community in Wisconsin, dairy farmers . . . and, more important, he really never was like the rest of us. It wasn't just the farm background in a class of city slickers that marked him off. Like a lot of us, he left the Jesuits after ordination to the priesthood and has spent much of the rest of his life working in a hospital for the chronically insane. He has never married, although he has a girlfriend of long standing and quite possibly of long suffering. I remember that he once visited my mother and father in his post-Jesuit days. My dad asked him how he was supporting himself and he replied without drama that he just went down to Manpower in whatever city he found himself, got in line, and took whatever job he was given. He didn't think it strange that after fifteen years of rigorous training and numerous college degrees that he might spend the day cleaning out waste baskets or scrubbing floors. Someone who knew him said, "Bill just doesn't take out insurance." He's still like that. I wonder if that was what Jesus had in mind.

I find myself thinking of *Mad Magazine's* Alfred E. Newman. Alfred E.'s motto, as you recall is "Me worry?" Is there some of that in what Jesus was looking for? But Alfred E. Newman's benign and smiling face is that of an idiot! He is not a responsible adult. I think I'm getting warmer here. The members of the kingdom described by Jesus seem to give pride of place to outcasts: wine bibbers, prostitutes, dishonest tax collectors, cripples of various kinds, blind guys, children, and some just plain crazy people, witness the man possessed by the Legion of devils. Did I forget to mention women? It is definitely an odd group. I'm not sure why these are his favorites, except that they don't seem to be anyone else's favorites, all of them living on the fringes of the system of both government and religion. I think some mysteries are best left as they are. I think it best to say that there are people who travel light, have few possessions, and seem out of step with the rest of the world who have a wisdom all their own.

Gifted people are often seen as crazy. Wise fools exist in the great literatures of history, from Shakespeare's jesters to Frederico Fellini's madmen and wise children. Somehow in their avoidance of respectability, they have a peculiar kind of wisdom and freedom that the rest of us lack. I think Jesus knew that. I think as well that almost everyone has a bit of this wise foolishness down deep inside themselves. If one can trick it out of hiding, then perhaps there will be a glimmer in one's life of the wise-fools and outcasts that Jesus held to be so sacred.

101. Luke 13:31-34
Lamenting over Jerusalem: A Feminine Man

The Passage

At that very hour some Pharisees came and said to him, "Get away from here, for Herod wants to kill you." He said to them, "Go and tell that fox for me, 'Listen, I am casting out demons and performing cures today and tomorrow, and on the third day I finish my work. Yet today, tomorrow, and the next day I must be on my way because it is impossible for a prophet to be killed outside of Jerusalem.' Jerusalem, Jerusalem, the city that kills the prophets and stones those that are sent to it! How often have I desired to gather your children together as a hen gathers her brood under her wings, and you were not willing!"

Commentary

I have written earlier about Jesus' approach to law, so much more a woman's approach than a man's, so much more merciful than heeding only the letter of the law, so closely tied to the people involved in the law rather than principle only. Here is another surprisingly feminine image of Jesus, lamenting his beloved Jerusalem, using the image of a mother hen protecting her brood as the image of his care for his people and the city whose walls summarized and distilled what it was to be a Jew down the centuries, David's town, the holy city of his people, the city of the temple. How surprising that this fiery man could show as well, compassion for his people and his heritage. I wonder if I will ever get to know him, so embracing and wide is his character. He is such a mixture of salt and honey that I can come to him as a child, fear him as a warrior, wonder at his recklessness and honesty, and see in him a woman's gift of compassion. He's tough to put into a category.

102. Luke 14:7-12
The Wedding Banquet (Being Small)

The Passage

When he noticed how the guests chose the places of honor, he told them a parable. "When you are invited by someone to a wedding banquet, do not sit down at the place of honor, in case someone more distinguished than you has been invited by your host; and the host who invited both of you may come and say to you, 'Give this person your place,' and then in disgrace you would start to take the lowest place. But when you are invited, go and sit down at the lowest place, so that when your host comes, he may say to you, 'Friend, move up higher;' then you will be honored in the presence of all who sit at the table with you. For all who exalt themselves will be humbled, and those who humble themselves will be exalted."

Commentary

I know well that the point of this parable has to do with not showing off or trying to be a big shot, yet it has always meant something different to me. I have thought many a time of myself as not being one of the great ones, not so much a question of pretense and subtle self-glorification, but just the plain unvarnished truth. And then to be welcomed at the banquet, almost because I am not much, that's something! I've imagined that table in a dream, all in browns and golds, and myself sitting way down at the end or not even having a chair or a setting to eat at all, just having barely squeezed into the great hall where the banquet is held. And then there comes this man down, taking me by the hand and knowing my name, letting me have a regular place with the good guys! It is an astounding vision of hope in the midst of a world often dark. It is an amazing voice to hear in the times when I find not much good within myself to be pleased with or happy about. As if out of the darkness and smallness of my life there would come someone who does not concern himself with the paltriness of my smallness but finds something very dear right there within it, allowing me to be there, and allowing me to go on with the smallness of my life with peace and a sense of abandon, not caring so much that I and my life are small. As if this sometimes bitter and provincial life which is mine, is seen by one person to be dear and good without regard to its narrowness of vision and even its pettiness of spirit. That means much to me.

103. Luke 15:8-10
The Lost Coin—God as Woman

The Passage

"Or what woman having ten silver coins, if she loses one of them, does not light a lamp, sweep the house, and search carefully until she finds it? When she has found it, she calls together her friends and neighbors, saying, ' Rejoice with me, for I have just found the coin that I had lost.' Just so, I tell you, there is joy in the presence of the angels of God over one sinner who repents."

Commentary

I have overlooked this parable most of my life. It is positioned next to its more famous companion, the parable of The Prodigal Son, which I shall treat in my next essay. It may well be that this image of God as a woman slipped right past my consciousness because I am not a woman myself. My wife Toni treated my ignorance over this parable with some scorn; it has not been popular for most of the centuries of the Christian tradition to have feminine images of God. Maybe this parable should be called, "The Lost Image".

In any case, here it is, appearing with the story of the Prodigal, told only in Luke's gospel. I have always thought of the gospels of Luke and John as the gospels aware of the primacy of women in Jesus' preaching. Here he speaks of a woman who has lost a silver drachma, worth an ordinary day's labor, say fifty dollars in our coinage. How carefully she looks for it, lighting the candle, sweeping the floor; how happy is she when she finds it.

I recall, in this regard, an evening at my home, a summer evening, in which my parents were entertaining a large number of guests. At the announcement of dinner, the guests forthwith left our brick patio in back of the house and trooped in for supper, many of them leaving their half-finished beverages behind on tables, the brick floor of the patio, or any flat surface that came to hand, in their desire to get at our dinner in their honor. I was left, aged twelve, with my older cousin, Buddy Smith to sample what remained of the cocktails, highballs and steins of beer left to our clutches by the grownups. We sampled vigorously without much regard to the potency of the contents of the goblets, glasses and steins left

so opportunely by the now vanished guests. As the evening wore on our imaginations became activated by the drinks we had consumed.

It seemed a good idea in our new found euphoria for the two of us to take an excursion to some far away place, like Texas, and to make that trip now while the iron was hot and our inhibitions dissolved. We scrabbled up two dollars and seventeen cents between us from my dad's cuff link box upstairs where he was wont to keep small change. I strapped on my machete, a huge knife designed for cutting corn or cane; for me it was the ultimate weapon. Lest we should somehow on our journey fall in with brigands or thieves. So armed, we went on foot into the shadows of that summer's night. We walked and talked of our coming adventures, first down the tar road in front of my house and then across a larger boulevard, thence into a group of houses under construction where we found shelter, having put several miles between ourselves and my home. We slept on the floor of an unfinished house in the warm air of the evening. We slept quite soundly despite the hard surface we lay on, covered only by our jeans and a tarpaulin left in the house by painters. Soon it was dawn, we awakened in the soft sunlight to find ourselves in a strange place, without the comforts of home. It didn't take us long to put our trip to Texas on hold for the time being, while we began walking home for breakfast in the dawn's early light. We were shortly accosted by a policeman, who offered us a ride home in his squad car. Suddenly we were home. The grownups were up, in fact both of our mothers were up, more than up, they were in high dudgeon having spent the night searching the house and grounds for two missing boys. They were certain we would not run away; not either of their thoughtful sons would pull such a trick. Surely we had been kidnaped by some sinister outsider. As they searched in wider and wider circles, it occurred to them that our lives might be at that very moment threatened by the kidnappers. The police were called, the neighbors alerted, search lights probed under every bush from the house to the creek a quarter of a mile away.

When we arrived home with our escorts in blue, the mothers were steamed. The lost darlings turned immediately into their more accustomed form of slippery rascals, heedless of their mothers' agony and search. I might add that both my father and Buddy's father had gone to bed with no particular concern, puzzled as they were by the fears of their spouses. We were the lost coins! I must admit that they did not throw a party in our honor, we the lost ones who had been found. I was grounded for weeks. I had to pull a thousand weeds from our lawn and be helpful to those who had been put out by our adventure. We lost coins had been searched for into the wee hours. Hills scoured, lanterns lit until we were found. Is God like our mothers? Concerned more than anyone else for our welfare? Willing to search us out, no matter how long the search? Well, that's what the story says. It's a comforting image for those of us who are prone to light out on unacceptable ventures without notice, with no thought of anything but the exaggerated joys of the journey. I hope Luke is right in quoting Jesus to this effect. God has, and will get, lots of practice, yes She will.

104. Luke 15:11-32
The Prodigal Son

The Passage

Then Jesus said, "There was a man who had two sons. The younger of them said to his father, 'Father, give me the share of the property that will belong to me.' So he divided his property between them. A few days later the younger son gathered all that he had and traveled to a distant country, and there he squandered his property in dissolute living. When he had spent everything, a severe famine took place throughout that country, and he began to be in need. So he went and hired himself out to one of the citizens of that country, who sent him to his fields to feed the pigs. He would gladly have filled himself with the pods that the pigs were eating; and no one gave him anything. But when he came to himself he said, 'How many of my father's hired hands have bread enough and to spare, but here I am dying of hunger! I will get up and go to my father, and I will say to him, "Father, I have sinned against heaven and before you; I am no longer worthy to be called your son; treat me like one of your hired hands."' So he set off and went to his father. But while he was still far off, his father saw him and was filled with compassion; he ran and put his arms around him and kissed him. Then the son said to him, 'Father I have sinned against heaven and before you. I am no longer worthy to be called your son.' But the father said to his slaves, 'Quickly, bring out a robe—the best one—and put it on him; put a ring on his finger and sandals on his feet. And get the fatted calf and kill it, and let us eat and celebrate; for this son of mine was dead and is alive again; he was lost and is found!' And they began to celebrate."

Commentary

I recall, years ago, teaching this parable to a class of eighth graders in a large public school tucked into the Gatineau hills of Canada's province of Quebec. After reading the story out loud, we dramatized it. One small and precocious boy wanted desperately to play the part of the fatted calf! A local priest played the part of the father of the prodigal. He embraced the boy who played the part of the prodigal son, heard his confession very briefly, and gave sacramental absolution to all the kids in the class. After that we played records of the Beatles and some Simon and Garfunkel, while the kids danced vigorously and naturally to the rock and roll beat of *Cecelia,* and a John Lennon tune about wanting to see the Lord. It struck me that no one of those kids seemed to think that we were doing anything out of the ordinary. The sequence of story, drama, confession, and dance seemed as natural as the rain to them. I wonder now, thirty years later, if any of them remember that hour as vividly as I do.

I wonder too, how it was that Jesus was able to tell such a story, he the fiery one, the radical, the one who did not censor or soften his words. As I do this I remember an ancient religious archetype, that of the wounded healer. And I wonder what it was that had earlier happened to this man who was capable of such tenderness towards scamps and wastrels. I wonder where in the years before he burst on the public scene in his early thirties—where was the tragedy in his own life? I do wonder that. We know nearly nothing of his childhood and youth, just hints in Matthew and Luke about his messiahship as what the Hebrew people called The Chosen and The Servant. The wounded healer comes by his compassion honestly. He is always in some sense a cripple, as the prophet Isaiah says:

> He had no form or comeliness that we
> should look at him,
> and no beauty that we should
> desire him.
> He was despised and rejected by
> others;
> a man of sorrows, and acquainted with grief;
> and as one from whom others hide
> their faces
> He was despised and we esteemed
> him not.[9]

I know that this and the other servant songs of Isaiah are linked to what we call the Passion of Jesus, his capture, torture, and crucifixion, but I know as well that the wounded healer has suffered prior to his work as healer. This, of course, is a story about a father who healed his son's broken spirit. What was there is in his childhood that marked him so? I don't know. There were many peasants as poor as he, scattered all over

---

9. Isaiah 53:3.

Roman Palestine, but there was only one Jesus. I'm sure there was something out of which was born his compassion and healing strength. I'll never know what it was. I can only imagine. Gifted children are often outcasts. The flinty hills of Galilee were good soil for suffering and hardship; that's true too. Was he truly illegitimate? Did everyone know that? I don't know. Was he deformed somehow? Was he of darker color than his neighbors? I know none of these things. What I do know as I have mentioned before, is that there was something which marked him off and made him different or he would never have been the healer he was. It is there that I myself find joy and hope, there in the dark and hidden early years which so clearly marked his later life, for he is my brother. There would have been no tale of a Prodigal's return to a loving father without a deep scar in the teller of the story.

105. Luke 16:19-31
The Rich Man and Lazarus

The Passage

"There was a rich man who was dressed in purple and fine linen and who feasted sumptuously every day. And at his gate lay a poor man named Lazarus, covered with sores, who longed to satisfy his hunger with what fell from the rich man's table; even the dogs would come and lick his sores. The poor man died and was carried away to Abraham's bosom. The rich man also died and was buried. In Hades, where he was being tormented, he looked up and saw Abraham far away with Lazarus by his side. He called out, 'Father Abraham, have mercy on me, and send Lazarus to dip the tip of his finger in water and cool my tongue; for I am in agony in these flames.' But Abraham said, 'Child, remember that during your lifetime you received your good things, and Lazarus in like manner evil things; but now he is comforted here, and you are in agony. Besides all this, between you and us a great chasm has been fixed, so that those who might want to pass from here to you cannot do so, and no one can cross from there to us.' He said, 'Then, father, I beg you to send him to my father's house—for I have five brothers—that he may warn them, so that they will not also come to this place of torment.' Abraham replied, 'They have Moses and the prophets; they should listen to them.' He said, 'No, father Abraham, but if someone goes to them from the dead, they will repent.' He said to him, 'If they do not listen to Moses and the prophets, neither will they be convinced even if someone rises from the dead.'"

Commentary

When I was twenty years old and a Jesuit novice I took the first of many years of speech courses that were part of Jesuit training. This particular course required that each of us write short adaptations of the stories of the gospels. One of my own early choices was the parable of the Rich Man and Lazarus. I made the rich man into an executive in a lumber company; his counter-player Lazarus was a country fellow who made railroad ties out of wood with an axe, as ties were made in the days before circular saws. It just so happened that my father was the president of a small business entitled Gross and Janes Company; the business of my dad's company was manufacturing wooden railroad ties. The company sometimes made deals with single tie-makers who worked alone in the forest hewing railroad ties from trees, which they themselves felled. They were called tie hackers. Many of these folks lived in the semi-wilderness of large forests, far from city life, with their families in rough-sawed shacks wallpapered with newspapers; they hacked those ties out of tree trunks, their only tools being great broad-headed axes. The finished ties were hauled by teams of horses to the railroad right of way where my dad's people could pick them up. There my dad's people payed the hackers for each tie, and then sold and delivered the same ties to the railroads for the upkeep of those long roads of steel. The steel rails were supported by wooden ties which together provided a reliable path for the great, black, steam locomotives and the cars they towed.

I didn't think it unusual to dub an officer in a tie manufacturing company as the rich man. My dad was a successful businessman and his company was prosperous. It didn't really occur to me that I was in effect consigning my own father to a place of considerable torment, far, as the story says, from Abraham's bosom. I didn't know any tie hackers personally, they being on the opposite end of the social scale on which my family lived. I knew about them because my dad often spoke of them with respect as well as some humor. He knew those people and he dearly loved dealing with them himself, sometimes walking miles to get to their homes deep in the woods of Missouri and Arkansas, where they would make deals on a handshake for the company to buy the ties they made. The hackers and their families were pretty basic folks, often without much if any education, carving their living literally with those great axes out of trees they themselves felled by hand. My dad loved those people, unlike the rich man in Jesus' story, who seems to have been quite indifferent concerning the plight of Lazarus, the beggar who was his neighbor.

I told my version of the story with a not very reflective righteousness. I could identify with Lazarus, of course, since I myself had shortly before left all my worldly possessions to enter a religious order where we did not own things individually but corporately. Well, you see, it was safe for me to tell the story. I never really thought my dad was going to hell, but I was very sure that I myself was a lot more like the tie hacker than the rich man of my story. Years of reflection have made it quite clear to me that the Jesuits I joined and loved for my entire young manhood lived and still live middle class lives with rare exception. When I left the Jesuits and married, my life-style improved a certain amount and I became more like the rich man in the story than is comfortable for me to admit. and I know now in my eighth decade of life, that never in my life, either in or out of the Jesuit Order have I been poor or missed a meal because there was no food in the pantry.

This story which so warmed my righteous heart at twenty years of age is not so comfy now. It's tough on the opulent ones, especially if they don't care about those who don't have much, like Lazarus. What can I make of that story today? Well, put it this way, I do hope it is not to be taken literally and totally; I wonder sometimes if I, like the rich man in the story, have already had my reward. And then, as I have told you before, it's not all bad if you are one of the ones less favored by the Lord in talent and virtue. I hope to have a little bit of Lazarus in me. And I do think of all of us as amalgams of these two starkly different people. I say to myself, "We are all The Rich Man and we are all Lazarus." We all need to nourish something of the beggar within us. I do believe that and I know it to be no easy task. And of course I know that a rich person without a social conscience is flat-out damned already, right now, right here, today.

106. Luke 17:20-21
Where is the Kingdom? Who is in the Kingdom?

Once, Jesus was asked by the Pharisees when the kingdom of God was coming, and he answered, "The kingdom of God is not coming with things that can be observed; nor will they say, 'Look, here it is!' or 'There it is!' For, in fact, the kingdom of God is within you.

Commentary

This word "kingdom" is a toughie. It is central to the gospel message. I'm aware that there were some people among the Jews of Jesus' time who thought of the kingdom as a political and sacred state, a holy country, like the kingdoms of David and Solomon in years gone by. I know as well that the early Christian community thought that Jesus would come down to earth again in a second and glorious coming, and very soon, changing the whole world, judging and glorifying those living at the time. I grew up in a generation of Roman Catholics that thought the kingdom and the Catholic church were one and the same thing, other Christian bodies being somehow in error, decidedly lesser and more marred versions of the kingdom than the Catholics. We've been centuries in the Christian tradition trying to make sense of the kingdom, often looking foolishly, almost always narrowly, at what Jesus meant by the kingdom.

Some translators don't like the word "kingdom of God" at all, but prefer the term the "Reign of God". I modestly state that I don't have *the* answer, only *an* answer. I love the passage above because it emphasizes a kingdom within, a kingdom of attitude and acceptance inside a person. It seems to me to open the kingdom's door to all the loving the people of the world, whether or not they are Christians. It's important to know that the people of Jesus' small corner of the Mediterranean world were not aware of the size of the world as we know it now. The wider and complete world was pretty much the Roman Empire. Nobody was aware that the vast majority of the world's people lived in the far East, beyond anyone's imagining in the West and Near East. No one knew that there were two huge continents which today we know as the Americas.

The world of Jesus' time was small flat as a plate. If you traveled too far, you'd fall off the plate into God knows what. We didn't really get a handle on the size of the earth until astronomers realized that the world was round and not flat and until explorers actually found out that there were a number of other worlds on the planet earth, the main ones being the older worlds of the far East and two whole continents in the West, not to mention a vast world south of the Mediterranean shores of Africa. Christianity is still struggling to admit the size and complexity of these other worlds. Most modern Americans still don't know that China, for example, really is a prosperous and burgeoning country of a size as large as our own, a population whose numbers we can't imagine, and a culture far older than our own.

So what? If the kingdom really is within, it can of course be everywhere and anywhere, among these people and those peoples, in this religious grouping and that one. I think of Jesus saying those shocking words to a Roman centurion, "You are not far from the Kingdom of God." Who knows what religion that soldier was. Can you say that the kingdom within is in every loving heart? I think so. Can you say that the kingdom can exist in many cultures and places and religious traditions? I think so, and what is more important, I think that the gospels themselves point to this, even if the vast majority of Christian churches still believe that these other worlds must still be converted to our own relatively small religion.

107. Luke 18:9-14
The Pharisee and the Tax Collector

See selection number 14.

108. Luke 20:45-47
Denouncing the Scribes

The Passage

In the hearing of all the people, he said to the disciples, "Beware of the scribes, who like to walk around in long robes, and love to be greeted with respect in the marketplaces, and to have the best seats in the synagogue, and places of honor at banquets. They devour widows' houses and for the sake of appearances say long prayers. They will receive the greater condemnation."

Commentary

I have typed this passage with some humor, because there was a period of my life when I often dressed in a long robe, a black cassock or soutande, which was once what American Jesuits wore pretty much everywhere except on the street. We wore them in the classroom; we prayed in them, we presided at liturgical services in them. The day I received my own cassock a week after I showed up at St. Stanislaus Seminary in Florissant, Missouri to enter the Society of Jesus, that day in which I took the cloth of a Jesuit was a day of great pride for me. I loved that long robe, the sash that held it in place at your waist, the long sleeves and the collar that fit your neck like a Nehru jacket's collar, an inch high, fitting snugly around the neck.

That garment carried with it considerable respect. I remember once striding into the beginnings of an ugly riot after a very close basketball game in the gym of the high school where I was teaching. I walked, wearing that robe, into the middle of a knot of young men, public high school students—I knew none of them—and told them to get out of the gym in no uncertain terms. They left like mice scurrying for their holes. One of them still holding a screwdriver with the business end sharpened at the tip like a knife. I, the unexpected slim figure in the long, black robe, scared them!

I drove kids injured in football practice to the hospital in that robe, knowing it would get us taken care of promptly in any Catholic hospital's emergency entrance. Wearing a black suit and Roman collar had much the same effect on people as did the long robe. You got respect, deference and reverence. When I was in graduate school at Fordham University in The Bronx borough of New York City, the drivers of public transport put a hand on top of the place where you normally paid your fare, letting you ride for free, if you wore the collar. I don't think I ever paid for my own lunch while traveling on a train in those years; whoever was opposite me at the dining table grabbed the bill and paid for "The Father." It was like that.

I remember well the first time I was stopped by a policeman after I left the order and the priesthood. There was none of this, "I know you're in a hurry, Father, but slow down a bit, would you please?" I got a surly and beefy cop leaning in the window of my car while reading me out for being so careless and daring to break the speed limit. And of course I got a ticket.

I missed that kind of treatment when I left the Jesuits. I was just one of the boys again, and it was a shock. Rank has its privileges; you don't know that until you get busted one way or another. We of course "said long prayers in public places" as well. Priests often read the Roman Breviary while on busses or trains or planes. That little black book of prayers marked you out as a man of God, whether you actually were one or not didn't seem matter much. Clothes make the man, so the old saying goes. I might add that I use the word "man" here advisedly. Men of the cloth in my church were always men, guys, fellas; there were no girls in the business of being priests.

I do wonder sometimes if that respect was all bad. It was surely shallow, coming from what you wore rather than what you were inside, but there were a lot of good priests. I knew that and I still know it. Jesus doesn't mention that the ones in the long robes were traveling ghettoes, never hearing rough language, eliciting politeness magically from almost everyone. People didn't cuss in front of you; they didn't tell dirty jokes; they often talked religion to you. You got the "priest record" reserved for your kind and experienced contempt only from your brothers and sisters on the rare times you went home. It was nice!—deserved or undeserved.

Jesus objected to the shallowness of professional religious people. He didn't like the holy ones cultivating that kind of respect either. I am reminded once again that he was not a priest in his own religion. He was an itinerant teacher and healer. He didn't get bowed down to much because of his clothing. He certainly didn't read the breviary or something like it, being most likely illiterate. Well, put that in your pipe and smoke it. You already know the gospel theme at work here. It's what's inside that counts, long robes or no long robes. The gospels aren't much on making a religious splash. They are not sympathetic to showoffs, especially religious showoffs. I might add here that you can show off piously in a number of ways. For example, instead of wearing a long robe, you might dress noticeably in rags, letting the world know how poor your are. You might act the humble servant too, with a hook. Smarmy and unctuous people often try for attention the same way the long robed ones do. Jesus didn't have much use for showy people who used their show to let the world know how holy they were. He was wary of the priestly caste. I think he was very smart about this, very smart.

109. Luke 22:1-6
The Plot to Kill Jesus

The Passage

Now the festival of Unleavened Bread, which is called the Passover, was near. The chief priests and the scribes were looking for a way to put Jesus to death, for they were afraid of the people.

Then Satan entered into Judas called Iscariot, who was one of the twelve; he went away and conferred with the chief priests and officers of the temple police about how he might betray him to them. They were greatly pleased and agreed to give him money. So he consented and began to look for an opportunity to betray him to them when no crowd was present.

Commentary

I have wondered, "What exactly happened at the betrayal of Jesus?" We don't know much. There was money involved; there was a betrayer. Both the Jewish hierarchy and the Roman overlords were involved. Judas, the betrayer, has sometimes been sympathetically portrayed. I think of the Judas of *Jesus Christ Superstar;* he's more important than Jesus in Andrew Lloyd Weber's musical, and more sympathetically portrayed .

I have certainly wondered whether, had I been one of the twelve, I would have been Judas. Judas knew that Jesus had made some very disturbing claims. None of his followers understood what he wanted. They looked for him to found a kingdom all right, a political one; knowledge of that didn't make the Roman governor happy one bit, even if this political version wasn't what Jesus meant by the kingdom. Ancient Israel, before the Roman occupation, was indeed a political entity, a state, occupying much of what is Israel today. During the period in their history when the country was governed by a king, the king was also its high priest.[10] Separation of church and state is a modern idea. I'm sure Judas was aware that the odds of founding such a state in the face of the Roman legions was ridiculous. Judas was a smart man. Several decades later when there actually was a revolt of the Jewish people of Palestine against

---

10. I note that the Herodian "kings" of Jesus' day were not kings at all, but puppets of the Roman overlords.

Rome, the Romans burned the city of Jerusalem, destroyed the temple, and slaughtered most of the city's inhabitants. They did it promptly, efficiently, and without a thought of mercy.

It seems quite logical that Judas came to think his Jesus had gone over the edge with his talk of a kingdom. There's a certain logic in Judas figuring that Jesus needed to be turned in to the Roman overlords before some terrible punishment was meted out on all of Jesus' followers. There was clearly a Roman involvement in the death of Jesus, although it seems strange to me that he was executed for something he seems never to have thought of himself, sedition against the Roman occupiers of his country. On one occasion, he said, "Give to Caesar the things that are Caesar's and to God the things that are Gods." Nobody got his message of an interior kingdom while he lived, not his followers, not his enemies, not the Romans. I'm not sure I would have been any different. Why didn't they get it? Well, if your vision of life is a narrow one, it's hard to understand something different. e.e. cummings has a wonderful poem about a stubborn and single minded man. I can't resist quoting it here.

> plato told
>
> him: he couldn't
> believe it(jesus
>
> told him; he
> wouldn't believe
> it)lao
>
> tze
> certainly told
> him,and general
> (yes
>
> mam)
> sherman;
> and even
> (believe it
> or
>
> not)you

told him: i told
him; we told him
(He didn't believe it,no

sir)it took
a nipponized bit of
the old sixth

avenue
el;in the top of his head:to tell

him

This poem has to be read out loud to be understood. It contains only complete sentences. It might help to know that General Sherman said, "War is hell." Lao Tze thought armed revolt against a Chinese emperor was worse than foolishness. The sixth Avenue el is or was an elevated commuter train in a large American city. The train is made almost entirely of steel as are the rails and superstructure which support it. The word *nipponized* is not in any dictionary I know, but I am aware that Nippon is a word for Japan. There was a war between Japan and the U.S. in the forties. America had sold a lot of junk steel to Japan before that war, which the Japanese obligingly used to make weapons of destruction. Enough said. I'm not sure what Plato said, but you get the point. Think of the man who was apprehended by the law for beating a mule over the head with a two by four. He said in self-defense, "I wasn't trying to hurt him; I was just trying to get his attention." During his public life Jesus might have been tempted to use a two by four or a piece of nipponized steel in the head to show his followers and his enemies what he meant by *the kingdom*. Like cummings' man, they didn't believe it.

Jesus did not get the understanding he wanted from his friends or his enemies. He still doesn't.

110. Luke 22:7-23
The Last Supper

The Passage

Then came the day of the Unleavened Bread, on which the Passover lamb had to be sacrificed. So Jesus sent Peter and John, saying, "Go and prepare the Passover meal for us that we may eat it." They asked him, "Where do you want us to make preparations for it?" "Listen," he said to them, "When you have entered the city, a man carrying a jar of water will meet you. Follow him into the house he enters and say to the owner of the house, 'The teacher asks you, 'Where is the guest room where I may eat the Passover with my disciples?'" He will show you a large room upstairs, already furnished. Make preparations for us there." So they went and found everything as he had told them: and they prepared the Passover meal.

When the hour came, he took his place at the table, and the apostles with him. He said to them, "I have eagerly desired to eat this Passover with you before I suffer: for I tell you, I will not eat it until it is fulfilled in the kingdom of God." Then he took the cup, and after giving thanks he said, "Take this and divide it amongst yourselves, for I tell you that from now on I will not drink of the fruit of the vine until the kingdom of God comes." Then he took a loaf of bread, and when he had given thanks, he broke it and gave it to them saying, "This is my body which is given for you. Do this in remembrance of me." And he did the same with the cup after supper, saying, "This cup that is poured out for you is the new covenant in my blood. But see, the one who betrays me is with me, and his hand is on the table. For the Son of Man is going as it has been determined, but woe to that one by whom he is betrayed!" Then they began to ask one another, which one of them it could be who would do this.

Commentary

Luke presents the last supper as a Passover meal. Passover was the Jewish feast that commemorates to this day the successful flight of the Israelites from slavery in Egypt, the crossing of the Red Sea and the beginnings of their long journey to the Promised Land, which was called Palestine in Jesus' time and is, as I have noted before, roughly the same territory as the Israel of today. In this context Jesus is seen as the New

Moses leading his people from a different kind of slavery to a different kind of freedom.

I want to speak a little about feasts of remembrance. When Jews today sit down at a Seder meal commemorating the flight from Egypt, a description of that famous journey is read from the book of Exodus. Bitter herbs are eaten in memory of the bitterness of their travail as slaves of the Egyptians. The story is told again in word and gesture and food. What I want to point out here is that there is more to this ceremony than telling a story of the olden days. There is a sense in which the event of God's leading his people to freedom happens all over again to those assembled at the Seder meal. Think of the celebration of a wedding anniversary, when a husband brings his wife a corsage of flowers very much like the flowers she wore on their wedding day. They go out together to a nice restaurant, away from kids, the telephone, and the thousand hooks of everyday living that make ordinary evenings noisy in many households: noisy, busy, and sometimes chaotic.

Well, what are they doing out there alone and dressed up in the quiet of an evening of good food and a bottle of wine? They are re-membering something they did long ago. They are putting a long ago event right back on center stage, they reminisce about that day and the days of their early marriage. They live it again in symbol and story. They hope, this celebration will bring back to them the commitment they made to each other long ago. They transcend the years and the place where they now live and are back again at their beginnings, their first promises, their first love. The first important celebration of their union happens again. They are young again; they are crazy about each other again, touched once more by something which happened long ago and now is put together another time. This is no ordinary meal and no unconnected story from somebody else's life. What happened long ago happens again to this couple, now.

So, when Jesus and his companions sat down for that Seder meal there was all the richness of their beginnings happening all over again. In this milieu he adds something new, a new passage, a new cup and bread, linked closely to the old one which they already share. When he says, "Do this in remembrance of me, he is saying it against the rich backdrop of the Exodus event and the Passover meal, adding a new layer, a new dimension. It is wider than the older one, even if it is essentially the same message of deliverance. It embraces a world beyond the boundaries of Judaism.

When Christian people of various sorts celebrate the Lord's Supper they do so against this backdrop of Passover with the addition of another Moses, namely Jesus of Nazareth. Down the centuries the learned ones in this tradition have argued over the meaning of the real presence of Jesus in these celebrations. I think it is useful to go back to the very basic idea of the celebration of any event of great and holy import: birthdays, anniversaries of any great past event from the fourth of July to one's own birth. When you celebrate your birthday or your marriage, if you do indeed re-member it in word and ceremony, that event comes again to you and yours, outside time and place, at the table or picnic ground, at an altar or sacred place. You don't have to be a philosopher or an intellectual to experience some great past event once more, feeling its power. This is why Christians still celebrate that old meal, to feel once more the vibrancy of the life and death of their Messiah, Jesus.

I might add, sticking to our text, that Jesus notes that the one who will betray him is present at table with him. We know that person as Judas Iscariot, the one who led an armed guard to take him away to a trumped up trial and eventually to his execution. In our own celebrations Judas is still there, still a part of it, still the traitor. Who is he now? He is you; he is me; he is whoever celebrates this meal, a part of us. It is important for me to know that there is now and always will be, right alongside the great beauty of my being, something sly and evil and traitorous. Wars and lies and deceit and injustice live right alongside the essential goodness that is ourselves. We need to know that Judas does indeed still live. It is important not to forget him, even at the feast of joy.

111. Luke 22:39-46
The Prayer and Agony on the Mount of Olives

The Passage

He came out and went, as was his custom, to the Mount of Olives; and the disciples followed him. When he reached the place, he said to them, "Pray that you may not come into the time of trial." Then he withdrew from them a stone's throw, knelt down, and prayed, "Father, if you are willing, remove this cup from me; yet, not my will but yours be done." Then an angel from heaven appeared to him and gave him strength. In his anguish he prayed more earnestly, and his sweat became like great drops of blood falling down on the ground. When he got up from prayer, he came to the disciples and found them sleeping because of grief, and he said to them, "Why are you sleeping? Get up and pray that you may not come in the time of trial."

Commentary

So, here he is in the garden at night, where he was accustomed to go to pray. His prayer this time is very human. "Get me out of this!" He knows things are coming to a head. I recall telling someone once that if Jesus actually *wanted* to get himself tortured and killed, then I had made a very bad choice for a religion. Have you ever had a sense of doom, a sense that something heavy was coming and there was no getting out of it? In my own world such things have been small on the scale of world events, but they are real. I dream sometimes of coming into a classroom as a student, knowing there was an exam to take, and being aware as well that I don't know my stuff. Somehow, some way I am not ready to take that test. I have a dream too that I was making a visit to my old Jesuit friends; they ignored me. When I walked up to one of them, he just turned away to someone else. I was no longer welcome to those men; I was shunned and there was nothing I could do about it. That sense of a present or impending doom was clear to Jesus. It is not foreign to me either.

I am reminded as well, that in daily living, there is often a sense of really not knowing what's going to happen. Every day brings with it a need to improvise, to adapt, to find new ways to deal with the things that get dropped in my path. Sometimes the thought of a new day is terrifying to me. I'm not up to it! I want to stay in bed. I remember a story about an

AFRAID

ordinary family one ordinary school morning in September. The mother has made breakfast. She calls her son to come down and eat before going off to school. The son has hidden his head under the pillow of his bed, trying to pretend that he hasn't heard her call. She calls again, "John, come down and eat your breakfast. You'll be late for school if you don't. John answers, "The kids don't like me! I don't understand what's going on in class. And my teachers don't understand me; I not going. I have a stomach ache! I want to stay home." John's mother replies, "John, you are forty years old, you're the principal of the school. You're good at your work. Now get up and get dressed! It's time!"

It's like that some days. You sweat it, old or young. You are afraid. It's a part of ordinary living. The agony in the garden is no ordinary scene, but there has been an inevitability to it. Jesus has been twisting the tiger's tail for a long time now. Both the Romans and some of his people are nervous about his outspokenness, his fire, his honesty. He is going to have to pay the piper and he knows it. Despite his fear there is his acceptance of whatever is coming. That's what makes him different from me.

Elisabeth Kübler-Ross has written perceptively about predictable stages people go through in the process facing death and dying.[11] Sometimes someone who knows she is to die, just denies that possibility. Sometimes, having faced death's reality, a person becomes enraged at the unfairness of it all. Sometimes, in the face of death, one tries to bargain one's way out of it. You try to make a deal. Sometimes there is a terrible depression . . . any or all of these typically happen before one accepts this or that unpleasantness, the most final of which, of course is death itself. I think Jesus is portrayed here as facing his own death. He asks to get out of it. He is angry that his best friends sleep while they might be comforting him. He sweats as though he were bleeding. The hour has come; he dreads it, even if he does accept it. His three best friends know as well that catastrophe is coming. They sleep, hiding their fears, hoping it will all be over when they waken. All of them dread what is coming. They are my brothers. I am like them.

---

11. *On Death and Dying* by Elisabeth Kübler-Ross.

112. Luke 22:47-53
The Betrayal and Arrest

The Passage

While he was still speaking, suddenly a crowd came, and the one called Judas, one of the twelve, was leading them. He approached Jesus to kiss him; but Jesus said to him, "Judas, is it with a kiss that you are betraying the Son of Man?" When those who were around him saw what was coming, they asked, "Lord, should we strike with the sword?" Then one of them struck the slave of the high priest and cut off his right ear. But Jesus said, "No more of this!" And he touched his ear and healed him. Then Jesus said to the chief priests, the officers of the temple police, and the elders who had come for him, "Have you come out with swords and clubs as if I were a bandit? When I was with you day after day in the temple, you did not lay hands on me. But this is your hour and the power of darkness."

Commentary

The sign of betrayal is a kiss. You the reader say, "What a despicable way to betray a friend!" And I agree with you. The kiss is a sign of friendship and intimacy. Judas the traitor, under a sign of friendship lets the police know whom to apprehend. Is this so rare a thing? Have you ever kissed anyone when that was the very last thing you felt? Have you ever shaken someone's hand when you didn't trust that person in any way? I think of talking to my dean at the university where I once taught, telling him what I knew he wanted to hear, because I could not afford to antagonize him. I needed his support to keep my teaching job. Being two-faced is not so strange a vice, even under the guise of friendship. Perhaps this scene is such a revolting one because we have all done it ourselves, one way or another. No one wants to admit having been a false friend, especially if being untrue to someone close to us is a part of our recent past.

We bring flowers to our wives and girlfriends when we have let them down. We gossip about those nearest and dearest to us. Family hatreds, often under the guise of friendship, are the bitterest hatred most people ever know. Jesus calls his betrayal "The hour of darkness" and I note that each of us has a dark and treacherous side like Judas, as I have mentioned earlier. Judas is not just the traitor who turned on his Lord; he is the dark side of everyone of us. We know him intimately even if we pretend not to. We are all Judas.

113. Luke 23:1-5
Jesus Before Pilate. Is He innocent?

The Passage

Then the assembly rose as a body and brought Jesus before Pilate. They began to accuse him, saying, "We found this man perverting our nation, forbidding us to pay taxes to the emperor, and saying that he himself is the Messiah, a king." Then Pilate asked him, "Are you the king of the Jews?" He answered "You say so." Then Pilate said to the chief priests and the crowds, "I find no basis for an accusation against this man." But they were insistent and said, "He stirs up the people by teaching throughout all of Judea, from Galilee where he began even to this place."

Commentary

There are political overtones to the death of Jesus. We see them here. He is accused of trying to cause a revolt against the Roman occupier. Jesus seems not to have been interested in kicking the Romans out of his country, even if his message of love might well have been regarded with suspicion by Pilate and those whom Pilate represented. Those who seek reconciliation are often hated by people in power. Martin Luther King, Jr. and Gandhi were both men of peace; both were assassinated. Dictatorships have never been held together by love, and those with great political power have seldom liked peaceful people. If your closest associates are outcasts and misfits, and Jesus surely was such a man, you will be held in suspicion in the corridors of power. I find nothing strange in Pilate's clear statement of Jesus' innocence of the charges made against him, while at the same time eventually putting his seal of approval on Jesus' torture and death.

As a boy I learned the epithet, "Nigger lover" as a term of contempt and suspicion. The "Niggers" in question were the wrong people for white folks to have for friends. Who knows what plots would be hatched by those who hung around with people of color treated them as equals. If you have lived any time at all here in the land of the free and the home of the brave, you know that story. American freedom is the possession of a small group of people. I won't comment about who lives in the neighborhoods of the free and the brave, except to say that the privileged free ones don't cotton to the brave ones, if the brave ones once lived on the wrong side of the tracks or are people of color, not now, not then, not there, not here. Jesus, you will remember, came from a class of people who had neither land, education, or privilege.

114. Luke 23:26-46
Crucifixion and Death

As they led him away, they seized a man, Simon of Cyrene, who was coming from the country, and they laid the cross on him, and made him carry it behind Jesus. A great number of the people followed him, and among them were women who were beating their breasts and waiting for him. But Jesus turned to them and said, "Daughters of Jerusalem, do not weep for me, but weep for yourselves and for your children. For the days are surely coming when they will say, 'Blessed are the barren, and wombs that never bore, and the breasts that never nursed.' Then they will begin to say to the mountains, 'Fall on us;' and to the hills, 'Cover us.' For if they do this when the wood is green what will happen when it is dry?"

Two others also, who were criminals, were led away to be put to death with him. When they came to the place that is called The Skull, they crucified Jesus there with the criminals, one of his right and one on his left. Then Jesus said, "Father, forgive them; for they do not know what they are doing." And they cast lots to divide his clothing. And the people stood by watching; but the leaders scoffed at him, saying, "He saved others; let him save himself if he is the Messiah of God, his chosen one!" The soldiers also mocked, coming up and offering sour wine, saying, "If you are the king of the Jews, save yourself!" There was also an inscription over him, "This is the King of the Jews."

One of the criminals who were hanged there kept deriding him and saying, "Are you not the Messiah? Save yourself and us!" But the other rebuked him, saying, "Do you not fear God, since you are under the same sentence of condemnation? And we indeed have been condemned justly, for we are getting what we deserve for our deeds, but this man has done nothing wrong." Then he said, "Jesus, remember me when you come into your kingdom." He replied, "Truly I tell you, today you will be with me in Paradise."

It was now about noon, and darkness came over the whole land until three in the afternoon, while the sun's light failed; and the curtain of the temple was torn in two. Then Jesus, crying with a loud voice, said, "Father, into your hands I commend my spirit." Having said this, he breathed his last.

Commentary

We are nearing the end of Luke's gospel and the end of this commentary on the four gospels. We see him now in extremis, walking the road to the hill called the skull outside the city, an outsider pressed into service to carry the cross. The women, so prominent in Jesus' life, are with him still, walking with the entourage of soldiers and mockers. His companions on the cross are outcasts, as we might expect, in this case criminals being crucified with him, one on his right, the other on his left. I think it is good to know that crucifixion was not an unusual punishment in the Roman empire of that era. It was a common form of execution used for those convicted of serious crimes, horrible but quite ordinary. Jesus' death is that of a felon. The soldiers cast lots to divide his clothing. Along with the few friends faithful to him at the end, a small crowd watches the slow death process of the three, much as a crowd of vengeance seekers and voyeurs watched the execution of Timothy McVeigh on television here in the United States. The ironic inscription on Jesus' cross, proclaims to the onlookers, "This is the King of the Jews."

Luke has Jesus say, "Father, forgive them, for they know not what they do." And to the criminal who has words of sympathy for him he says, "Truly I tell you, today you will be with me in Paradise," favoring, as always, one who was an outcast, condemned by society. And at the end, we see nature echoing the malice and treachery that surround the death of Jesus of Nazareth. Luke says that darkness covered the earth for three shrouded hours and that the veil of the great temple in Jerusalem was torn in two. In all this, it is very clear Jesus died; there is no question about it; it was a public death. All four gospels are clear about this. There is no masking of death, no tricks, no seeming demise of this man. There is torture, mockery and death. There is a glimmer of hope there at the end of his life, expressed in his words spoken to the one we have come to know as *the good thief*, a promise of paradise, paradise being the word used in the Jewish Scriptures in their Greek form for the garden of Eden, the place where Adam and Eve lived in earthly delight before eating the forbidden fruit.

We are left then, in a scene of disarray, his followers in shock. On the morrow they will keep the sabbath rest, and then the women will come to the tomb early in the morning of the first day of the week, to anoint the body.

115. Luke 24:1-12
The Resurrection

The Passage

But on the first day of the week, at early dawn, they came to the tomb, taking the spices that they had prepared. They found the stone rolled away from the tomb, but when they went in, they did not find the body. While they were perplexed about this, suddenly two men in dazzling clothes stood beside them. The women were terrified and bowed their faces to the ground, but the men said to them, "Why do you look for the living among the dead? He is not here, but has risen. Remember how he told you, while he was still in Galilee, that the Son of Man must be handed over to sinners, and be crucified, and on the third day rise again." Then they remembered his words, and returning from the tomb, they told this to the eleven and to all the rest. Now it was Mary Magdalene, Joanna, Mary the mother of James, and the other women with them who told this to the apostles. But these words seemed to them an idle tale, and they did not believe them. But Peter got up and ran to the tomb; stooping and looking in, he saw the linen cloths by themselves; then he went home amazed at what had happened.

Commentary

So, who were the first witnesses? The women among his disciples; there is no surprise here, for they alone of all his followers were there at the crucifixion itself. It was they who came to anoint his dead body according to Jewish custom.

I remind the reader of a quotation from the wise man of the Sioux nation, Black Elk, whom I have quoted before in this book, "I don't know whether these things happened or not, but I know that they are true." The men in the band of Jesus' erstwhile friends called the witness of the women "An idle tale." They are still that way, in the person of the vast majority of those who interpret the meaning of the resurrection . . . glued to the fact of his death without imagination. If you want to understand the Resurrection of Jesus, you must use your imagination as well as your faith. The male disciples, we note, still have not seen him at this juncture of the story.

We have been to the resurrection scene four times now, at the end of each of the gospels; this is the last account, that of Luke. We have seen that the women played a primary role in believing Jesus had risen. We have suggested that the resurrection itself took a long time and that its meaning was and is that Jesus is still present with his people. I want to remind the reader that the resurrection stories are as much the stories of the people of the early church as they are lessons about the life of Christ. The men of the early church were slow to believe his continued presence. In my own opinion, they still are. The presence of Jesus among his people is still more recognized by women than by men.

It is clear still that those who are the possessors of power and pelf have the hardest time cottoning to the gospel. I am talking about church office here. For most of the history of the Christian movement women have not had the grace of office and power. They have only rarely been priests or ministers or bishops, never a pope. Only in the early centuries of the Christian movement have they had the power of office, except for today when a strange transformation is taking place in Christianity. Priscilla the dyer of purple, Prisca, Mary Magdalene, Joanna the mother of James, The Beguines of old, and an occasional mitered abbess are finding company in a Czechoslovakian Catholic female priest, in women priests in the Protestant bodies of Christianity, among Episcopalians and Anglicans, Presbyterians, Methodists, ministers and priests in a variety of African-American churches just to name a few of the churches who have returned to the ancient practice of women priests. The Quakers and Shakers are getting some company! They have, of course, had to fight for church leadership. Martin Luther King, Jr. was right when he once said that no one in power ever gives up that power willingly. Dr. King was speaking of the power of White America, but he could have been speaking of the power of men (sic) in the Christian movement. The apostles, you will recall, were all men and, after the death of Jesus, uncomfortable with both the resurrection and with the fact that they grudgingly came to believe in it because of the witness of the women in their community.

I realize that the remarks above, not to mention much of the whole course of this commentary, may be seen by some as intemperate and exaggerated. I am content with that; it does not bother me. There's never been anything temperate and measured about the gospel message. It's just like that.

116. Luke 24:13-35
The Walk to Emmaus
(A Very Long Walk Indeed)

The Passage

Now on that same day two of them were going to a village called Emmaus, about seven miles from Jerusalem, and talking with each other about all these things that had happened. While they were talking and discussing, Jesus himself came near and went with them, but their eyes were kept from recognizing him. And he said to them, "What are you discussing with each other as you walk along?" They stood still, looking sad. Then one of them, whose name was Cleopas, answered him, "Are you the only stranger in Jerusalem who does not know the things that have taken place there in these days?" He asked them, "What things?" They replied, "The things about Jesus of Nazareth, who was a prophet mighty in deed and word before God and all the people, and how our chief priests and leaders handed him over to be condemned to death and crucified him. But we had hoped that he was the one to redeem Israel. Yes, and besides all this, it is now the third day since these things took place. Moreover, some women in our group astounded us. They were at the tomb early this morning, and when they did not find his body there, they came back and told us that they had indeed seen a vision of angels who said that he was alive. Some of those who were with us went to the tomb and found it just as the women had said; but they did not see him." Then he said to them, "Oh, how foolish you are, and how slow of heart to believe all that the prophets have declared! Was it not necessary that the Messiah should suffer these things and then enter into his glory?" Then beginning with Moses and all the prophets, he interpreted to them all the things about himself in all the scriptures.

As they came near the village to which they were going, he walked ahead, as if he were going on. But they urged him strongly saying, "Stay with us, because it is almost evening and the day now nearly over." So he went in to stay with them. When he was at the table with them, he took bread, blessed and broke it, and gave it to them. Then their eyes were opened, and they recognized him; and he vanished from their sight. They said to each other, "Were our hearts not burning within us while he was talking to us on the road, while he was opening the scriptures to us?" That same hour they got up and returned to Jerusalem and they found the eleven and their companions gathered together. They were saying, "The Lord has risen indeed, and he has appeared to Simon!" Then they told what had happened on the road and how he had been made known to them in the breaking of the bread.

Commentary

This story has been etched in my heart for a very long time. None of the other gospels tell it, only Luke. I have imagined a Spring day, mist rising from the ground, and a forlorn couple trudging down a dirt road leading away from Jerusalem. We know the name Clopas is a man's name, but his companion may well have been a woman. They meet a stranger and continue their journey in his company. The stranger explains the scriptures about how the Messiah (Christ) must suffer before entering into his glory. He stays with them, after having made a gesture that he might go on alone. And then, at meal time, they recognize him as Jesus in the breaking of the bread. They hurry back to Jerusalem to tell the others, who have already learned. He is back with them.

There are a number of old motifs here. One of them is the compressing of time. The story makes sense to me if I see the early Christian community, crystalized in Clopas and his companion. These early Christians are seeking to find the meaning of the suffering Messiah in the scriptures of their ancestors, and at the same time experiencing the presence of Jesus in their midst in new and different ways than when they walked with him on the dusty roads of Roman Palestine before his death.

Another recurring theme is the rich imagery of recognizing him in the breaking of the bread. Indeed to this day, the breaking of the bread is one of the chief ways Christians have of knowing the risen Christ. We call it the Eucharist, the Lord's Supper, the meal he requested his people to eat in his remembrance. So then in this story we see his presence in the church after his death: in scripture and in Eucharist. This is not just the experience of the early days of the church. It is ours as well. There are other ways of knowing him, to be sure, but these are among the central ones.

I want to add a note here about my delight in the emphasis of the role of women in the gospel message. You might think that I, whose gender is masculine, would be less pleased at the prominent place of women in the gospels and in the early church, not to mention the slow rising of women to prominence in Christian leadership in the Christian churches of today.

My gender is not female; that's a fact. Put it this way. My understanding of the gospel is born of my own life experience. I grew up in a household of strong women. My father and I were the only male figures in a house with my mother, my two sisters, and a number of other salaried women who helped my mother run the house. These other women lived right with us in my home. They were part of the household. I learned my earliest ways of knowing primarily from women. All my teachers through kindergarten and seven years of primary school were women. A lot of women's ways rubbed off on me. Years later when I read Carol Gilligan's *In a Different Voice* and Mary Belenky et al's *Women's Ways of Knowing* I was struck by my own kinship to a woman's way of knowing and a woman's way in making moral decisions, going first to the case and then to the principle.

I've told you about that before, but I want to underline it here at the end of this commentary. I was struck in turn that it seemed to me that the morality of Jesus of Nazareth was of a more compassionate, case-centered kind than the abstract and principled morality I had learned in a very male seminary. Furthermore, when I read about women's ways of learning as being long on intuition in contrast with more linear and logical thinking and more cooperative than competitive, I recognized my own preferred ways of learning throughout a lifetime. You have already seen that the intuitive ones in the gospel were mostly women and that Jesus himself was a very intuitive person. Intuition is far more the language faith than logic is, loving cooperation is the ideal of the gospel far more than a more competitive mode of living. That's how I see it.

117. Luke 24:50-53
The Ascension of Jesus

The Passage

Then he led them out as far as Bethany, and, lifting up his hands, he blessed them. While he was blessing them, he withdrew from them and was carried up into heaven. And they worshiped him, and returned to Jerusalem with great joy; and they were continually in the temple blessing God.

Commentary

And so, he was and is to be seen no more except in the scriptures and the breaking of the bread, and of course where two or three are gathered together in his name. If you visit sick people, or people in prison, if you have a hand in feeding those who are hungry or providing a drink for one who thirsts or a shirt for somebody who needs one, then you will see him as well. It gets down to whether you care for people who need to be cared for. If you are a caring person, you are part of the kingdom of nuisances and nobodies he once spoke of. You'll find them good company, but likely not much help for getting into the country club.

118. Summary and Conclusion—Prayer

I want to ask a question, here at the end of the book. It concerns the heart of any religion; it is prayer. Did Jesus pray? How did he pray? Let's try to put together a picture from the scattered references in the four gospels. He does withdraw from other people at key times in his life. He goes to the desert or to a mountain or some other lonely place. In doing this he is a good Jew, very much in the tradition of Moses receiving the law from God alone on top of Mount Sinai or confronting God in a burning bush, alone with his sheep at pasture in the country. It is quite clear that he didn't trust people who made a great show of their piety and prayers. "Pray to the Father in secret," he says.

What goes on within Jesus himself during these times of being alone? Well, he is certainly tested; he comes up against the powers of evil there— his own ambition, his own hunger, his ego. He finds comfort as well— he is consoled by an angel after his time of temptation in the desert. It is clear that he does not use many words in his prayer and that solitude is vital for his prayer. Trust is at the heart of Jesus' prayer, epitomized in the gospel prayer we have come to call the *Our Father*. He puts a premium on acceptance of what his Father wants from him. Remember the prayer in the garden on the mount of olives just prior to his passion. He was afraid; he asked to be freed from what he knew was coming, but he recognized that he must do what the Father wanted. His prayer was, "Father, let this chalice pass from me, yet not my will but thine be done." He is forgiving in his prayer. On the cross he says, "Father, forgive them, for they know not what they do."

On a different note his prayer seems to me that of a wildman, the one who was at home outside, climbing the craggy hills, braving the desert. He is as well the wounded healer who asks the Father to make sick and possessed people well. At the end of his life he prays in the desperation of his suffering, "My God, My God why have you abandoned me." He is a priestly person, though not a member of the clergy of his people. He is at home with the ritual of the Seder meal, the celebration of Passover. He is descended from the greatest of the Jewish priests before his time, David. He numbers Abraham among his ancestors, Abraham, whom we know as the Father of All Believers.

His prayer is allied to trust—always, always, always. He calls the one to whom he prays, "Abba." I don't think there is an exact English word for the Aramaic word he used for his Father. Still, the English slang words that children use for their dads give the idea. I think of the words "Daddy" and "Poppa." These words are close to Jesus' word "Abba", because they are children's words for their fathers. They imply both trust and love. There's nothing formal about them.

You may be tempted to say that any sophisticated word for God should echo an understanding of God's vastness, God as above and beyond, far above gender, whether male or female. As Alice Walker's character Shug puts it, "God is a It." Well, what about that? Was Jesus a grossly superstitious Jewish peasant who used a child's pet name for God in hopes of making things easier for himself? His human father Joseph, as far as we know, was long gone by the time Jesus began his teaching years. So maybe Jesus got himself another Daddy in hopes of remaining a child himself, irresponsible, impulsive, and given to tantrums, as all children are.

That's exactly what Freud said about Jesus, as well as anybody else who regarded God as an all powerful father. And I have pondered at times whether all our prayers, including those of Jesus, are basically neurotic exercises that we adults use as excuses not to grow up, stand on our own feet and be poppas and mommas ourselves. How about it? There's no question in my mind that some people use their prayers precisely to hope against hope that the Dad in the sky will do their own work for them.

I think that Sigmund Freud's cutting criticism of prayer poses a question that you and I will have to answer first and foremost for our own prayers as well as measuring the prayer of Jesus. Does a religious sense of trust find its origins in superstition and a refusal to grow up? I'll leave that one for you to answer. This, after all, is the end of a book on Jesus and the gospel. You've had a look here. You have your own thoughts formed in the crucible of your childhood, and your own days which followed it. You have the rest of your life as well to ponder this and to act on it.

Still at the end of this book, I can't resist telling you a story about prayer in the life of a small boy. Robert Coles, perhaps America's greatest interpreter of the world of children, tells of interviewing a small Muslim boy, perhaps eight years of age. In the course of the interview the young one told Coles that when he grew up, he wanted to be a pilot. Furthermore the boy noted that he wouldn't be any good as a pilot without the help of Allah. Coles quizzed him about Allah's role in the future life of this aspiring pilot and asked the boy if Allah would help him keep track of all the minutiae of flying an airplane. "Oh no, the small one replied, "That's *my business.*"

Returning to the gospels on prayer and finishing this essay and this book, I might add by way of conclusion that I do not find mch of the nuts and bolts of prayer in the gospels. The gospel is not a "how to" book about forming a prayer life. What we have is a sketch of Jesus' prayer as well as the prayer of the first Christian community. Where he went, how he was accompanied or alone, and some broad strokes of attitudes. There's no instruction on the minutiae of how one gets on with contacting God. That has been the task of the centuries of the Christian tradition. There have been and are many styles of Christian prayer. You will recall, of course, the story of the tax collector and the Pharisee at prayer in the temple. The tax collector sat in the back, he was not obtrusive, and didn't brag. There's a hint for you, regardless of your cultural tradition of prayer.

In closing I will quote a revered figure in my tradition of Christianity, a contemporary thinker, only recently in his grave. His name: Karl Rahner. He is a giant among contemporary thinkers on religion. He said, toward the end of his life, "If Christianity is to survive, it will have to become a religion of mystics." I believe that.

The End

Part Five

References You Might Find Useful to Read, See or Hear, Listed According to Gospel Theme (Confer Index)

119. Heavy References

Celtic Spirituality by John O'Donohue
>   Hope and Joy
Contemplation by Francis Kelly Nemeck and Marie Coombs
>   Prayer
On Death and Dying by Elisabeth Kübler-Ross
>   Hope and Suffering
In a Different Voice by Carol Gilligan
>   Law and Morality
The HarperCollins Study Bible (New Revised Standard Version)
>   All Gospel Themes
Jesus, a Revolutionary Biography by John Dominic Crossan
>   Poverty, Women, Midrash
Memories, Dreams and Reflections by C.G. Jung
>   Women, Faith, Prayer, Doubt
In Over Our Heads by Robert Kegan
>   Bureaucracy
Reflections on the Psalms by C.S. Lewis
>   Evil, Prayer
When Women Were Priests by Karen Jo Torjesen
>   Women

Will and Spirit by Gerald May
        Prayer, Surrender
The Women Around Jesus by Elisabeth Moltman-Wendel
        Women, Servant
Women's Ways of Knowing by Mary Belenky, et al.
        Law, Surrender

120. Novels and Biographies

The Color Purple by Alice Walker
        Suffering, Presence, Hope, Prayer
Deep River by Shusaku Endo
        Suffering, Healing, Servant
The Ground Beneath Her Feet Salmon Rushdie
        Fear, Trickster, Tenderness
I Heard the Owl Call My Name by Margaret Craven
        Doubt, Faith, Wildmen, Servant
Legend of the Baal-Shem by Martin Buber
        Faith, Healing, Joy, Prayer
Monsignor Quixote by Graham Greene
        Doubt, Evil, Hope, Bureaucracy

121. Movies

Agnes of God directed by Norman Jewison
        Love, Faith, The Kingdom
The Apostle directed by Robert Duval
        Faith, Love, Evil, Trickster, Karma, Servant
Babette's Feast directed by Gabriel Axel
        Presence, Food
Cotton Patch Gospel written and directed by Tom Key, music by
Harry Chapin
        Trickster, Midrash, Abba
Fannie and Alexander directed by Ingmar Bergman
        Trickster, Fear, Evil
Godspel film version directed by David Greene
        Trickster, Servant, Tenderness
The Gospel According to Saint Matthew directed by Pier Paulo Passolini
        Wildman, Anger, Poverty

The Passion of the Christ directed by Mel Gibson
        Suffering
Jesus Christ, Superstar directed by Norman Jewison, music and lyrics
by Andrew Lloyd Weber and Tim Rice
        Women, Doubt, Evil, Bureaucracy
Jesus of Montreal directed by Denys Arcand
        Healing, Love, Law, Kingdom, Resurrection
Monty Python: The Life of Brian
        Trickster, Play
Monster's Ball directed by Marc Forster
        Suffering, Love
No Man's Land directed by Danis Tanovic
        Suffering, Evil, Bureaucracy

122. Poetry

100 selected poems by e.e. cummings
        Love, Play, Tenderness
A Coney Island of the Mind by Lawrence Ferlinghetti
        Trickster, Play, Law, Life
Gerard Manley Hopkins: Poems and Prose edited by W.H. Gardner
        Suffering, Transfiguration, Hope
Selected Poems by T.S. Eliot
        Presence, Hope
Collected Poems by W.H. Auden
        Presence, Hope, Love

Index

Reference here is to the number attached to each passage and commentary, not to page number.